The Magic of Our Universe

Beyond the Facts

by
Kent Davis Moberg
1999

Camelot Productions, Inc.
P.O. Box 1709
Blowing Rock, NC 28605

Publisher's Cataloging-in-Publication

Moberg, Kent.
       The magic of our universe / Kent Moberg. -- 1st ed.
       p. cm.
       Includes bibliographical references and glossary.
       Preassigned LCCN: 98-071051
       ISBN: 0-9663797-2-1

       1. Curiosities and wonders. 2. Parapsychology. 3.
Supernatural. I. Title.

     AG243.M63 1998   001.9'4
                                       QBI98-561

*The most beautiful thing we
can experience is the mysterious.
It is the source of all science.*

— **Albert Einstein**

The universal message of this book is conveyed with great hope and love to all of those whose curious eyes and open minds wander among its pages. This work has been written in honor of my parents, Claus R. and Jean D. Moberg, whose love, wisdom, devotion, creativity, and faith have immeasurably fortified and inspired my direction.

Table of Contents

Preface

Other titles were considered for this book such as *The Secrets of Our Universe, Our Hidden Universe, Mysteries of Our Universe,* or *Our Secret Universe,* all of which nicely convey the premise that there are countless fascinating discoveries yet to be explored and revealed.

The Magic of Our Universe was finally selected because it implies an appropriate sense of dynamic interactivity. Dramatic, permanent changes in human behavior have occurred as a result of our interaction with extra-terrestrial life and the realm beyond death. "Magic" conveys the essential element of enchantment in this exploration. This book fills the void between the general population's understanding of anomalies and that of the scientific community researching this fascinating realm of cutting edge science. Science is filled with intrigue that often gets lost in the black-and-white, disciplined, technical arena of scientific research.

The word "magic" is used primarily in the context of any extraordinary or mystical power, influence, or attraction, such as the magic of the sea, or the magic of winter, or the magic of the Grateful Dead (for Jerry and for Steve and Valerie). To some degree, magic implies "illusion" in that paranormal, supernatural, and unexplained phenomena may at first seem like illusions until the facts are gathered and the evidence is analyzed and the magic begins to take on a more definable context — perhaps not always in human terms. In fact, in the next century I suggest humans will be reevaluating their perspective to better fit the universal picture.

The purpose of this book is threefold: First, to enlighten humans about the genuine existence of the fascinating mysteries hiding within our universal living space, and then to inform them of the facts surround-ing these anomalies; second, to do something with this knowledge, to pick it apart, to analyze it, to put it back together, to derive meaning from it, to apply this meaning to the human condition to reveal both immense potential benefit and the interconnectedness of the Universe; and third, to illustrate the tremendous learning potential of high quality documentary television. This book is a think tank for those interested in the unexplained. If more questions than answers remain at its conclusion, it will have served its purpose well.

Why television? Why not books or the Internet? Because television is dynamic, it is in color, it is in motion, it is alive, and it moves the human spirit. I believe it is the most effective and least expensive untapped educational resource currently available to ninety-eight percent of all American households. Television represents the culmination of human thinking. The Internet is an exceptional resource for specific information, but as a source for information on general topics, the Internet is a nightmare. You sift through mountains of fat to get to the meat. I used television for general, categorical, and specific information, and the Internet and books for specifics and for verification of details. Moreover, the quality of television information is exceptional because producers are motivated by "time is money," so they must produce very complete, very succinct, very informative programs. They employ top-notch research personnel, sometimes up to twenty for one single documentary, and as many as fifty if you add the associated network personnel.

So, how did I become interested in this subject? Since childhood, I have always marveled at the stars, at what lies beyond, and at what lurks beneath the surface of the world's oceans. But what really grabbed me up out of my chair was a television documentary I stumbled upon while channel surfing on a crisp fall afternoon in 1989 (*UFO Cover Up?* Live, Fall, 1988). For two hours I sat glued to the tube as actor Mike Ferrell of *MASH* fame hosted a riveting exposé about Area 51, Russian UFO history, and the ongoing research being conducted by top scientists regarding United States UFO cases and others worldwide. Ferrell interviewed a U.S. intelligence agent whose voice and appearance were of course camouflaged.

Nicknamed "Condor," he revealed the U.S. government and military cover-up, some details about Area 51, and specific details about alien anatomy. From that day forward I was hooked and became intrigued with the notion of extraterrestrial life as well as with the plethora of possibilities hiding in our unseen Universe.

Little did I know, however, exactly where my curiosity might lead. The impact writing this book has had on my life has been permanently profound to say the least. Evidence of extraterrestrial life, life beyond death, and extrasensory perception all suggest that humans are far more than little ants running around in cars or on golf courses on some planet in an endless sea of space. All evidence collectively suggests that life is interconnected through an invisible Universe.

The Magic of Our Universe does what television can't do. You can't take your TV on a cruise ship. In book form, the most enlightening information from all sources can be delivered to the reader in a complete, detailed format that tells an amazing story about human evolution. In general, each paranormal subject reviewed in this book is explored according to the Anomaly Presentation Format found on the following page. Some categories do not apply to some anomalies, so each chapter may vary slightly in format. Modern Language Association guidelines have been used to cite multimedia sources, and documentary opinions and views may not necessarily be those of the networks. The information herein, though believed to be entirely factual, is not guaranteed as accurate because so much remains unknown about paranormal occurances. Therefore this information should not be independently acted upon. This book shall be revised every few years to include current discoveries regarding unexplained phenomena.

And now, I hope you enjoy your journey through *The Magic of Our Universe...*

Kent Davis Moberg

Anomaly Presentation Format

Name of Anomaly

Definition of Anomaly
> Etymology is provided to allow the reader to trace the word back to its origin. This reveals much about the origin of the anomaly.

Anomaly Statistics
> The Number and Dates of Books in Print on Each Anomaly
> Frequency of Television Documentaries
> Event Frequency
> Event Frequency Change over Time
> Event Locations
> Event Hot Spots
> Other Applicable Statistics

History of Anomaly

Best-Documented and Most Fascinating Cases

Hard Evidence

Beyond the Facts

Resources for Further Investigation
> Leading Research Scientists and Investigators
> Recommended Television Programs and Networks
> Recommended Books
> Recommended Videotapes and CD-ROMS
> Recommended Internet Sites
> Organizations
> Other Applicable Resources

Endnotes
> Television Documentaries
> Books
> Other Sources

Note: Above categories may apply to some anomalies and not to others.

Credits

Editor	Peter Bumpus
Cover Design	Kent D. Moberg
Cover Production	Chris Pearl & Associates
Text Format	Kent D. Moberg
Typesetting and Text Design	Rosamond Grupp
Principle Word Processing	Kathy Roark
Word Processing	Beth Keeney at Creative Printing
Documentary Transcriptions	Anita DiLeonardo
Principle Internet Research	Amy Sloat
Internet Research	Cheryl Chase
Intellectual Property Law	Olive & Olive, P. A.

My heartfelt appreciation is extended to the kind individuals listed above who have assisted me in this venture. With immense gratitude I also acknowledge the networks, documentary producers, writers, editors, and their staffs for creating such informative programs of outstanding quality, and for bringing the Universe into our homes. Television truly can be a phenomenal library. Without all of these invaluable human resources, these pages would never have made it to press.

The original manuscript for this publication was written entirely by hand. Through this process, certain conviction, a better sense of purpose, and deeper meaning all flow with greater strength from your brain, through your heart and on through the pen, as if the ink were your blood, pouring onto the pages, a part of your soul.

Humanity is giving up an important part of humanity to the machine.

Now, on with the magic ...

Kent Davis Moberg

Introduction

THIS IS A BOOK OF ENLIGHTENMENT

One common thread connecting all humans is the curiosity that makes us go out into the night, gaze up through the clear heavens to the stars, and try to imagine the mysteries that lie among them, and beyond the farthest one. What a contemplative experience this is. Yet, in the pursuit of financial security, we seem to become lassoed by our workaday world, settling contently into a routine earthly existence.

Do we dare consider venturing outside of our routine zone of comfort? Here on Earth, a few have only just begun to explore the unknown with intelligent scientific prowess. But has the human race evolved enough to comprehend the potential wealth of beneficial knowledge hiding therein? Are humans able to consider, with open minds, the Universe in its magnificent diversity? Are we aware that we may be living in a time of unparalleled enlightenment?

In the beginning of the second century A.D., the Greek astronomer Ptolemy described an Earth-centered Universe. Some 1,400 years later, Copernicus proposed for the first time that the Earth rotated around the Sun. Then in 1610, Galileo found evidence for the Copernican system by using one of the first astronomical telescopes. But the religious inflexibility of the Middle Ages would not hear of such a preposterous concept, and in 1633, the Roman Catholic Inquisition forced him to retract his contention. He recanted in a cathedral before the people. It has taken nearly 50,000 years for *Homo sapiens sapiens* (modern humans) intelligence to evolve enough to comprehend the Universe even in its most primitive relationship to Earth. Although our evolution continues exponentially with time, it appears that unwarranted skepticism continues to limit our advance.

Why are humans so skeptical? Is skepticism born of caution? Scientific caution is good, but to what point? The hard evidence strongly supporting the existence of extraterrestrial life is way beyond overwhelming, yet many scientists continue to ignore it. Why? Is caution a by-product of fear? What are we afraid of? Is fear innately human? Could this fear have evolved from the millennia of human conflict in the struggle for dominance. Will the human race ever grow up?

Today, the "inquisition" consists basically of two groups. First, there are the skeptics who believe that humans are the only intelligent life among the billions of galaxies similar to our own throughout the Universe, or that other life exists, but it could never travel across the vast distance to Earth. These people attempt to explain the unknown purely by citing current scientific, religious, or human understanding. The other group is of course the military, who believe they have our best interest and safety in mind when they conceal the truth. This is an interesting notion—they know the truth, but they are acting like skeptics. Perhaps they believe they must preserve our social stability by slowing down the exponential curve of learning and intelligence, releasing new technology only when they believe we are capable of meshing it into our social fabric. Or, perhaps they wish to prevent it from falling into hostile hands. Regardless of their reasoning, military behavior regarding top-secret leaks or witnesses to UFO crashes can be directly compared to the harsh and sometimes fatal treatment of heresy during the Roman Catholic Inquisition of the 1600s. Hollywood has dramatized this most effectively in the *X-Files* series.

Both groups, for different reasons, try to explain the unknown in terms of current human knowledge. One example of this is the attempt to explain extraterrestrial transportation (UFOs) in terms of rocket propulsion technology, instead of in terms of a more probable, advanced type of propulsion such as the manipulation of gravitational and electromagnetic fields that could instantaneously transport matter to new locations. I personally believe this is how some UFOs get from A to B in seconds with little or no sound. Though currently just a theory, try to imagine for one moment the impact of such advanced technology on human transportation here on Earth and throughout space.

Galileo was theoretically and scientifically correct. However, closed-minded seventeenth-century religious fervor superceded scientific proof. The lesson for our generation is that it is unproductive for humans to explain away the incomprehensible with a closed or biased mind. In essence, we may become skeptics simply because we are unwilling, perhaps out of fear, to expand our level of comfort with the unknown.

The *Magic of Our Universe* is a revealing collection of mysterious anomalies that pervade our universal living space, such as extraterrestrial life, ghosts, miracles, angels, and so forth. In general, the best-documented and best-researched cases are reviewed; then, the potential human benefit from understanding these anomalies is explored in a section called "Beyond the Facts." A comprehensive interactive reference list completes each anomaly presentation, which lists the top research scientists and organizations as well as the best books, videos, television programs, and internet web sites. Readers are encouraged to further explore the magic of our Universe through this resource section and through the "Reference Section" in the back of the book, which includes a Statistical Synopsis of Our Universe, a Directory of Television Networks, and a Glossary. Some anomalies such as "Vampires" are historical, while others such as "Extraterrestrial Life" are more contemporary. Perhaps if we see how we have tried to understand anomalies throughout history, we may be able to formulate a more effective approach to the complex enigmas of the twentieth and twenty-first centuries.

The ultimate purpose of this book is to increase our awareness of the sheer magnitude and diversity of our universal living space and of the high probability that there is other intelligent life and fascinating phenomena therein. Significantly, some of these mysterious anomalies, such as extraterrestrial contact, are becoming more frequent and widespread throughout the world. The Universe is sending us a wake-up call—it is very much alive and teeming with potentially useful knowledge.

It is time for us to learn from the "inquisitions" of our past. We must expand our intellectual, physical, and psychological comfort zone so that, perhaps, we may begin to comprehend the true magic of our Universe. We must not be intimidated by the unknown, but rather must embrace it with great hope and courage, for therein may lie the simple answers to our most incomprehensible problems.

THIS IS A BOOK OF IMPECCABLE TIMING

There is perhaps no greater barometer of events in our universal living space than television. Ninety-eight percent of all households in America have TV sets. Only about forty percent own computers. More houses have televisions than have running water or telephones, and the average 65-year-old will have watched nine years of television in his lifetime (Gorham, Joan, ed. *Mass Media 95/96.* 2nd ed., 1995).

Cable networks such as The Learning Channel, The Sci-Fi Channel, A&E, and The Discovery Channel, in their eternal battle for advertising dollars, continue to air the best-researched, most comprehensive prime-time documentaries about universal anomalies such as UFOs and the existence of life beyond death. PBS airs exceptional educational programs about our Earth and the Universe, and CNN keeps us posted on news and breakthroughs. Weekly documentaries such as *Sightings, Unsolved Mysteries, The Unexplained, SciTrek, Science Mysteries, Arthur C. Clarke's Mysterious Universe, Into the Unknown, In Search of History, Ancient Mysteries,* and *Mysteries of the Bible* continue to draw upon the world's top experts in their open-minded exploration of the unexplained.

A myriad of reflective science fiction television shows such as *Touched by an Angel, The Visitor, Dark Skies, X-Files, Millennium,* and *Star Trek* continue to dramatically increase in number and frequency. Some of Hollywood's contributions are the movies *Ghost, Independence Day, Men in Black,* and George Lucas's millennium debut of the continuing *Star Wars* saga. This expanding exploration of the unknown, whether fiction or nonfiction, is highly indicative of increasing human interest in universal anomalies.

Television has been used in several ways to research this book: first, as an indicator of public interest in mysteries of the unknown as revealed by the frequency of related programming; second, as an indicator of public disposition regarding the unknown through program interviews; and third, as perhaps the most comprehensive source of current information regarding the unknown.

The frequency of broadcast and the continuous content revision of some of these programs, as they are now aired again after several months, indicates the degree of the astuteness of program research. A prime example is The Learning Channel series *Alien Invasion Week,* which aired in my area in March 1997 and again in January 1998. Revisions within the order of documentaries and the 1998 addition of startling new footage of UFO sightings were deliberate programming alterations that reflected recent extraterrestrial discoveries.

Information regarding case files presented in documentaries is researched by the most highly respected research scientists throughout the world. These people devote their lives to uncovering the truth, and they do. Research organizations and scientists are listed in the "Resources for further Investigation" section following each anomaly. Another prime objective of this book is to demonstrate the value of good television. The TV is among the finest libraries available to mankind. But as with all libraries, we must first learn how to use it.

Nothing since the dawn of civilization would have a greater impact on humanity than the discovery of enough evidence, both hard and soft, that proved the existence of extraterrestrial life, allowing us to realize the implications. Officially, for the average human, that moment is drawing near. Unofficially, for a detached top-secret government organization, that moment arrived back in 1947 with the Roswell UFO crash. Their base of operations is likely Nellis Air Force Base, home of Area 51 and S-4, in the Nevada desert.

Phenomenal new discoveries such as the cloning of sheep and cattle and the almost daily revelations regarding black holes, other star systems similar to our own, and the origin of the Universe, all flood into our homes through television. Are we being conditioned for the wonderment awaiting us in the new millennium? Are we being conditioned for the truth?

Prophets such as Edgar Cayce, messages from UFO abductees, new crop circle theories, increased UFO sightings, fascinating evidence of life beyond death, new hard evidence of extrasensory perception, and recent discoveries regarding global warming all suggest that some very significant event or events may be imminent for the human race.

The Magic of
Our Universal
Living Space

Extraterrestrial Life

UFOs
The UFO Cover-up
Area 51 and Area S-4
Alien Abductions
Crop Circles
Cattle Mutilations
The Timeline of Extraterrestrial
and Human Interactivity

Extraterrestrial Life

Definitions

Extraterrestrial Life. Any life-form originating or existing beyond the boundaries of Earth. The word *extraterrestrial* was created around 1858 by combining two words: *extra* and *terrestrial.*

UFO. Any object moving through the Earth's atmosphere that cannot be identified or explained as either natural or as an object manufactured by humans. Many unidentified flying objects are eventually identified as either natural phenomena such as the planet Venus, or as known human craft. But a percentage of sightings remains unexplained. Some UFOs are suspected to be of extraterrestrial origin. The term "Unidentified Flying Objects" was invented and then shortened to UFO between 1950 and 1955.

UFO. A UFO is the reported sighting of an object or light seen in the sky or on land, whose appearance, trajectory, actions, motions, lights, and colors do not have a logical, conventional, or natural explanation, and which cannot be explained, not only by the original witness, but by scientists or technical experts who try to make a common sense identification after examining the evidence. (*This definition is provided by the Center for UFO Studies or CUFOS; see Resources for Further Investigation*)

Statistics

* As of 1998 there were 242 books in print on the subject of extraterrestrial life, including all categories listed on the title page. Annual publications in print begin with 1 in 1958, 1 in 1973, 1 in 1975, 2 in 1976, 2

in 1977, 3 in 1978, 3 in 1979, 1 in 1980, 3 in 1982, 1 in 1983, 1 in 1984, 3 in 1985, 4 in 1987, 2 in 1988, 8 in 1989, 9 in 1990, 7 in 1991, 11 in 1992, 13 in 1993, 12 in 1994, 15 in 1995, 18 in 1996, 37 in 1997, and 17 through the summer of 1998. A steady increase occurred in the late eighties with dramatic increases in the 1990s culminating in thirty-seven books printed in 1997, doubling from the previous year. This increase unquestionably suggests a dramatic increase in both interest and activity (Numbers derived from *R. R. Bowker's Books in Print*, the 1998 list).

• In 1997 there were approximately 63 hours of documentaries aired on the subject of extraterrestrial life, which includes all categories listed on the title page. In 1998 there were 176 hours aired on the subject. This threefold increase suggests a phenomenal increase in activity and interest (Numbers obtained from Gissen, Jay. ed. *The Cable Guide*, 1997, 1998).

• According to a September, 1998 Gallup Poll, around fifty percent of U.S. adults believe in the reality of UFOs, and seventy-one percent believe the U.S. government knows more about UFOs than it has disclosed (Lindemann, Michael. ed. *CNI News*.<http://www.cninews.com>. 26 August 1998).

• Most Americans think there is intelligent life on other planets — more intelligent than on Earth (AP Washington. *AP The Wire*. December 15, 1997. <http://www.nacomm.org/news/1997/qtr4/ etpoll.htm>. 26 August 1998).

• Eighty percent of Americans think the government is hiding knowledge of the existence of extraterrestrial life forms (CNN Interactive, *CNN/ Time Poll*, June 15, 1997, <http://www. nacomm.org/news/1997/qtr2/ cnnpoll.htm>, 26 August 1998).

• Twenty-seven percent of Americans believe extraterrestrials have visited Earth, and eighty percent believe the U. S. government is covering up the existence of extraterrestrials (Inter Press Service, *CNN/Time Poll*, 10 June 1998, <http://www.nacomm.org/news/1998/qtr2/cnntime .htm>, 26 August 1998).

• Fifteen million Americans claim to have seen a UFO (*"UFO's: Above and Beyond,"* 16 July 1998).

• The Drake equation, formulated by Ohio State Professor Frank Drake, is widely used by scientists and others to calculate the number of detectable intelligent civilizations in the Universe:

$N = R \cdot fp \cdot nefl \cdot fi \cdot fc \cdot L$, where the variables are as follows:

R = The rate of star formation in our galaxy. Obviously, the more stars, the more potential abodes of life there will be.

fp = The fraction of those stars that have planets.

$nefl$ = The number of planets in each system that are potential abodes of life.

fi = The fraction of systems of living things that give rise to intelligence.

fc = The fraction of systems of intelligent creatures that develop detectable high technology.

L = The length of time a civilization is typically detectable. Civilizations may be destroyed by cosmic accidents or nuclear war. More likely, civilized technology becomes so sophisticated that no energy is wasted. Since no energy is released into space, there is no detectable sign of their existence.

N = The number of detectable civilizations in space. To calculate N, the rate of production ($R \cdot fp \cdot nefl \cdot fi \cdot fc$) is multiplied by the length of time a civilization is detectable (L).

By using the Drake equation, a conservative estimate of detectable intelligent civilations in the universe is 100 million million, or N = 100,000,000,000,000 (*"UFO* Reason to Believe," 8 Dec. 1997).

• The official position of the United States government regarding UFOs remains that they neither confirm nor deny their existence ("Deliberate Deception," *Sightings*, 25 March 1998).

• Until events at Gulf Breeze, FL, ninety percent of all reported UFO sightings occurred at night. The remaining ten percent occurred during daylight hours and were less often captured on video or film ("Gulf Breeze Encounters," *Sightings*, 10 May 1998).

• "Renowned psychiatrist Carl Jung observed that the disc or mandala is a shape familiar to many cultures. He speculated that when people see them in the sky they are expressing the human desire for transcendence and harmony" ("*UFO's*: Above and Beyond," 16 July 1998).

• Researchers have found that most UFO sightings can be explained as natural or man-made phenomena. Roughly one third turn out to be celestial bodies such as stars, planets, or meteors. Less than 5 percent are hoaxes. The remainder of cases are the subject of worldwide fascination, mystery, and research ("*UFO's*: Above and Beyond," 16 July 1998).

• Most UFO sightings are of saucer-shaped objects ("*UFO's*: Above and Beyond," 16 July 1998).

• UFO sightings increased more than one thousand percent after World War II ("*UFO's*: Above and Beyond," 16 July 1998).

• Many UFO sightings led to stage-one alerts during the 1950s ("*Sky Watchers*, We Are Not Alone," 3 May 1998).

• As of 1994 there were 4,500 worldwide physical trace cases of UFO landings where UFOs left some form of environmental impact such as anomalous chemical residue or metallic material, burn marks, or imprints at the landing site (Randle, Kevin, Capt. Air Force Reserves, Interview with Larry King, *The UFO Cover-Up?*, Live from Area 51, A TNT Larry King Special, 13 Sept. 1998).

• "If you look at the ancient history of the Near East and consider the Sumerians and Babylonians, you'll find these people believed their civilizations were given to them by beings that came down from the heavens" (Thompson, Dr. Richard L., Interview, "*UFOs*: The First Encounters," 19 July 1998).

- "UFOs seem to have a keen interest in places where atomic weapons are stored or where atomic energy is being generated" (Fowler, Raymond E., Interview, "UFOs: Japan," *Sightings*, 19 March 1998).

- "I'm convinced beyond doubt, we have recovered alien vehicles, that we have made contact with aliens, that we are communicating with them in some way or form, and that we have vehicles and bodies in preservation" (Stevens, Lt. Col. Wendelle, Foreign Technology Division, Wright-Patterson A.F.B., Interview, "*Alien Secrets:* Area 51," 8 Dec. 1997).

- "Since at least 1947, elements of our government have been absolutely aware that we have non-human highly advanced intelligence visiting this planet. If the secret is impossible to keep, then we must find a way to adjust to this extraordinary oddity. Bottom line is, at all cost, preserve the social order" (Lindeman, Michael, UFO Investigator, Interview, "Gulf Breeze Encounters," *Sightings*, 10 May 1998).

- "I was told by one intelligence source here some years ago that they had up to thirty alien bodies underground at Wright-Patterson field alone up to 1966" (Stringfield, Leonard, UFO Researcher, Interview, "What's Inside Hanger 18," *Sightings*, 10 Feb. 1998).

- In a period of five years between 1983 and 1988, the residents of New York State's Hudson Valley region and surrounding areas racked up over seven thousand UFO sightings (Imbrogno, Phillip, UFO Researcher and Author, Interview, "Extraterrestrial Life," *The Unexplained*, 9 March 1998).

- The five official categories for describing close encounters with extraterrestrials or with their craft were first published in 1972 by J. Allen Hynek and are listed as follows:

    CE-1: A close encounter of the first kind, the most common type, occurs when a UFO is observed within 150 yards.

    CE-2: A close encounter of the second kind occurs when an alien craft leaves physical evidence of visitation. Examples are landing imprints or burns, or crash debris.

CE-3: A close encounter of the third kind involves the actual sighting of a UFO occupant. Less than one percent of all encounters fall into this category.

CE-4: A close encounter of the fourth kind is the rarest — the alien abduction experience.

CE-5: A close encounter of the fifth kind is the phenomenal and currently final category of alien contact, which is communication with these beings.

• "The best and rarest UFO reports occur when groups of people see the same thing" (*"UFO's:* Above and Beyond," 16 July 1998).

• Every month there are between four and five hundred UFO reports in Australia, of which about ten percent prove to be genuine mysteries (*"Oz Encounters,* UFOs in Autralia", 27 Sept. 1998).

• Between 1989 and 1990 there were roughly two thousand UFO reorts in Belgium (Good, Tim, Interview,"*UFOs:* The 100 Year Cover-up," *Sightings,* In Depth and Beyond, 1 Jan. 1998).

• "Over two thousand hours of video were filmed documenting the July 11, 1991 Mexico City event" (*"UFO's:* Above and Beyond," 16 July 1998).

• UFOs, in particular UFO "strings," are sometimes sighted just before or during major Earth or atmospheric events. Some ufologists believe that these UFO sightings are linked in some fashion with Earth changes. Concurrent UFO–Earth events have been documented during the Korean War in the early fifties, in Utah in 1952, in Mexico City in 1992, and recently in Seoul, South Korea in October of 1994. Researcher Lee Elders claims there have been as many as seven hundred such sightings since the Mexico City sightings of 1991 and 1992. In many situations Elders believes the UFOs are delivering messages of destiny ("Cluster UFO," *Sightings,* 17 March 1998).

- "It is a commercial judgment that pilots shouldn't speak about UFOs. Unfortunately it's a fact of life that any UFO, alliance with a UFO sighting, or anything unusual about a particular crew member will downgrade the potential of that airline to earn maximum profits" (Sheppard, Graham, Commercial Pilot, Interview, "Idaho UFO Flap," *Sightings*, 2 Feb. 1998).

- Over 100,000 UFO cases are archived at the Center for UFO Studies (CUFOS) headquartered in Chicago ("*UFO* Reason to Believe," 8 Dec. 1997). *(For information on this and other organizations, see the Resources for Further Investigation in the back of this chapter.)*

- Eleven hundred pages of documents were released through the Freedom of Information Act, proving the involvement of the FBI, the CIA, the Department of Naval Intelligence, the Department of Army Intelligence, and the National Security Agency, all of whom denied any interest in UFOs (Good, Tim, Interview, "*UFOs*: The 100 Year Cover-up," *Sightings*, In Depth and Beyond, 1 Jan. 1998).

- There is a thirty-four-billion-dollar black budget in the United States of which one half is spent on technology, the other half on spying (Friedman, Stanton, Interview with Larry King, *The UFO Cover-Up? Live from Area 51*, A TNT Larry King Special, 13 Sept. 1998).

- "The government is not a monolith. It is a hugely complex entity and there are activities in the government which many people at the top are not even aware of. The people have to help the executive branch and Congress become aware of this in a way that is credible. That is what we are trying to do at CSETI" (Greer, Dr. Steven, Director of CSETI, Interview with Larry King, *The UFO Cover-Up? Live from Area 51*, A TNT Larry King Special, 13 Sept. 1998).

- Project Bluebook Special Report 14 is a little-mentioned government project where 3,201 UFO sightings were categorized and evaluated for quality. Twenty-one percent were listed as "unknown." An additional ten percent were listed as "insufficient information." Yet the Secretary of the Air Force still announced to the public: "On the basis of this report we believe that no objects such as those popularly described as flying saucers have overflown the United States" (Friedman, Stanton, Interview with Larry King, *The UFO Cover-Up?* Live from Area 51, A TNT Larry King Special, 13 Sept. 1998).

• Area 51, located on Groom Dry Lake Bed, and Area S-4, on Papoose Dry Lake Bed, are both contained within the Nellis Air Force Base Complex, which is roughly the size of Switzerland, or 15,900 square miles. President Harry Truman commissioned the base in the 1950s as a top-secret test facility for black-project and next-generation aircraft. It is home to the longest runway in the world. Area 51 is protected by unmarked black helicopter gunships and armed guards in unmarked white jeeps, all of which are authorized to use deadly force. The perimeter is further protected by motion detectors, cameras, and signs. The base perimeter is ten miles down Groom Lake Road from Nevada State Highway 375. The guard house is one-quarter mile from the perimeter and the base is thirteen miles in from the perimeter. The entire complex is located in Nevada, 118 miles to the northwest of Las Vegas ("*Alien Secrets*: Area 51," 8 Dec. 1997).

• "Clear as day in the last of nine hangers was the disc.... The work that I did basically entailed back-engineering the power and propulsion system.... With the clearance I had, known as "majestic clearance," there were only twenty-two people at S-4 with that clearance to work on the craft" (Lazar, Robert S., Alleged former Area 51 and Area S-4 Research Engineer, Interview, "*Alien Secrets*: Area 51," 8 Dec. 1997)

• The one genuine U.S. government document that in my opinion lends credibility to Bob Lazar's claim of having worked at S-4:

Robert Lazar's Federal W-2 Tax Document:
Employer's Name: United States Department of Naval Intelligence
Washington, D.C. 20038
Number above employer's identification number:
E-6722MAJ (highly classified)
Employer's identification number: 46-1007639 (highly classified)
(*"Alien Secrets*: Area 51," 8 Dec. 1997).

• "When you go to work out at those locations, you sign away your constitutional rights. You sign a piece of paper saying if you violate your security agreement and you discuss programs you are working on, without a trial, without right of appeal, you will go to Leavenworth penitentiary for twenty years" (Goodall, James, 133 Airlift Wing, Interview, *"Alien Secrets*: Area 51," 8 Dec. 1997).

• The following document title refers to the actual security agreement routinely executed by employees of Area 51: "Oath Upon Inadvertent Exposure to Classified Security Data or Information" refers to Sections 793 to 798 of The United States Code (*"Alien Secrets*: Area 51," 8 Dec. 1997).

• "In the last fifteen years, tens of thousands of people have come forward to describe their experiences at the hands of alien abductors" (*"UFO* Great Balls of Light," 23 Jan. 1998).

• "What makes alien abductions hard to dismiss is the close similarity of the experiences described" (*"UFO* Great Balls of Light," 23 Jan. 1998).

• "When I began studying abductions, I expected these cases to turn out to be some kind of psychological phenomenon, possibly hoaxes, but certainly nothing more serious than that. There was something really peculiar here. I kept seeing a consistency in these things that I didn't expect to see, and the people seemed so sincere and so normal that it became very difficult to attribute these reports to anything other than a genuine experience" (Bullard, Dr. Thomas, Indiana University, Conducted twenty-year academic study, Interview, "The Secrets of Alien Abduction," *Sightings*, In Depth and Beyond, 14 March 1998).

- "The UFO abduction phenomenon appears to be worldwide. Quite early there were cases coming out of South America, out of Britain, in particular. The numbers of cases have been growing exponentially" (Bullard, Dr. Thomas, Indiana University, Interview, "The Secrets of Alien Abduction," *Sightings*, In Depth and Beyond, 14 March 1998).

- A Table of UFO Reports in Canada since 1989:

1989: 141	1992: 223	1995: 183
1990: 194	1993: 489	1996: 258
1991: 165	1994: 189	1997:284

The total through 1997 is 2,126 (Rutkowski, Chris A., ed., Ufology Research of Manitoba, *The 1997 Canadian UFO Survey*, Winnipeg, Manitoba, 1998,<http://www.geocities.com/Area51/rampart/2653 97survey.html>, 26 August 1998).

- A 1992 Roper Poll of 5,947 adult Americans indicates that at least two percent of the U.S. population have experienced the alien abduction phenomenon (Hopkins, Budd et al., "*The Roper Poll, Budd Hopkins*," 1992, <http://www.spiritweb.org/spirit/abduction-roper-poll.html>, 28 August 1998).

- "Although crop circles have been sighted worldwide, more than ninety percent of the world's total have been found in southern England within forty miles of Stonehenge" ("Winchester, England, Crop Circles," *Sightings*, In The News, 4 March 1998).

- 1997 International Crop Circle Formations:

Australia: 1	The Netherlands: 5
Brazil: 1	Romania: 1
Canada: 1	United Kingdom: 92
Czech Republic: 1	United States: 9
Denmark: 1	

(International Crop Circle Database, Enigma Publications, 1997, <http://www.interalpha.net/customer/puigay/dbase/1997.html>, 26 Aug.1998).

• U.S.A. Crop Circle Formations:

Pre-1990 : 6	1997 : 9
1996 : 17	1998 : 15

(International Crop Circle Database, Enigma Publications, 1997, <http://www.interalpha.net/customer/puigay/dbase/1997.html>, 26 Aug.1998).

• "In over twelve thousand documented cases of cattle mutilation, not one single person has been brought up on charges or has ever been implicated publicly as being one of the mutilators" (O'Brien, Chris, UFO Researcher, Colorado, Interview, "San Luis Valley, Colorado, Mysterious Valley," *Sightings*, In The News, 9 April 1998).

A list of UFO hot spots worldwide in order of activity:

1. Mexico City, Mexico
2. Gulf Breeze, Florida, U.S.A.
3. Baturite, Brazil, South America
4. Avebury, England, U.K.
5. San Luis Valley, Colorado, U.S.A.
6. Bonnybridge, England, U.K.
7. Hudson Valley Area, New York State, U.S.A.
8. Ruwa, Zimbabwe, Southern Africa
9. Hakui, Japan
10. Fairfield, Idaho, U.S.A.

A partial chronological list of UFO incidents involving a cover-up:

Roswell incident: July 2, 1947

Mantell incident: January 7, 1948

Iceland incident: 1951

DesVergers incident: August 19, 1952

The *U.S.S. FDR* case: 1952 through 1962

Lake Superior incident: November 25, 1953

Eureka, Utah incident: April 28, 1962

Socorro, New Mexico incident: April 24, 1964

Vandenberg missile test: November, 1964

Exeter, New Hampshire incident: September 3, 1965

Edwards Air Force Base: October 7, 1965

Apollo Astronaut McDivitt photographs: June, 1966

Shag Harbor incident: October 4, 1967

Mansfield, Ohio incident: October 18, 1973

U. S. and Canada military base flyover: October–November, 1975

Iranian incident: September 19, 1976

The Valentich Pine Gap incident: October 21, 1978

The Cash–Landrum case: December 29, 1980

The Bentwaters case: December 20, 1980

"Fast Walker": May 5, 1984

The Wytheville–Gordon case: October 7, 1987

The S-4–Lazar case: 1989

Discovery pilot Blaha conversation: March, 1989

British military–crop circle spheres: 1991 through 1994

Varginha, Brazil: January 20, 1996

The Phoenix Lights: March 13, 1997

• Two Wright-Patterson engineers, upon retiring from their military obligations, applied for three patents based on flying saucer technology ("What's Inside Hangar 18," *Sightings*, 10 Feb. 1998).

• "I do believe there is a growing pattern of contact which suggests that we are getting closer to actually meeting the neighbors. Gulf Breeze is part of that pattern" (Lindemann, Michael, UFO Investigator, Interview, "Gulf Breeze Encounters," *Sightings*, 10 May 1998).

• "If Earth is being visited by people from other places, from other worlds, from other dimensions, they are speeding up the process right now. Something major is happening" (Dilletoso, Jim, Interview, "Cluster UFO," *Sightings*, 17 March 1998).

- "If this is true, it is the biggest event in all of human history" (Hopkins, Budd, Interview with Larry King, *The UFO Cover-Up? Live from Area 51, A TNT Larry King Special*, 13 Sept. 1998).

History

UFOs

The ancient history of UFOs dates back twenty thousand years, while modern ufology began on June 24, 1947 with the Kenneth Arnold sighting. UFOs appear in many shapes including saucers, discs, boomerangs, spheres, diamonds, cigars, triangles, and chevrons. Some UFOs also have running lights or strobes flashing in red, white, and sometimes green. UFOs range in size from small probes only a few meters in diameter to huge ships several football fields in length or width. One likely source of power might be a matter–antimatter reactor, and a likely source of propulsion might be gravitational field manipulation. This would explain why many eyewitnesses hear no sound from hovering or gliding UFOs. UFO maneuverability ranges from a perfectly motionless hover to an instantaneous shot out of sight. Speeds have been clocked on radar at several thousand miles per hour. The number of eyewitness sightings of UFOs probably now runs well into the millions. Video evidence likely numbers into thousands and thousands of feet.

The UFO Cover-up

Intentional concealment of evidence, data, photographs, and other documentation related to the existence of UFOs and extraterrestrial life began in 1947 with the crash of at least one saucer near Roswell, New Mexico. Evidence now suggests the United States military was involved in the recovery of at least one Roswell disc and its extraterrestrial occupants. Since the Roswell incident, thousands of pages of documents have been uncovered indicating a strong, ongoing, unofficial government interest in, and investigation of, all matters pertaining to extraterrestrial life. The

UFO cover-up is not limited to United States boundaries. A top-secret NATO UFO investigation was launched in 1961 and culminated in a report entitled "The Assessment," which disclosed shocking, overwhelming evidence that Earth and humans have been the subjects of a long-term study by several highly intelligent extraterrestrial civilizations ("Top Secret Projects," *Sightings*, 3 Feb. 1998).

Theories regarding the motives driving this concealment are:

1. That sudden proof of extraterrestrials and their visitations to Earth would completely disrupt the socioeconomic fabric of many human societies worldwide,

2. That the government wishes to control such highly advanced and potentially dangerous technology, and

3. That the military, which is responsible for the safety of U.S. citizens, does not wish to admit they have little or no control over extraterrestrials and their advanced technology. Some UFO researchers believe the government has implemented an ongoing disinformation campaign designed to discredit UFO research and mislead the public.

The Alien Abduction Experience

The first reported alien abduction occurred in 1961 with Betty and Barney Hill. A 1992 Roper Poll suggested that as many as 3.7 million Americans may have experienced an alien abduction.

An alien abduction usually begins with a sighting of a UFO or a bright light, along with an awareness of missing time. Usually months or even years pass before the abductee realizes that something may have happened that night. Nightmares or dreams about their experiences may trigger memories. Also individuals may notice a scar that appears overnight. These scars usually fall into three categories: scoop marks, puncture marks, or patterned wounds.

Unable to pinpoint the problem, alien abductees eventually turn to a physician who often recommends regressive hypnotherapy after hearing the symptoms. Under hypnosis, these people usually reveal their amazing experiences at the hands of extraterrestrials, which nearly always include a medical examination with specific interest in the reproductive system. Once one family member is abducted, it is not uncommon for the entire family to become involved in a multi-generational experience that may last decades.

One prevailing theory regarding extraterrestrial motives is that they are creating a human–alien hybrid, possibly because they need a DNA infusion. Testimonial evidence suggests these beings communicate telepathically with humans during the experience. Some typical messages are:

1. "Don't worry, we won't harm you. Just do what we say."

2. "We bid you peace."

3. Some abductees return from their journey with new abilities such as new scientific perspectives or the power to heal.

4. Some return with warnings of environmental catastrophes and concern for the human race.

Perhaps the most remarkable aspect of the abduction phenomenon is that it occurs to individuals from every walk of life, every color, every creed, and every country. Abductions seem to be random in nature. Nearly all of the victims independently report similar events and describe similar beings.

Crop Circles

The crop circle phenomenon is perhaps the most enigmatic and controversial component of the extraterrestrial picture. Simple circles began appearing in the United Kingdom around 1975 with a peak of 203 authenticated entries in 1992. As circle numbers increased, so did the complexity of the patterns, ranging from simple connected circles to complex snowflakes, to pinwheels, and to patterns resembling entire solar systems complete with the asteroid belt. Although this phenomenon has been plagued with hoaxes, the two most infamous being "Doug and

Dave" in Great Britain, "genuine" crop circle formations usually feature one or more of the following characteristics: genetic cell mutation within the crop stems, microwave stem node damage blown out from the inside, anomalous electromagnetic and geomagnetic readings inside the circles, and very strong psychic and dowsing activity inside formations. Crop circles are now appearing around the world, with the most frequent incidents by far in southern England near Avebury.

Theories of how crop circle formations are formed vary nearly as much as the number of different patterns, but the most popular follow:

1. Extraterrestrial origin
2. Plasma vortex
3. Whirlwind vortex
4. Earth energies
5. Hoaxes

Several vidoes now exist of metallic spheres hovering in and around crops prior to or after formations. Army helicopters have been videoed chasing and observing metallic and illuminated spheres in southern England.

Cattle Mutilations

Beginning around 1965, bizarre animal mutilations began to appear across America along the U.S.-Canadian border. Animals' sex organs, lips, tongues, and ears were surgically removed with a high-heat precision instrument. Oddly, no tracks of any kind have been found near the animal, and no blood has been found on or around the animal. Crop circles are occasionally discovered nearby. Three main theories prevail regarding this phenomenon:

1. Extraterrestrial origin
2. Covert black project of U. S. government
3. Natural or predator causes

To date there have been over twelve thousand precision mutilations.

History of Documented Cases

Following is a chronology of signifcant events from prehistory to the present time where humans and extraterrestrials have interacted. The events presented here are real. They truly happened, and in most cases they affected those individuals involved very deeply, catalyzing complete changes in thinking, in lifestyle, in human behavior, and in some cases, even changes in human capacity or human ability. The following cases are recounted as they occurred, as they were investigated and researched by the finest scientific minds, and as reported to the world by esteemed television documentary producers.

This chronology is far from being complete, but it provides a clear and fascinating overview of the long history and pervasive depth of the phenomenon as it continues to impact the human condition. The cases presented here are among the strongest, involving highly credible witnesses such as military, municipal, or professional personnel, radar-tracking audio and video tapes, medical documentation, photographic evidence, and other strong physical evidence such as actual UFO debris and landing site grounds that have been analyzed. Prior to their involvement, most of the participants in these events had little or no interest in UFOs or extraterrestrial life. In fact, some were die-hard skeptics.

As we delve further and further into the timeline, a truly amazing story begins to unfold. It is a simple story, one that affects every human, everywhere, every day. It is the next chapter in the continuing saga of human evolution. It is a story of human behavior, of how we approach and deal with the unfamiliar, with the unknown, with those parts of our shared Universe that are, perhaps, outside of our human comfort zone.

20,000 years ago
Cave art depicting flying saucers appears in France and Spain.[1]

15,000 years ago
Cave art depicting saucer-shaped objects appears in southern France.[2]

5,000 years ago

Cave art depicting extraterrestrial creatures appears in Australia and in the western United States.[3]

5,000 years ago

Sumerian texts refer to bizarre aerial craft and their occupants.[4]

3,500 years ago

One of the earliest written records of an unidentified flying object is penned in Egypt by Pharaoh Tutmosus III.[5]

1000 B.C.

A clay figure from the Japanese Dogu Period is sculpted with the appearance of an alien being.[6]

865 B.C. to 850 B.C.

A *possible* Biblical reference is made to an alien abduction when Elijah, after crossing the Jordan River, "went up by a whirlwind unto heaven…" (2 Kings 2:11)[7]

550 B.C.

A *possible* Biblical reference is made to Ezekiel's encounter with UFOs: "They moved in any four directions never swerving from their course." (Ezek. 10:8)[8]

329 B.C.

Alexander the Great witnesses a UFO during his invasion of Asia. Witnesses record the event in art form.[9]

322 B.C.

Alexander the Great encounters UFOs again during his invasion of the Phoenicians in the eastern Mediterranean. Multiple witnesses record the event in art form.[10]

A.D. 682

An empress in Hakui, Japan witnesses UFOs shooting across the sky in zigzag fashion. This event is documented in a scroll of A.D. 682.[11]

A.D. 1100 to 1200

A Russian icon is painted depicting two flying discs in the background of the crucifix.[12]

A.D. 1250

A Yugoslavian monastery fresco is painted depicting a flying vehicle and its occupant.[13]

A.D. 1463

Artist Herman Shatton witnesses and draws a bizarre elongated object flaming through the sky over medieval Europe.[14]

A.D. 1558

A UFO is sighted by multiple witnesses over La Spezia, Italy.[15]

April 14, 1561

Huge round cylinders with smaller circular objects emerging from them appear over Nuremberg, Germany.[16] This event is documented in a German woodcut.[17]

1566

A very similar extraterrestrial event occurs above Basel, Switzerland.[18]

1680s

A French metal token is forged depicting the underside of a UFO.[19]

April 17, 1897

A silver cigar-shaped object reflecting the morning sun glides in over Aurora, Texas and crashes just on the edge of town. The occupant is dragged from the burning wreckage and is later described in *The Dallas Morning News* as "…not an inhabitant of this world."[20] The extraterrestrial is laid to rest among the ancestors of Aurora in the Aurora Cemetery. The tombstone, simply marked with a crude single line sketch of the occupant's "air ship," is eventually stolen from the grave site.[21]

Summer, 1908

Eight hundred square miles of desolate forest in Tunguska, Siberia are instantaneously obliterated, sending a shock wave twice around the

Earth. Russian scientist Uri Lavbin proposes that an extraterrestrial craft may have been involved because unusual metals and x-ray radiation, by-products of a nuclear blast, were unearthed at ground zero. Russian nuclear weapon technology did not exist in 1908. This event continues to be researched by Professor Nikolay Vasilyer of the Russian Academy of Sciences and by Uri Lavbin, among others.[22]

1942
"Foo Fighters" invade the skies throughout World War II. Some appear as red or white glowing balls of light, while others are solid structured objects. The military secretly records hundreds if not thousands of wartime sightings.[23]

February, 1942
Thousands of people are startled by unexplained white lights in the night skies over Los Angeles. Assuming they are under attack by the Japanese, the city unleashes spotlights and anti-aircraft guns on the objects. The guns blaze for hours with absolutely no effect. The incident remains unexplained.[24]

1942
One of the first photographs of a UFO is snapped in China.[25]

July 16, 1945
The first nuclear weapon ever detonated on Earth is tested at Alamogordo, New Mexico,[26] releasing a very strong electromagnetic pulse into space.[27]

August 6, 1945
The very first nuclear weapon is dropped on a populated area of planet Earth. More than seventy thousand Japanese people are killed in Japan's southwestern city of Hiroshima.[28] This event releases a strong electromagnetic pulse into space.

August, 1945
The United States obliterates the inner city of Nagasaki, a port in southwest Japan, by dropping the atomic bomb.[29] This ultimate statement of technological achievement ends World War II with the

Japanese. The explosion kills more than seventy thousand people and sends a strong electromagnetic pulse into space.

1946 to 1956

Atomic bombs are tested on the Bikini atoll in the northern Pacific Ocean.[30] These numerous nuclear detonations not only obliterate and irradiate the Bikini atoll, the Marshall Islands, and surrounding ocean,[31] but also bombard space with a series of intense electromagnetic pulses.

June 24, 1947

Private pilot Kenneth Arnold, flying along the Cascade mountain range in Washington state, witnesses a line of nine shiny, silver, wing-shaped craft traveling at 1,200 miles per hour.[32] A newspaper headline writer describing Arnold's experience coins the term "flying saucer."[33]

July 2, 1947

A UFO crashes on the Brazel Ranch near Roswell, New Mexico. Saucer debris is first discovered by rancher Mack Brazel. The saucer and alien bodies are stumbled upon by an archeology crew and are then recovered by military personnel.[34] To the present day this incident remains controversial with respect to the number of saucers and bodies recovered, but it launches the modern era of ufology.

Summer, 1947

The "Majestic 12" group is allegedly assembled by President Harry Truman to control and supervise the recovery of a crashed UFO and its occupants from Roswell, New Mexico.[35]

July 8, 1947

For the first and only time, the military officially announces the existence of flying saucers, to the public, in a front page article in the Roswell Daily Record. The press release is authorized by U.S. Air Force General R. L. Chandler. This declaration is retracted in the very next edition of the Roswell paper and the cold war of secrecy is born between the United States government and its people.[36]

January 7, 1948

Over Franklin, Kentucky, Captain Thomas F. Mantell, Jr. becomes the first victim of a human-provoked UFO–military confrontation. Gutman Airfield air traffic controller, Quinton Blackwell, along with a host of majors and generals, the base commander, and the base intelligence officer all witness the UFO encounter. In his last minutes, Captain Mantell describes the craft as a metallic disc roughly two hundred feet across, seventy-five feet in height, with an observation area on top. *Sightings* has thoroughly investigated this case and was instrumental in bringing closure to this event for the Mantell family, and also uncovered military documents proving the air force summoned a special UFO investigator from Wright-Patterson Air Force Base in Ohio.[37] No one ever saw Mantell's body or found any blood at the crash site.[38] Because of this evidence, Mantell is listed here as a victim and not necessarily a casualty.

December 8, 1948

A classified military project called "Project Sign" is launched with a 2A classification of secrecy. The project officers report to the chief of staff of the air force that UFOs, flying saucers, and flying discs are extraterrestrial in origin.[39]

December, 1948

"Project Sign" is renamed "Project Grudge" signifying both a negative turn in the top brass's attitude towards UFOs as well as their continued frustration with respect to the appropriate approach in dealing with the American public regarding the UFO issue.[40]

September 22, 1949

The Soviet Union tests its first atomic weapon sending a strong electromagnetic pulse reeling into space.[41]

Early 1950s

The first covert United States government project to track, film, and document UFOs begins with camera-equipped planes in the skies over

Alaska. Reel after reel of UFO footage is handcuffed to military personnel and flown to the Pentagon several times per month.[42]

1951

Near an Iceland military base, U. S. Navy Commander Graham Bethune and thirty-one other aviation officials fly over and very near a group of enormous UFOs with fluorescent rings. These objects are tracked on military radar.[43]

1951

Numerous UFO sightings are reported in Lubbock, Texas. Photographer Carl Hart, Jr. records the event with a series of startling photographs.[44]

1952

"Project Grudge" becomes "The Arial Phenomena Group," code-named "Project Bluebook," which investigates, classifies, and assesses twelve thousand UFO reports.[45] Ultimately, seven hundred incidents will be listed as unexplained, another four thousand listed as insufficient data for classification, which can be construed as unexplained.[46]

1952

A UFO formation is photographed over Salem, Massachusetts.[47]

Summer, 1952

Perhaps the largest wave of UFO sightings in the history of the phenomenon ripples across the United States from coast to coast. This nationwide incident climaxes with the July, 1952 mass sighting over Washington, D.C.[48]

July, 1952

A squadron of UFOs is viewed by thousands of people over the U.S. Capitol in Washington, D.C. They are captured on both movie film and in photographs, and are recorded on radar stations at three airports in and around Washington. The event is well covered by newspapers and news organizations around the world.[49] The radar operators clock the craft at 7,000 miles per hour.[50]

July 7, 1952

While traveling with his family through Tremonton, Utah, navy photographer Delbert Newhouse films a string formation of UFOs maneuvering at high altitudes. This event is of particular significance because of Newhouse's credibility and professional military expertise. It is also some of the first UFO film on record.[51]

August 19, 1952

Boy scout leader Sonny DesVergers encounters a UFO on the ground in a wooded area off a military trail in West Palm Beach, Florida. Physical evidence from the landing site and photographs taken by another witness are confiscated by the military.[52]

November 1, 1952

The first nuclear fusion or thermonuclear device, the hydrogen bomb, is tested.[53] This detonation sends a very strong electromagnetic pulse into space.

1952 to 1962

UFOs carry on a ten-year vigil with the aircraft carrier *U.S.S. FDR* which is the only carrier commissioned to carry advanced nuclear weapons. Numerous crew members with different ranks and tours of duty witness and record this event.[54]

January, 1953

A top-secret air force memorandum states that if reports of UFO speed and maneuverability are accurate, the technology must have come from another world.[55]

November 25, 1953

Two pilots in an F-89 fighter pursue a UFO as it is tracked on radar over Lake Superior. Either the F-89 and its occupants are abducted by the UFO or the F-89 crashes and rapidly sinks into Lake Superior. No crash debris is recovered. This case remains controversial.[56]

July, 1959

A UFO is filmed over Corpus Christi, Texas.[57]

1960

Dr. Frank Drake conducts the first modern radio search for extraterrestrial life using a radio telescope.[58]

September, 1961

While driving in the New Hampshire countryside one night, Betty and Barney Hill unknowingly launch the alien abduction phenomenon by becoming the first reported abductees. A 1963 hypnosis session uncovers their shocking experiences.[59]

1961

The Brookings Institute conducts a survey entitled "The Implications of a Discovery of Extraterrestrial Life." Results suggest that among all professionals, scientists and engineers would be most devastated by the confirmation of extraterrestrial life.[60]

April 18, 1962

A massive UFO is tracked across the United States from New York to Utah. The craft illuminates the entire town of Eureka, Utah so brightly that it trips photoelectric cells and turns off the street lights. Jet fighters from Nellis Air Force Base in Nevada and from Luke Air Force Base in Arizona pursue the craft as it is tracked by both surveillance and height-finding radar. It crashes mysteriously in Mesquite not far from the Nellis Air Force Test Range.[61]

April 24, 1964

Lonnie Zamora, a highly credible police officer in Socorro, New Mexico encounters a white egg-shaped UFO and its occupants on the ground. This event gains immediate national news coverage, is well documented, and is thoroughly investigated by air force investigator J. Allen Hynek. Physical evidence is recorded on site. As a result of this convincing case, Hynek becomes very dismayed when the air force attempts to cover up the incident. He eventually quits the official government investigation and becomes an ardent critic of the government and military cover-up.[62]

November, 1964

Military cameraman Dr. Robert M. Jacobs of Vandenberg Air Force Base in

California films a secret missile test launch with a secret, new, high-powered telescopic camera. Military officials are astonished when the film is played back: It reveals that a saucer-shaped UFO approached the missile, which was equipped with an unarmed warhead, and danced around it at thousands of miles per hour, scanning it from several different angles. Jacobs is told by his commanding officer that as far as he was concerned, the event never occurred.[63]

September 3, 1965
A UFO projecting a bright red light is sighted over a forest in Exeter, New Hampshire by local resident Norman Muscarello. Two police officers join Muscarello as on-site witnesses. The number of witnesses ultimately reaches six, all of whom file reports with the Exeter Police Department. In spite of the strong evidence, air force investigators intimidate Muscarello and others into silence.[64]

1965
Animal mutilations performed with high-tech, laser-like precision, around which there are no tracks, footprints, or blood, begin to appear across farms in the United States and Canada.[65]

September 8, 1965
Sheriff deputies Billy McCoy and Robert Goode encounter a UFO on Highway 36 in the rural Texas town of West Columbia, near Houston. The object hovers silently over the deputies' car, then instantaneously flies off. Two days later Deputy Goode is confronted and harassed by two "Men in Black." This incident is significant because the witnesses are highly credible sheriff's deputies, and because it is the first documented case involving the Men in Black. This event was investigated in depth by *Houston Chronicle* reporter Stephen Johnson and can be pulled up on the *Houston Chronicle* web site.[66]

October 7, 1965
A squadron of twelve UFOs infiltrate Edwards Air Force Base in the California Mojave Desert triggering alert status and ultimately involving

five other air force and military bases. Edwards is one of the largest aircraft test facilities in the world. Producer Sam Sherman condensed six hours of declassified audio tape into a dramatic audio documentary.[67]

April 5, 1966

A congressional hearing is held regarding the overwhelming number of public complaints about how the United States Air Force is dealing with UFO reports. In the case of the Exeter, New Hampshire sighting of September 3, 1965, the air force admits the reported UFO remained unidentified and that the event did take place, thus confirming their initial cover-up of the truth.[68]

June 1966

Apollo astronaut James McDivitt photographs a cylindrical UFO in space. The photos disappear after being turned over to NASA.[69]

July 4, 1966

The Freedom of Information Act is passed, opening doors to the tens of thousands of pages of UFO-related documents that strongly suggest an ongoing cover-up by the FBI, the CIA, army intelligence, naval intelligence, and the NSA, all of which have categorically denied any interest in UFOs.[70]

May 20, 1967

While rock-hunting approximately one hundred miles east of Winnipeg, Manitoba in Canada, Stephen Michalak encounters a "flawless" silver saucer that lands on a hill several yards away. As he approaches the craft, a door opens revealing the interior but no occupants. Soon the hatch closes and the saucer begins to take off. Michalak is blown back on the ground by a discharge from grid-like vents in the craft. The grid pattern is burned onto his torso. These burns baffle physicians to this day. It has been determined that they are primarily from a chemical source. Strangely, every three months they subside, then reappear, reviving the pain from the burn. This case has been thoroughly documented medically.[71]

October 4, 1967

A UFO is witnessed in the evening skies by several villagers from the fishing community of Shag Harbor on the island of Nova Scotia, Canada. Suddenly the saucer turns forty-five degrees and plunges into the water, which illuminates the water's surface. Fishermen race to their boats thinking it may have been an aircraft, but are surprised when they reach the site and find no debris, only a thick yellow fluorescent foam floating on the surface. In a covert operation, investigators from nearby Shelbourne Military Base track the UFO as it travels underwater for days after its plunge.[72, 73]

September 14, 1969

A Department of the Air Force training manual is printed including protocol on how to greet and deal with UFOs and extraterrestrial beings.[74]

December 17, 1969

Project Bluebook is officially closed by the military. Of the twelve thousand sightings, seven hundred are listed as unidentified, another four thousand are listed as insufficient data for scientific analysis.[75]

September 8, 1973

Two army MPs encounter a UFO with a brilliant red light on the perimeter road at Hunter Army Airfield in Savannah, Georgia. This event is confirmed with the county sheriff's office. On the night following the incident, MP Burns and MP dispatcher Al Murray return to the same location and again witness the same UFO.[76]

October 18, 1973

Returning in a helicopter from their annual physical, four army reservists encounter a UFO over Mansfield, Ohio. The unidentified craft suddenly projects a green cone-shaped light down over the chopper, which begins to pull the chopper up towards the craft. The tractor beam is released after a few minutes. All four men file military reports detailing the incident.[77]

November 9, 1974

Dorothy Izatt of Vancouver, British Columbia in Canada films UFOs in her backyard, accumulating more than twenty-five hours of 8mm film over a period of years. She eventually has three thousand single frames enlarged showing light patterns that suggest inconceivable speed and maneuverability. Her photography is authenticated by experts.[78]

1975

Crop circles begin to appear in England.[79]

January 28, 1975

Edward Billy Meier is witness to the first of over one hundred UFO encounters in Hinwil, Switzerland. Some of his photographs are among the first ever to be authenticated by optical computer enhancement. Metal allegedly obtained from extraterrestrials is analyzed and found to be "intricately machined, cold-fused, and from a place other than Earth." The Meier incident remains controversial.[80]

Late October to Early November, 1975

UFOs fly over a dozen U.S. and Canadian military bases in a three-week period, including Malstrom Air Force Base in Wyoming, Wurtsmith Air Force Base in Michigan, and Loring Air Force Base in Maine, all of which are Strategic Air Command bases housing nuclear weapons. At Malstrom during the first week of November, according to one military witness, an object hovers over a missile silo and somehow changes the tracking numbers. The missile has to be removed and retooled.[81]

November 5, 1975

Travis Walton is abducted by extraterrestrials in the White Mountains of Arizona. Fellow loggers witness this event. All pass lie detector tests. Travis is found five days later.[82]

1976

The *Viking* space probe surveys the surface of Mars revealing objects bearing close resemblance to pyramids and a carved human face.[83]

1976

The Ahrens family multi-generational alien abduction experience
begins in West Plains, Missouri.[84]

August, 1976

Four friends, Charlie Foltz, Chuck Rak, and twins Jim and Jack Weiner,
all have the experience of their lives while night-fishing on Smith Pond
in the Allagash Wilderness of Maine. From their canoe, all four watch a
huge bright ball of light rise from the forest. The object responds
instantaneously to a flashlight signal from the men and chases them
toward shore with an intense light beam. The four then find themselves
back on shore staring up at this thing. After having strange nightmares
in 1978, the Allagash four find help from UFO researcher and
hypnotherapist Ray Fowler. Under regressive hypnosis, all men independently reveal the same chilling but fascinating story of missing time,
of being beamed up to an alien craft, and of being examined by
creatures with large eyes and four-fingered hands.[85] Jim and Jack
Weiner's traditional artistic styles are transformed after the experience.
Both artists began to express a compelling interest in science, mathematics, and multidimensional space.[86]

September 19, 1976

Iranian military, pilots, and civilians witness what is perhaps Iran's best-
documented UFO encounter. The object is pursued by Iranian Imperial
Air Force F-4 fighters for hours over Mehrabad Airport in Tehran. Every
time the jets approach the object within seven miles, all electronic
instruments, communications, and weapons systems cease to function.
Amir Kamyabipour, former lieutenant general of the Imperial Air Force
and Abdollah Azarbarzin, former deputy commander, both thoroughly
investigate this incident and report back to Iranian and United States
military advisors that the high velocity and electronic jamming capabilities of the UFO are unprecedented. United States reconnaissance
satellite tracking data confirm the location of the object over Iran and
that the event lasted over an hour. The former deputy commander

personally believes that extraterrestrials in general are trying to find some way to communicate with humans. The UFO is then tracked over Cairo, then Portugal, then into space.[87]

August 15, 1977

Dr. Jerry Ehman of Ohio State University discovers a very strong transmission signal on the Ohio State radio telescope called "Big Ear." He writes the now famous "Wow!" in the margin of the printout. Unfortunately the signal never resurfaces.[88]

The Late 1970s

The handheld video camcorder is introduced to consumers and begins to replace home movies with instantaneous playback technology.[89] This audiovisual revolution forever changes the human documentation of extraterrestrial events and exponentially accelerates the accumulation of filmed evidence of extraterrestrial life.

1978

Astronaut Gordon Cooper proclaims his personal belief in the existence of extraterrestrials to the United Nations Panel on Unidentified Flying Objects.[90]

October 21, 1978

Australian Air Training Core pilot Frederick Valentich is allegedly abducted along with his plane by a UFO just off the southern coast of Melbourne, Australia. A previously top-secret audio tape between the control tower and Valentich is eventually leaked to a UFO investigator. In dramatic detail the tape reveals the final conversation between Valentich and the control tower where the pilot describes every move the craft makes as well as its dimensions and shape. The UFO is "…a wingless tube maybe a one hundred feet long with a green blast, sometimes green vapor…."[91, 92]

April, 1979

Russian Cosmonaut Victor Afanasyer is followed in space by a UFO.[93]

November 20, 1980

British police officer Alan Godfrey is abducted from his police vehicle in Todmorden, England as other eyewitnesses look on. He reveals his experience with extraterrestrials in a hypnotherapy session.[94]

December 20, 1980

What is certainly one of England's best-documented cases occurs when a UFO is encountered in Rendlesham Forest at the joint British–American Royal Air Force Base in Bentwaters, England. The event is dramatically documented on an audio tape made by United States Air Force Col. Charles Halt, who investigates with several other military personnel. Several different types of intelligently controlled craft are involved in this incident, including one pyramidal object that actually lands in Rendlesham Forest and leaves landing gear soil imprints, and another craft that flies in above the team, hovers at around two thousand feet, then suddenly illuminates the ground just in front of their feet. Holt describes this light beam in detail as a very narrow, concentrated, white shaft of light about eight to ten inches in diameter, like a laser beam. As quickly as it appeared, the light beam retracts and the ship is gone. This event is also witnessed by civilians in Bentwaters.[95]

December 29, 1980

On an isolated two-lane road just outside Dayton, Texas, Betty Cash, her grandson, and a friend witness a diamond-shaped UFO land on the pavement directly in front of their car. The UFO is surrounded by twenty-three unmarked, black helicopters. Soon after the incident, all three witnesses begin to show symptoms of radiation sickness such as nausea, headaches, skin rashes and burns, and hair loss. Assuming the military is somehow involved, Betty Cash and her friend attempt to sue the United States government, but the case is dismissed. This case is well documented by physicians.[96]

1983 to 1988

Seven thousand citizens of the Hudson River Valley in New York State and surrounding East Coast areas witness continuous UFO activity.

Witnesses include police officers, scientists, airline pilots, educators, attorneys, doctors, and CEOs of major corporations. One object in particular is described by many as a massive chevron-shaped craft, one to two football fields in width, that glides slowly overhead. The book *The Hudson Valley UFO Sightings* details these accounts.[97, 98, 99]

1984

Los Angeles film producer Jaime Shandera receives a collection of documents from an anonymous source in Washington, D.C. Among them are the MJ-12 documents signed by Harry S. Truman. He also receives two encrypted postcards suggesting other document locations in Washington.[100]

May 5, 1984

Twenty-two thousand miles above the Indian Ocean, a fast-moving, intelligently controlled object, code-named "Fast Walker," is detected and tracked for nine minutes by a United States Defense Support Program satellite. Top-secret details including verifiable hard evidence is leaked to UFO investigator Joe Stefula.[101] (*See hard evidence section.*)

1985

In upstate New York, Whitley Strieber experiences his first abduction encounter with alien beings and writes his best-selling book *Communion*, which describes his experience.[102]

January 29, 1986

An alien probe crashes at Height 611 in Delnivorsk, Siberia. The crash is witnessed by both military personnel and civilians. The retrieval of hard physical evidence makes this one of the most important UFO incidents in Russian history. After the crash another UFO is sighted at night searching for the crashed probe. Its spotlight has no beam; rather it lights only the ground it touches.[103] (*See Hard Evidence section*)

1987, on the eve of Rosh Hashana

A multiple UFO event occurs in Shikmona, Israel. Soil with unusual chemical and physical characteristics is retrieved from one landing site.

Another UFO is witnessed by several people and is documented on film by one with a camera. Yet another object is witnessed by former Chief of Police Yitzhakk Mordechai of Bet Shean. Finally, a UFO is chased by three hundred Israeli soldiers to the Jordanian border and back.[104]

October 7, 1987
Wytheville, Virginia news director Danny Gordon of station WYVE becomes involved in a UFO experience that changes his life. The UFO is first witnessed by three Wythe County Sheriff's Deputies, all of whom were military men. Two weeks later, Gordon, very much a UFO skeptic, encounters, with a friend, a saucer two football fields in diameter. The night before a planned press conference announcing these UFO events, Gordon receives an anonymous phone call warning him that the CIA and the FBI are very interested in this case and that he should back off. By the end of December the number of sightings of UFOs of several different sizes and shapes in Wytheville escalates to over fifteen hundred. Danny Gordon finally calls the Pentagon and talks to a spokesman for all branches of defense who tells him, "We do not deny UFOs exist, but we deny they pose a threat to the populous of Wythe County." After Gordon asks him how he knows this, the spokesman replies, "I can't tell you, but they are no threat to you." By the end of his encounter, Danny Gordon and his family receive numerous threatening phone calls, he is visited by two bogus reporters, and he has one of his UFO negatives stolen. His last sighting occurs in December of 1990.[105]

November 11, 1987
The Gulf Breeze, Florida UFO event begins with UFO sightings and photographs taken by builder Ed Walters.[106]

1989
Communism ends in Eastern Europe and *Glastnost* opens a floodgate of previously classified documents regarding Russian UFO encounters. *UFO Xtro*, a weekly Russian TV documentary program, is launched featuring UFO cases and other Soviet paranormal experiences.[107]

1989

In an interview with George Knapp of KLAS-TV in Las Vegas, physicist Robert S. Lazar brings international attention to the most top-secret military test site in the world, known as S-4, where Lazar allegedly worked on reverse-engineering the power and propulsion systems of nine alien saucers.[108] Area S-4 on Papoose dry lake is several miles from Area 51 on Groom dry lake, both of which are contained within Nellis Air Force Base in Nevada, which is about the size of Switzerland.

March, 1989

While talking on a secret NASA channel, space shuttle *Discovery* pilot Col. Blaha is monitored from Earth by a ham radio operator and is heard to say: "Houston, we still have the alien spacecraft under observance." After the tape of this conversation is made public, NASA begins scrambling all shuttle transmissions.[109]

November 29, 1989 to March, 1990

Several hundred Belgian citizens from all walks of life, including many officers from the Belgian police and the Belgian military, all follow a huge, black, triangular UFO that has white lights beneath its three corners and a red center light. After being tracked by four NATO radar stations, the UFO is eventually pursued by two Belgian Air Force F-16 fighters. The jets attain radar lock for a period of five seconds, after which the UFO disappears at an unconventional speed. Hard evidence of this event is in the video record of the pilots' onboard radar screens, which illustrate the UFO maneuvering at velocities that would crush a human in seconds under conventional flying conditions.[110]

1990 to 1991

The military moves their saucer test site from S-4 in the Nellis Air Force Range, possibly to Area 6413 in the White Sands launch complex in eastern Utah.[111] This information remains unconfirmed.

1990 to 1995

Whitley Strieber invites friends and colleagues to join him in his ongoing experiments with alien encounters at his cabin in upstate New York.[112] Strieber writes another book that details these experiences entitled *Breakthrough.*

November 7, 1990

In Montreal, Canada, over forty people stand on a hotel rooftop and gaze up at a massive UFO as it hovers for almost three hours in the night sky. This event is believed to be the largest mass sighting in Canadian history, and later is thoroughly investigated by Dr. Richard Haines and others.[113]

1991 to 1994

Metallic spheres by day and glowing, rotating orbs at night are filmed over and around crop circles in the vicinity of Avebury, England. British military helicopters are seen monitoring these events.[114]

July 11, 1991

The last total solar eclipse of this century darkens the skies over Mexico City and triggers perhaps the largest mass sighting of unidentified flying objects in human history. Over two thousand hours of videotape are filmed.[115]

September 16, 1991

Eyewitness videographers in Mexico City record a round, silver UFO dancing amidst the annual military air show.[116]

1992 to 1995

Over 1,050 pages comprising seventy top-secret UFO documents created between 1962 and 1979 are declassified and released by the Spanish government. Spanish ufologist Vicente-Juan Ballester Olmos announces this achievement at the 1995 UFO conference in Sheffield, England. Olmos explains simply that since the Spanish government was unable to effectively deal with the complex UFO issue, they decided to release these photographs, reports, and other related material to the public. Olmos was instrumental in this accomplishment, having argued with the Spanish government that this information should be made available for public scientific investigation.[117]

June, 1992

A quorum entitled "Alien Discussions. Proceedings of the Abduction Study Conference" is held at MIT in Cambridge, Massachusetts. Esteemed MIT physicist Dr. David E. Pritchard and Pulitzer Prize–winning Harvard psychiatrist John E. Mack organize the conference. Five days of seminars and debate transpire, including contributions from world leaders in alien abduction research such as Thomas E. Bullard, John Carpenter, David Gotlib, Richard Hall, Budd Hopkins, David Jacobs, Pam Kasey, Joe Nyman, Mark Rodeghier, Michael Swords, and Walter Webb. Twenty abductees reveal their very real and fascinating experiences. In the audience, C.D.B. Bryan, a respected journalist, author, and ardent skeptic, is hoping to gather material for a spoof article in the *New Yorker*. However, he is so entirely captivated by the sincerity of the abductees and by the potential reality of the phenomenon that he instead writes a book entitled *Close Encounters of the Fourth Kind: Alien Abduction, UFOs, and the Conference at MIT*.[118]

July 28, 1992

A midair collision nearly occurs between a UFO and a Mexican jet over Mexico City. The incident is tracked on radar.[119]

September 16, 1992

Eyewitness videographers in Mexico City record a round, silver UFO dancing amidst the annual military air show. This object is identical to the one filmed at the air show exactly one year earlier.[120]

October, 1992

A vertical string or cluster of UFOs is recorded on video over Mexico City. UFO investigator Lee Elders views the tape and claims he has investigated hundreds of identical sightings, including one in Utah in 1952 that had been filmed with a movie camera.[121]

October 14, 1992

The Search for Extraterrestrial Intelligence (SETI) is launched by the United States government with a congressional endorsement of 100 million dollars. One year later SETI is dismantled and Project Phoenix rises with private funding. Some UFO investigators speculate that the government shut SETI down because they found evidence of extraterrestrial life; they continue to provide an operating location and stay close to Project Phoenix.[122]

1993
Ray Santilli of Great Britain acquires the now controversial Roswell autopsy film from a former United States military cameraman. Stills from the film can be found at two hundred sites on the Internet.[123]

March to June, 1993
Five separate UFO visitations occur in Qadima, Israel, a quiet rural area near the Mediterranean Sea. During this event, which is believed to be Israel's biggest modern UFO encounter, five women, unrelated and unknown to one another, all encounter a very tall alien being in a flight suit. They all claim the being communicated with them telepathically. Hard physical evidence is discovered at landing sites. Fifty-nine crop circles are attributed to this event. Some ufologists believe that today's UFOs may be the angels of the Biblical era.[124]

August 8, 1993
A fascinating piece of Australian UFO history is written on a country road leading north from Melbourne, Victoria in the southeastern point of Australia. Two groups of people, unknown to one another and traveling in separate cars, pull off the road for a better view of a UFO that had landed in a field. Alien beings disembark from this craft in shafts of light and approach Kelly Cahill and her husband and the other group of three individuals slightly further up the road. Those three, Jane, Glenda, and Bill, later draw sketches of the craft and its occupants that are nearly identical to those drawn by Kelly. Jane, Glenda, and Kelly are all left with triangular marks just beneath their navals. Jane and Glenda are marked with three equidistant tiny round scars on their inner thighs as well. All remember few details of

their actual abduction experience. Other physical trace evidence is recovered in the form of burn marks where the craft landed. This case is well documented and has been thoroughly researched.[125]

September 16, 1993

Eyewitness videographers in Mexico City record a round, silver UFO dancing amidst the annual military air show. This object is identical to the one filmed at the air shows of 1991 and 1992.[126]

October 18, 1993

The United States government purchases Freedom Ridge and Whitesides, two mountain vantage points used by hikers and ufologists for viewing Area 51 in Nevada.[127]

November 28, 1993

Ed Walters of Gulf Breeze, Florida, videotapes a bright UFO during the day. His tape along with other videos and still photographs of rare daylight UFOs are confirmed as authentic and are considered very significant by Jeff Sainio, the MUFON international photo and video analyst. Daylight sightings by highly credible eyewitnesses such as doctors, lawyers, and law enforcement officials dramatically increase during the winter of '93. Sainio points out that the videos corroborate one another and corroborate eyewitness testimony. In two videos, UFOs are caught hovering and then instantaneously darting off at four thousand miles per hour.[128]

January 12, 1994

Retired USAF pilot Col. Jimmie W. Lloyd witnesses a formation of seven bright green orbs streaking across the San Luis Valley of Colorado. This sighting is tracked by NORAD and the objects are covertly pursued by military jets. An anomalous explosion recorded by satellites may also be related to this sighting.[129]

March 2, 1994

Post Falls, Idaho is pelted with a mass UFO sighting, much of which is videotaped. Cattle mutilations are also reported. Washington state

MUFON director, retired Col. Jerry Rolwes, investigates the incident and helps educate and calm eyewitnesses.[130]

March 5, 1994
Videotape facility owner Jose Escamilla begins taping UFOs over Midway, New Mexico near Rowell. He eventually amasses a library of over five hundred hours of UFO video, many of which have been authenticated by internationally respected video and photo analyst Jim Dilletoso.[131]

September 14, 1994
A UFO is videotaped by an eyewitness in Southern Africa.[132]

September 16, 1994
Sixty-two schoolchildren of the Arial School claim to have close encounters of the first, second, third, and fifth kinds in Ruwa, Zimbabwe in southern Africa. The event is first investigated by South African UFO expert Cynthia Hind and more recently by Pulitzer Prize–winning Harvard psychiatrist John E. Mack, who is producing a television documentary about the event. Mack believes the children are truthfully conveying a real event. In describing their experience, the children claim that an alien ship landed and alien beings telepathically conveyed to them an urgent message that the Earth is environmentally endangered.[133, 134]

October 1, 1994
From just beyond the perimeter of Area 51 near Rachel, Nevada, Larry King hosts a two-hour program on TNT network entitled *"The UFO Coverup?,* Live from Area 51." His guests are Kevin Randle, Stanton Friedman, Dr. Steven Greer, and Glenn Campbell.[135]

October 1, 1994
In Baturite, Brazil, Reginaldo Athayde and his UFO investigation team record a very strong electromagnetic field in their vicinity along with increased atmospheric static electricity. Shortly thereafter, they photograph six flying saucers hovering soundlessly in a very thin, pastel, blue-

white fog. On the first Saturday of each month these UFOs seem to reappear with uncanny precision at 2 P.M. Thousands show up for the vigil. Some Brazilians believe they are witnessing an apparition of the Blessed Virgin Mary. This event is also researched by John Saliba, PhD, a professor of comparative religion at Columbia University, and by South America's leading ufologist, Irene Granchi.[136]

December 30, 1994

Community leader Herzel Csantini encounters an alien craft and its large occupant in a field in Yatzitz, Israel. "Its face was glowing intently; its face was projecting something."[137] Csantini provides a description of this being regarding its size and telepathic communication that is nearly identical to that given by the five women of the Qadima incident of Spring, 1993. Hard physical evidence is recovered from the Yatzitz site in the form of a plaster cast of foot or boot prints left in the mud. The *Sightings* team, currently in possession of the plaster casting, investigated this incident along with Israeli investigator Doron Rotem, who also worked on the Qadima case.[138]

May 26, 1995

An America West Boeing 757 encounters a UFO estimated to be three hundred feet in length flying at thirty thousand feet above New Mexico around midnight. This UFO is tracked by NORAD radar. The three highly trained pilots are recorded on audio tape as they witness the UFO. This event is investigated by Dr. Richard Haines, retired pilot and researcher of UFOs.[139]

Summer, 1995

An elaborate crop circle is discovered in Winchester, England that depicts our inner solar system of the Sun, Mercury, Venus, and Mars. The Earth's orbit is there, but the planet Earth is conspicuously missing. This formation is surrounded by a string of interconnected bodies believed to be the asteroid belt. Peter Sorensen, a crop circle videographer discovers this relationship and believes the missing Earth is a possible warning from our extraterrestrial neighbors that Earth may be in danger of an asteroid collision.[140]

July 21, 1995

Ed Walters, living in international UFO hot spot Gulf Breeze, Florida, videotapes a UFO from his office. Ed's tape is analyzed by research physicist and UFO photo analyst Dr. Bruce Maccabee and by Jeff Sainio, MUFON international photo and video analyst. Both researchers rule out a hoax and proclaim the tape very unique because the UFO's shadow appears in the film along the distant tree line.[141] Since 1987 Gulf Breeze sightings occur almost daily with thousands of feet of videotape shot and hundreds of still photos taken. Gulf Breeze remains one of the most active UFO hot spots in the world.

August 27, 1995

Tim Edwards records on video a bright, shimmering UFO over Salida, Colorado. The event is investigated by MUFON and Colorado investigator Michael Curta, and the video is analyzed and pronounced authentic by video and photo analyst Chip Pedersen. The San Luis Valley of Colorado is a known UFO hot spot. UFO investigator Christopher O'Brien has investigated over one hundred cattle mutilations and their relationship to UFO activity.[142]

September, 1995

The Nevada State Assembly passes Bill #533 officially renaming State Highway 375, The Extraterrestrial Alien Highway.[143] The road leading to Area 51 branches off of Highway 375.

September, 1995

A solid UFO appears over a small town to the northeast of Seoul, South Korea. The craft then breaks up into a vertical string of numerous silver balls of three different sizes, the largest of which is one hundred feet in diameter, traveling at an altitude of ten thousand feet. All craft are traveling at speeds of eight to nine hundred miles per hour, according to a professional analysis of the videotaped incident by Jim Dilletoso. H. David Froning, a forty-year aerospace engineer, suggests the probable mode of propulsion is a field propulsion system. This sighting is believed to be related to identical sightings in Utah in 1952 and in Mexico City in 1992.[144]

September 26, 1995
President Clinton signs Presidential Determination #95-43 into law, which declares that in the interest of the United States, disclosure or release of classified information concerning "that operating location" is exempt from the Freedom of Information Act. "That operating location" refers to Area 51 in Nevada.[145]

December, 1995 to January, 1996
Along the east coast of New South Wales, just north of Sydney, Australia, hundreds, if not thousands, including police officers and a former air traffic controller, witness a metallic silver sphere maneuvering soundlessly in coastal areas around Gosford. On several occasions, the object is seen probing the water with five shafts of light projecting from beneath.[146]

January 20, 1996
A UFO roughly the size of a small bus is sighted floundering above the village of Varginha, Brazil located to the northwest of Rio de Janciro. The incident has been compared to the Roswell crash of 1947 in that allegedly a UFO crashed, alien beings were recovered, and a military cover-up ensued. The Varginha fire department claims they captured an alien being and turned it over to the military. Eventually as many as five humanoid aliens with leathery green skin and large red eyes were "taken into custody" by the authorities. Reports indicate the United States government not only alerted the Brazilian military about the flailing UFO, but flew in to aid in the covert recovery of the craft and its occupants. This incident was thoroughly investigated in Varginha by Vitorio Pacaccini.[147]

June, 1996
Ray Muniz of Austin, Texas is approached by several Men in Black who trick him into thinking he is being audited by the IRS. They hand him

a summons to appear downtown with his records. He arrives for his meeting only to be greeted by another Man in Black who simply says "Thank you, you can leave now." Surprised by the suspicious activity, Muniz returns home to find that his house has been broken into and his video collection has been ransacked. He then realizes the Men in Black had plotted to steal his remarkable video of a UFO hovering over Georgetown, Texas.[148]

July 4, 1996
A crop circle ninety-three feet in diameter is discovered on the farm of Don and Sue Arend in Pauline, Ohio. It is confirmed authentic by Professor W. C. Levengood when microwave damage to wheat shaft nodes is discovered.[149]

Fall, 1996
A UFO wave sweeps across Texas with events videotaped in West Columbia, New Braunfels, and Cleburne, Texas. This flap is investigated by Houston MUFON senior investigator Dale Musser who believes it may be the beginning of an annual pattern.[150]

Fall, 1996
A Pepsi Cola advertising campaign continues, wherein a UFO beams up a Pepsi machine instead of any other machine. This successful campaign triggers a host of other UFO or alien ads that promote cars, vodka, and so on.[151]

Early 1997
The Japanese UFO museum is opened in Hakui, Japan. Financed from both government and private sources, the saucer-shaped facility archives one of the most complete collections of UFO-related objects and information in the world.[152]

1997
Spiritual healer and therapist Elizabeth Robinson of Perth in Western Australia is interviewed for the Australian documentary *"Oz Encounters, UFOs in Australia."* She reveals her fascinating symbiotic association

with extraterrestrials, which began in 1992. Although it has taken her
five years to accept her alien abduction experience as a real fact of her
life, she also realizes they have given her the power to heal. Elizabeth,
who has experienced close encounters of the first through fifth kinds,
suggests that "Grays" are coming to Earth "to help us awaken"; they are
also here to help their own civilization by creating a "new race of beings
or a hybrid race of beings." Elizabeth currently leads a support group
for other women having similar experiences, and she is writing a book
based on her own detailed journal entries.[153]

March 13, 1997
A line of UFOs in V-formation flicker on and off in the night sky over
Phoenix, Arizona. The event triggers thousands of eyewitness sightings
and numerous video recordings from Phoenix, nearby Prescott, and
other surrounding locations. Video evidence obtained of the "Phoenix
Lights" has been scrutinized by internationally esteemed video analyst
Jim Dilletoso and his partners in their Phoenix labs. Their extensive
database of known flying objects was compared to the digital signature
of the Phoenix Lights. Finding no match, plotting their vectors, and
ruling out all other possibilities, Dilletoso found these objects to be
UFOs under intelligent control.[154]

June 24, 1997
A press conference is held by Col. John Hayes of the Department of
Defense presenting the military's "final word" on the Roswell Crash
entitled "The Roswell Report: Case Closed."[155]

August 6, 1997
One of the most dramatic videos to date of a large saucer is filmed over
Mexico City. Since 1991, Mexican TV journalist and serious UFO
investigator Jaime Mausson and his associates have documented
hundreds of thousands of sightings and have made hundreds of
videotapes.[156]

June 27, 1998
X-Files, the movie, debuts depicting agents Mulder and Scully violating

FBI orders to uncover a vast worldwide cover-up of the existence of extraterrestrials.

July 3, 1998

In the *Journal of Scientific Exploration,* a publication of the Society of Scientific Exploration, scientists such as Professor Peter Sturnock and Professor Von Eshleman, both of Stanford University, along with others from respected bastions such as the University of Arizona, all conclude that the physical evidence backing UFO sightings should be researched and that the study of UFOs should be funded in the same fashion as mainstream science.[157]

Hard Evidence

For Earth visitation from extraterrestrial civilizations:

As of 1994, there were 4,500 physical trace cases in sixty-five countries throughout the world where UFOs had interacted with the environment of the Earth (Randle, Kevin, UFO Researcher, Stanton Friedman, Nuclear Physicist and UFO Researcher, Interviews with Larry King, *The UFO Coverup? Live at Area 51,* a TNT Larry King Special, 13 Sept. 1998). Examples are the Zamora case on April 24, 1964 and the August, 1993 Australian case of Kathy Cahill where anomalous burn marks were photographed and analyzed at the landing site.

For a close encounter of the second kind (physical evidence of visitation):

The grid-like burns on the torso of Stephen Michalak from alleged close-range exposure to a UFO are the same as the grid of vents on the UFO that Michalak meticulously sketched. The bizarre medical history of Michalak's recurring burns is well documented and photographed (Rutkowski, Chris, UFO Researcher, Interview, UFO Encounter, *Unsolved Mysteries,* 19 Sept. 1998).

For close encounters of the fourth kind (evidence of an alien abduction):

A T-shaped implant encased in a dense gray membrane was removed from an alien abductee. Because of its unusual properties and because highly sensitive sensory nerves were uncharacteristically found deep in the toe area from which it was removed, the object is believed to be of extraterrestrial origin. It is being tested at Stanford University. This evidence is documented with x-rays, surgery witnesses, and video, and by the object itself.

A tiny egg-shaped eye implant with one open end fell out of a woman's eye while she was at work. This event was witnessed by her boss. The woman, an alien abductee, believes the implant may have been attached to her retina for the purpose of monitoring our world through her eye. The object is believed to be of extraterrestrial origin and is being tested at Stanford University. Other very small objects of various shapes have been removed from alleged alien abductees. These objects are believed to be extraterrestrial implants, are being tested at Stanford University, and are in the possession of Derrell Sims. (Sims, Derrell, Investigator, and Dr. Roger Leir, California Foot Surgeon, Interview, "*Alien Hunters*, We Are Not Alone", 3 May 1998).

For a close encounter of the second kind (physical evidence of alien visitation):

The object code-named "Fast Walker" was tracked at very high speed twenty-two thousand miles above the Indian Ocean on May 5, 1984. The object came from deep space into Earth's atmosphere, then vectored suddenly back out into space. It triggered an alert at the North American Air Defense Command and was tracked for nine minutes by a United States Defense Support Program Satellite. Top-secret documentation of this event listed its time, place, infrared signature, and its orbital path, which was less than fifteen miles from the satellite. Hard evidence for this event exists in the form of verifiable satellite printouts leaked to a UFO investigator (Stefula, Joe, UFO Investigator, Interview, "*UFO* Deep Secrets," 4 Jan. 1998).

For a close encounter of the second kind (physical evidence of alien visitation):

Metallic wreckage of a UFO that crashed at Height 611 in Delnivorsk, Siberia, near the east coast of Russia, has been scientifically analyzed and found to be of an unearthly origin. A 300-page report determined that an alien probe crashed on January 29 of 1986 and left extraordinary debris that contained elements of unearthly purity and technological sophistication, such as net-like material comprised of quartz insulation wrapped around gold wires thinner than a human hair. Three hundred grams of material including bits of magnetized lint were collected ("*UFO* Uncovering the Evidence," 4 Jan. 1998).

Paired with multiple eyewitness accounts, the debris collected from Height 611 unquestionably provides some of the strongest physical evidence for extraterrestrial visitation on Earth. Extraordinary combinations of precious metals, quartz, silicones, and unidentifiable alloys were discovered along with promethium, an element that does not occur naturally on Earth. The microscopic quartz mesh found wrapped around gold mesh filaments was only seven microns thick. A human hair is fifty-six microns thick. Human technology does not yet exist that could interweave this microscopic netting. This event has been researched by biologist Valeri Dzuzhilnyi of the esteemed Russian Academy of Science, by Paul Stonehill of the U.S. - based Russian Ufology Research Center, by George Knapp, one of America's leading UFO investigative reporters, and by the *Sightings* investigative team among others ("Height 611," *Sightings*, 24 May 1998).

For a close encounter of the second kind (physical evidence of an alien visitation):

In March of 1990, a UFO was tracked by four different NATO radar stations in Europe. Two Belgian Air Force F-16 fighters pursued this object in an attempt to identify it. Their onboard radar videotape shocked the Belgian military when it was replayed. The radar that was locked on the UFO showed that within a matter of five seconds it climbed from seven to ten thousand feet then dropped to five hundred feet. It then instantaneously accelerated to over one thousand miles per hour. Although this velocity was more than three times the speed of sound, no sonic booms were heard by witnesses on the ground. This acceleration would have easily killed a human pilot in a conventional aircraft. The hard evidence of the onboard F-16 radar video becomes irrefutable when coupled with hundreds of eyewitnesses from the Belgian military, the Belgian police, four NATO radar stations, and civilians from Belgian villages (The Belgian Air Force, The Belgian Gendarmerie, Interviews, *Unsolved Mysteries*, 17 June 1998).

For close encounters of the first and second kind together (the sighting of an alien ship and physical evidence of that same alien visitation):

During the multiple-UFO, multiple-witness event in Shikmona, Israel in 1987, charred soil samples recovered from a landing site where a UFO launch was eyewitnessed were tested by biophysicist W.C. Levengood and were found to contain a zinc level 104 times greater than normal. He also discovered a level of hydrocarbon coating on the charred soil sample far above that found in nature on Earth. Moreover, this coating began to melt as Levengood prepared a slide for a photomicrograph (Levengood, W. C., Biophysicist and Barry Chamish, Investigator, Interviews, "UFO Encounter: Shikmona," *Sightings*, 18 Feb. 1998).

For close encounters of the second, third, and fifth kinds (physical evidence of a visitation, the sighting of a UFO occupant, and communication with the UFO occupant):

Between March and June of 1993, in the quiet community of Qadima, Israel, located near the Mediterranean Sea, five women unknown and unrelated to one another, all encountered a very tall alien being on separate occasions. Fifty-nine crop circles were discovered at the same time. High levels of electromagnetic energy, an anomalous red residue, and small, 99.8-percent-pure silicon nuggets were all discovered in or very near the crop circles. The silicon nuggets were analyzed and tested by the National Geological Survey Laboratories in Jerusalem. The nuggets were found to be pure silicon, which doesn't exist naturally on Earth. All five women independently described the same alien creature in a flight suit. This being was massive and stood three meters tall. The women claim he communicated with them telepathically. Laser precision animal mutilations were also associated with these encounters. This case is considered to be Israel's most significant alien encounter. It was researched by Israeli ufologist and horticulturist Doron Rotem, by Barry Chamish, journalist and ufologist, and by the *Sightings* investigative group (Rotem, Doron, and Barry Chamish, Interviews, "UFO Contact: The Holyland," *Sightings*, 6 June 1998).

For a close encounter of the first, second, and third kinds (the sighting of a UFO, physical evidence of alien visitation, and the sighting of the UFO occupants):

On April 24, 1964, a highly credible police officer, Lonnie Zamora, encountered an egg-shaped UFO and its occupants on the ground just outside Socorro, New Mexico. Zamora raced back to his patrol car as the two alien crew members quickly boarded their craft, which then launched with a fiery blast shooting from beneath. Physical evidence in the form of landing gear imprints and launch burn marks on the ground were sampled and photographed. Another independent civilian film also recorded this event and was later obtained by *Sightings*. The landing site was inspected and documented by J. Allen Hynek, acting air force investigator, by the FBI, and by international news crews. This case is of special interest because it is at this investigation that the esteemed Dr. Hynek became dismayed by an obvious attempt by the air force to cover up such a strong case and quit their UFO investigation team to become a private ufologist and author ("Contact at Socorro," *Sightings*, 5 March 1998), ("Socorro, New Mexico, UFO Investigation," *Sightings*, In The News, 25 March 1998).

For close encounters of the first, second, third, and fourth kinds (the sighting of a UFO, physical evidence of alien visitation, sighting of the

UFO occupants, and the ensuing physical interaction between humans and these occupants):

On August 8, 1993 two groups of people unknown to one another and traveling in separate cars, pulled off a country road for a better view of a UFO that had landed in a field. This event transpired just north of Melbourne, Australia. Alien beings disembarked from their craft in shafts of light. One group approached Kelly Cahill and her husband while another group moved towards the other three individuals who were watching from slightly further up the road. Jane, Glenda, and Bill later drew sketches of the craft and its occupants that were nearly identical to those drawn by Kelly. This alien abduction is evidenced by photographs and medical documentation on Kelly, Jane, and Glenda. All three women had identical triangular incision marks below their navals. Jane and Glenda were also marked with three equidistant tiny round scars on their inner thighs. Other physical trace evidence was recovered at the site in the form of burn marks on the grass where the UFO had landed. Kelly Cahill now travels to UFO conferences lecturing about her experience. This event was investigated, documented, and researched by ufologists in both Australia and the United States (Cahill, Kelly, and Others, Interviews, "Oz Encounters, UFO's in Australia," 27 Sept. 1998).

Beyond the Facts

The possibility of neonatal interaction between extraterrestrial life and human life is without question the most pervasive, most enlightening, and most fascinating of all paranormal phenomena currently challenging human life. A complete and detailed perusal of the timeline of extraterrestrial and human interaction reveals several incredible stories.

The most interesting of these is the unwitting, unintentional, and certainly serendipitous method in which we may have sent a message to our celestial neighbors that we had arrived at the atomic age — that humanity finally understood, albeit in basic form, the workings and shear power of the atom.

By looking at the human activities that preceded the birth of modern ufology, we may find the mechanism that triggered it. The first atomic bomb test detonated on July 16, 1945 sent a strong electromagnetic pulse reeling into space for the first time in the history of Earth. Then in August of 1945 all of humanity witnessed the absolute, deadly power of the atom when the United States effectively and ironically ended World War II bloodshed with the mass annihilation of the two Japanese seaports, Hiroshima and Nagasaki. Again, strong electromagnetic pulses were projected into space.

Still more nuclear fission reactions were set off in 1946, practically obliterating the Bikini atoll in the north central Pacific Ocean. Each blast exploded with a force of two hundred thousand tons of TNT and every blast sent an electromagnetic pulse into space. This atomic weapons testing proceeded for ten years in the Marshall Islands. Then in 1952, the humans of Earth witnessed the climax of nuclear power in the detonation of the first thermonuclear device, the hydrogen bomb. With the force of forty-five nuclear fission bombs or 15 million tons of TNT, this nuclear fusion device released the greatest ever electromagnetic pulse into space, a pulse forty-five times stronger than the previous ones.

Considering the highly advanced level of intelligence we are probably dealing with, one wonders whether highly intelligent and sensitive life-forms, who may rely completely on pollution-free matter-antimatter reactors for power and on gravitational and electromagnetic field manipulation for transportation, detected these electromagnetic pulses and responded with visits to Earth to investigate. Nuclear weapons testing began in July of 1945. Modern ufology was born on June 24, 1947 with the sighting of nine flying saucers by Kenneth Arnold. The Roswell UFO crash occurred on July 2, 1947 almost on top of what was at the time the world's only atomic bomb air base, the Roswell air base in New Mexico. Could our deployment of this breakthrough technology have inadvertently brought our curious extraterrestrial neighbors to us in droves?

As we examine the timeline further, we can see this highly developed form of intelligence interact peacefully and at times even playfully with our human war machines. Even before the atomic age, the "Foo Fighters" of World War II literally danced around war planes, and the mysterious lights over Los Angeles in February of 1942 remained motionless in the night sky, without aggression, without reprisal, as they were fired upon relentlessly. Could these UFOs have been messengers of peace trying to persuade the inhabitants of such a promising planet to cease their fighting.

Then, in the summer of 1952, our celestial neighbors showed up en masse, apparently to bid greetings to the new atomic Earth. Could the squadron of UFOs over Washington, witnessed by thousands in July of 1952 and filmed in broad daylight, have been harbingers of peace tipping their hats to us perhaps in mild celebration that our wars were finally over. Could this very real event in human history have been the proverbial "landing on the White House lawn" or as close to it as extraterrestrials thought we could handle at the time.

As bizarre as all of this may seem to some, we must continuously remind ourselves that these events are real. They occurred to real people in real places and have become well-documented segments of real human history.

Soon after the UFO wave of 1952 swept the country, our alien visitors apparently began a survey of Earth's atomic knowledge. They launched a ten-year vigil around the *U.S.S. FDR*, the only United States warship commissioned at the time to carry the atomic bomb. In November of 1964 a flying saucer was filmed dancing around a Vandenberg test missile equipped with a nuclear warhead. One year later on October 7 a fleet of up to twelve UFOs flew over Edwards Air Force Base, one of the largest aircraft test facilities in the world. Then in late October and early November, UFOs carefully inspected over a dozen U.S. and Canadian Strategic Air Command military bases housing nuclear missiles. At Malstrom Air

Force Base in Wyoming, an object hovered over a missile silo and changed the tracking numbers. Could this event have perhaps been both a gesture of peace and a peaceful, maybe even playful, demonstration of their superior technology?

And then there were the cases of humans flaunting military might at these remarkable beings and their "magical" craft. It began with the Mantell incident of 1948 where "hot guns" were ordered on other P-51 Mustangs in Mantell's squadron going after a UFO. On November 25, 1953, two pilots and their F-89 mysteriously disappeared as they aggressively pursued a UFO over Lake Superior. More jet fighters followed a squadron of UFOs over Edwards Air Force Base in 1965 only to be left in the dust as their targets raced to the heavens with instantaneous eloquence. In Iran on September 19, 1976, two Imperial Air Force F-4 fighters relentlessly pursued a UFO. Within seven miles of the object, their electronic instruments and their communications and weapons systems were all rendered inoperable. They were not fired upon or aggressively chased by the UFO. Instead they were playfully sent the message that perhaps aggression is not the most effective road to understanding.

Reviewing the timeline reveals a very significant fact: in hundreds of thousands of UFO sightings and encounters, not once has a UFO been seen brandishing weapons of any kind or in an unprovoked way aggressively pursuing or threatening humans. Remarkably, just the opposite seems to be the case. One exceptional example is the peaceful UFO that has been videotaped at the annual military air shows over Mexico City on September 16 of 1991, 1992, and 1993. Also, the Pentagon may have alluded to their knowledge of peaceful extraterrestrials in a conversation with Danny Gordon during the Wytheville mass sightings of 1987. (*see the timeline: October 7, 1987*)

Indeed, it is my theory that as sophisticated and technologically adept as these amazing creatures are, they could at any time empower weaponry beyond our imagination, *Independence Day* stuff, that could obliterate humans at will. But it seems we are dealing with highly intelligent beings who possibly spend much of their time exploring the Universe learning about other life-forms like us. Intelligence in this case implies peace, altruism, and symbiosis, and the peaceful application of highly evolved skills such as telepathy and other extrasensory abilities. Intelligence implies medical and light technology and knowledge of composite materials far beyond human understanding. Can humanity benefit from encounters with extraterrestrials? What do you think?

And then there are the alien abductions. Thousands and thousands of humans, many female, have had their human and civil rights violated with unsanctioned medical probing and experimentation.

As horrible a nightmare as this experience must be to those randomly selected to journey down that path, let us understand that after their experiences all of these people seem to be neatly tucked back in their beds or back in their cars as though nothing ever happened. They are gently and carefully put back into the nest of Earth. In some symbiotic cases, humans are compensated for their humiliating contribution to what may very well be a worthy cause of alien DNA embellishment.

Cases such as that of Elizabeth Robinson in Australia illustrate this symbiotic relationship: Elizabeth was given the power to heal in exchange for her DNA contributions to the "Grays." Other abductees have been granted enhanced extrasensory powers of perception. The artistic styles of Jack and Jim Weiner changed dramatically after they were abducted in the now-famous Allagash incident in 1976. Jack, a very traditional painter of still lifes and landscapes prior to his experience, became obsessed with science, mathematics, and physics, and began drawing and painting in three dimensions on a two-dimensional surface. Jim Weiner also became obsessed with incorporating scientifically proportioned elements into his clay work in order to produce fascinating structural pieces, where his pre-abduction pottery was rather mediocre in style (Michaels, Susan, *Sightings: Beyond Imagination Lies The Truth*, 1996, Photographs 58 and 59).

Reviewing the chronology of the interaction of humans and extraterrestrials, certain timeline inconsistencies become clear with respect to United States government and military activity. The attempt to conceal real extraterrestrial events seems obvious and out of place when viewed alongside other worldwide events of the same period. At the outset, the Freedom of Information Act was passed on July 4, 1966, unlocking the doors to document upon document implicating the CIA, FBI, army intelligence, naval intelligence, and the NSA in an ongoing cover-up of UFO-related events and information. Practically every page of the extraterrestrial chronology in this book contains some reference to concealing the truth.

A prime example of official concealment being completely disjoined from worldwide events occurred in 1997 when the United States Department of Defense revealed its thousand-page, million-dollar "final word" on the Roswell incident, entitled "The Roswell Report: Case Closed," wherein they skillfully changed their story about what transpired for the third time. In a much more mature, realistic, and appropriate gesture earlier in 1997, the Japanese unveiled their mammoth UFO museum in the seaside city of Hakui. The museum, built in the shape of a flying saucer, was financed by both government and private funds and houses one of the world's largest collections of UFO-related objects and information. This somewhat embarrassing revelation, I must admit, makes me feel like just one sheep in the entire American flock that certain factions of our government and military continue to drive in the direction of their choosing.

There was a time back in the fifties, sixties, and seventies when we humans simply hadn't evolved enough to mesh the reality of the extraterrestrial phenomenon into our social fabric. But considering the exponential revelations of the information age and the inevitable exponential progression of human understanding, it seems it is time for the government to meet the American people halfway with the truth. In the interest of United States security it is understandable that they would covet and shroud some military secrets.

One very reasonable solution to the cover-up dilemma would be to establish a working relationship between military and other intelligence groups, and civilian research organizations such as MUFON and CUFOS (*see Resources for Further Investigation*). Russia, Belgium, Australia, and Spain all benefit from shared military and civilian research regarding extraterrestrial life. The technological implications of a shared-research relationship that included U.S. government-controlled knowledge are infinite in scope.

In the United States another rift in the approach to extraterrestrial research exists between two groups of scientists: those who believe we have not been visited, and those who know we have. One member of the first group is Dr. Thomas R. McDonough, SETI coordinator for The Planetary Society. Many scientists like Dr. McDonough seem to be married to the concept of radio telescope detection of extraterrestrial civilizations. For some unknown reason they seem unwilling to consider the hard evidence such as the twelve cases presented above. They tend to be limited in vision. I believe this group of humans is attempting to explain away the unexplained or the unknown by citing the limits of current human technology. For example, they might believe deep space travel is constrainted by both rocket technology and the speed of light, both concepts of current human perspective.

The other group of scientists, such as nuclear physicist Stanton Friedman, have reviewed the evidence and know that not only have we been visited, but that extraterrestrial visitation of Earth is an ongoing process. I believe this group of humans considers the Universe in more universal terms, and they conduct research with an open mind. Since they have seen evidence of alien visitation of Earth, they probably think projects like SETI are a big waste of time and money. Congress also thought SETI to be a waste of time as they cancelled not part, but all funding in 1993, only one year after launching the endeavor. Could certain members of Congress be privy to government-concealed knowledge that extraterrestrials have been visiting Earth for some time?

For decades humans have been trying to fight gravity with more powerful rocket technology. Perhaps it might be easier to work with gravity instead of against it. Or better yet, have it work for us.

That is precisely what members of a highly elite third group are doing. They are far beyond SETI, far beyond the acceptance of extraterrestrial life, and as intelligent capitalist Americans, they may be developing alien technology for human use. One such researcher is space physicist John Hutchison of Vancouver, Canada who has actucally developed and demonstrated anti-gravity technology through electromagnetic field manipulation.[158] It does seem silly for humans to invent future technology when all we may have to do is inherit it.

Consider the Gulf Breeze events of 1993 to 1994, and more specifically the switch from nocturnal UFO sightings and photography to daylight sightings and photography. I believe this switch may have been a deliberate event, planned and implemented by our intelligent celestial neighbors to gently and gradually provide further evidence of their peaceful and perhaps even playful existence. Also of great interest are the daylight videos from two different sources of the same UFO accelerating from a motionless hover to a 4,000 mph vector in a matter of only two or three frames of film. Such speed would indicate that the occupants of this craft have not only mastered field propulsion, but have also mastered the interrelated elements of space and time, since the G-forces of an instantaneous acceleration from 0 to 4,000 mph would otherwise obliterate a living being.

Taking these observations one significant step farther, imagine the technological leap those intelligent and seemingly peaceful beings could share with humans. Imagine what they could teach us if we would first be willing to openly consider the evidence of their existence and their visits to Earth, and I believe of their peaceful and perhaps symbiotic intentions. I believe we as a world population of all colors and creeds are being gently signaled, nurtured, and beckoned like an infant to stand up for the first time on feeble legs and take our first step into the universal community. My fellow humans, it is time for us to consider the Universe from a universal perspective instead of a human one.

Another technology extraterrestrials seem to have mastered is the use of light. After the 1986 crash of a UFO probe, another UFO searched for it with a beamless light that lit only the ground it touched. In most abduction cases light is used to somehow transport humans and aliens into a hovering craft. Green, yellow, and multicolor vapors surround some UFOs, and in Baturite, Brazil a blue-white glowing fog projected in rays from a craft. The Gosford sphere witnessed by hundreds just north of Sydney, Australia around January of 1996 was seen probing the water with five shafts of intense light. Light energy may very well be a pertinent universal element, the possibilities of which are only now beginning to be made clear to us through our gradual introduction to extraterrestrial life.

Based on an open-minded observation of the historical evidence as it has been written into human history by the sincere individuals involved, and as it has been documented, investigated, and researched by some of the leading scientific minds in the world such as nuclear physicist Stanton Friedman, Pulitzer Prize–winning Harvard psychiatrist John Mack, biologist W. C. Levengood, and many many others, I submit the following deductive theories regarding our current state of affairs with respect to extraterrestrial life:

1. That several highly intelligent extraterrestrial civilizations may have detected strong electromagnetic pulses emitted by human nuclear explosions, and because of their highly advanced understanding and utilization of the entire electromagnetic spectrum, these civilizations may have identified the specific types and origination points of such explosions, resulting in initial and subsequent visits to Earth to verify and to investigate.

2. That these civilizations possess a working knowledge of the space–time continuum and can manipulate it along with gravitational and electromagnetic fields for the purpose of transportation through space. Furthermore these craft likely rely on 100-percent-efficient matter–antimatter reactors (with no exhaust) to fuel their field propulsion system. These technologies would allow them to travel through deep space with no ill effects from G -forces and time loss. Electromagnetic field manipulation also explains why car and aircarft electronic systems shut down during close encounters with UFOs. Nuclear missle tracking numbers were altered by a UFO hovering over Malstrom Air Force Base in the fall of 1975, and in September 1976 Imperial Air Force fighters lost all electronic instruments, communications, and weapons systems while persuing a UFO over Iran.

3. That it is time to develop research around the thousands of feet of video evidence that indicate UFOs manipulate gravitational and electromagnetic fields, instead of assuming that highly advanced extraterrestrial civilations could be even remotely interested in human-based radiowave technology.

4. That these civilizations are peacefully and perhaps even playfully trying to communicate with humans through both aerobatic demonstrations of their field propulsion technology and their artistic and perhaps symbolic crop circle displays.

5. That some of these civilizations value some human characteristics enough to carefully and skillfully attempt to harness human DNA through what humans refer to as the alien abduction experience.

6. That these civilizations demonstrate their sensitivity, their good will, and their altruism through respectful handling of humans during meticulous DNA-transfer procedures. That during these procedures they telepathically convey messages of concern for our environment and concern for our lack of attention to our life-giving and life-sustaining Earth. That they telepathically communicate their peaceful will to help enlighten humans.

7. That it is time for humans through open-minded observation of the overwhelming evidence to stop questioning the existence of extraterrestrial life and to begin to understand these life forms:

    a. Do they have emotions?

    b. Do they have a religion?

    c. Do they like music, and how do they express it?

    d. Do they have pets, and what do they look like?

    e. What does their world look like?

Resources for Further Investigation
Leading Research Scientists and Investigators

To better understand extraterrestrial life, it is immensely beneficial for us to familiarize ourselves with those international professionals who are engaged in ongoing research of the phenomenon. Though it is not possible to list the thousands of scientists, researchers, and investigators, the following individuals well represent the field, and many are frequently interviewed for television documentaries.

Colin Andrews

Perhaps the leader in crop circle research, Colin Andrews has battled the hoaxers for years, insisting that evidence of wheat shaft molecular damage proves that crop circles are more than hoaxes.

Reginaldo Athoyde

Reginaldo Athoyde is head of CPU, one of Brazil's oldest and most-esteemed organizations currently tracking paranormal activity. Unquestionably, the most active Brazilian UFO hot spot, Baturite, has been the focus for Reginaldo and his associates. Here, they have compiled exceptional evidence such as anomalous atmospheric and electromagnetic readings and exceptional UFO photographs.

Kinichi Arai

He has researched UFOs since his service in the Japanese Air Force in the 1940s. Over the years, he has amassed an extensive collection of UFO material, which he has made available to the public in a library opened in 1979.

Keith Basterfield

One of Australia's top ufologists, Keith Basterfield has studied the behavior of multiple abduction experiences and has found an emerging pattern of messages relating to environmental concerns, improved healthier lifestyles, and a keen interest in conveying the reality of the abduction phenomenon.

Dr. Thomas Bullard

A professor of folklore at Indiana University, Dr. Bullard conducted a twenty-year academic investigation into alien abductions. Once a die-hard skeptic, he now believes the experiences are genuine due to the sincere consistency throughout the thousands he has studied worldwide.

Glenn Campbell

He is the founder of the Area 51 Research Center in Rachel, Nevada. A former computer programmer, Glenn Campbell now runs a one-man mission to find out what makes Area 51 tick. He gathers information, interviews former or current employees, and is fascinated by the human behavioral aspect of the whole Area 51 mystique. He has found that any Area 51 employee, former or present, simply will not discuss anything. In fact, if he mentions "Area 51," they simply walk away, and he has discovered that the United States government can and does keep secrets. He has unearthed many fascinating stories about recovered alien spacecraft. Campbell believes some secrets may soon be revealed because we no longer have to concern ourselves with a Soviet threat.

John Carpenter

An alien abduction researcher and a hypnotherapist, John Carpenter focuses on worldwide alien abduction cases such as that of Elizabeth Robinson in Perth, Australia in 1997. He lectured at the MIT Conference on Alien Abductions and also investigated other UFO cases such as the suspected crash and recovery incident in Varginha, Brazil.

Barry Chamish

Mr. Chamish is a journalist and ufologist in Israel. He has developed a controversial theory around the history of extraterrestrial contact as it correlates to Biblical history. Chamish believes that the Qadima abduction cases and the Shikmona UFO encounters are part of the ancient Biblical story: Today's aliens of Israel are the angels of the Bible returning to Earth. He claims that the Bible is a continuing UFO story as exemplified by the "pillar of fire" and the "glowing cloud" that led the Hebrews out of bondage. He believes these events will all culminate in the revelation at Jerusalem.

Jerome Clark

Based in Detroit, Michigan, Jerome Clark has compiled one of the most extensive scholarly collections of modern UFO encounters available anywhere. He is often interviewed on television documentaries because of his knowledge and reputation.

Dr. William Cole

A clinical psychologist, Dr. Cole is a quintessential skeptic who believes that any human who has experienced an extraterrestrial encounter is delusional and that all experiences are derived from television and movie fiction. He also believes that all UFO abduction researchers rely on the same preconceived list of alien abduction symptoms; when a patient comes through his door with these symptoms, he is automatically labeled an abductee.

Robert Dean

A retired United States Army sergeant major and a former NATO attaché in Paris during the 1960s, Dean has been involved with United States covert military operations for thirty years and has acquired extensive knowledge of the depth and worldwide breadth of the UFO cover-up. He has violated the terms of his NATO security agreement by revealing the amazing details of a massive UFO that crashed in the Baltic in 1963 where twelve alien bodies were recovered. Dean states that more like him will step forward with the truth once they receive congressional immunity for violating their national security oath.

Jim Dilletoso

A computer scientist and a partner of Village Labs in Phoenix, Arizona, Jim Dilletoso is respected internationally as a digital image processor who specializes in the digital enhancement of video and still UFO images. He has analyzed and authenticated nearly all of the Ed Walters UFO film from Gulf Breeze, Florida, along with countless others from sightings worldwide. For over twenty years, Village Labs has amassed an extensive image archive of known and unknown aircraft for comparative analysis.

Professor Frank Drake

An astronomer at Indiana University, he formulated the Drake equation for estimating the number of detectable intelligent civilizations in the Universe, and he launched the first radio telescope search for extraterrestrial life in 1960.

Lee Elder

A UFO investigator and video analyst, Elder lives in Colorado and analyzes UFO videos and is especially well versed in UFO "string" formations.

Raymond E. Fowler

A UFO researcher and author, Mr. Fowler has been investigating UFO cases for over thirty years. His background as a former NICAP member and his thorough, meticulous, scientific approach have brought him worldwide respect. He is perhaps most famous for his research and his book on the Allagash abduction case. Fowler is interviewed regularly on documentaries, primarily for his work on the Allagash case.

Stanton Friedman

A nuclear physicist of worldwide esteem and an author, Dr. Friedman has researched and investigated UFO cases for forty years. He worked on classified projects for fourteen years. He has reviewed evidence at fifteen archives. Stanton has delivered over seven hundred lectures in fifty states and nine provinces. He has lectured at six hundred colleges. He was the original investigator of the Roswell incident and is certain, based on overwhelming evidence, that alien bodies were recovered from at least one and more likely two extraterrestrial craft. Based on his tenured UFO research, Stanton asserts "(1) The evidence is overwhelming that planet Earth is being visited by extraterrestrial spacecraft; (2) we are dealing with some kind of cosmic Watergate — that means a few people know what's going on, not everybody; (3) none of the arguments made by the debunkers like Carl Sagan or Phil Klass who never refer to the relevant evidence stand up under careful scrutiny; and (4) we are dealing with the biggest story of the millennium" (Friedman, Stanton, Interview with Larry King, "*The UFO Cover-Up?*" Live from Area 51, A TNT Larry King Special, 13 Sept. 1998).

Timothy Good

A thorough British UFO researcher and author, Tim Good has focused primarily on worldwide cover-up issues. One of his greatest discoveries was the Majestic 12 documents. He has uncovered thousands of pages of information that demonstrate a cover-up by the FBI, the CIA, and others going back to the 1940s.

Irene Granchi

She is a leading UFO researcher in South America, an author, and the director of CESNI. Members of her society believe that science, mysticism, culture, and religion should all be considered together with respect to extraterrestrial life and UFOs as they are perceived by South Americans. Granchi believes some Catholic apparitions of the Virgin Mary may be UFO-related.

Barry Greenwood

A UFO researcher and author, over the years Barry Greenwood has focused on exposing concealed information regarding UFOs and extra-terrestrial life.

Dr. Steven Greer

Dr. Steven Greer is a researcher of extraterrestrial life, an ER Physician, and the international director of The Center for the Study of Extraterrestrial Intelligence (CSETI). Greer and CSETI, a nonprofit international scientific organization, are dedicated to establishing communication between humans and extraterrestrials. Their current method is to direct extraterrestrial craft into a landing area through light signaling. If this kind of communication is achieved, it would be a close encounter of the fifth kind or CE-5. Greer has been successful in vectoring alien craft to hover ten feet above the ground within only a few hundred feet of his location. Greer believes humanity will soon evolve from national societies into a global one.

Dr. Richard Haines

An aerospace engineer and UFO researcher, over the past forty years, Dr. Haines has independently amassed the world's largest archive of pilot encounters with UFOs.

Richard Hall

He is a UFO researcher, historian, and author and is chairman of the Fund for UFO Research (FUFOR). He also organized and contributed to "The Briefing Document on Unidentified Flying Objects: The Best Available Evidence," which was compiled to provide world leaders with a factual perspective on the reality of the phenomenon. One of the top researchers worldwide, Hall believes humans are very poorly educated regarding the reality, evidence, and history of the UFO phenomenon. He has gravitated from being an ardent critic of the government cover-up to being more sympathetic to their complex logistical position in dealing with the extraterrestrial issue. Richard Hall is often interviewed for television documentaries.

Robert Hastings

For twenty-five years, Hastings, a UFO researcher, has observed the American military and civilian interaction with the UFO phenomenon. He has observed that there is increased UFO interest in nuclear missile bases.

Cynthia Hind

A MUFON investigator in Africa, Cynthia Hind was the leading investigator of the Ruwa, Zimbabwe encounter between an occupied alien craft and the schoolchildren of the Arial School.

Budd Hopkins

Mr. Hopkins is a top researcher of the alien abduction experience and the founder of The Intruders Foundation. Among his most notable case studies is that of the Copley Woods incident where an Indiana family experienced a thirty-year multi-generational alien abduction experience. After a three-year study of this case Hopkins concluded that the extraterrestrial agenda is to create alien–human hybrids. Hopkins has conducted numerous surveys to determine the extent of worldwide alien abduction involvement. A 1992 Roper Poll put the United States figure at 3.7 million. Hopkins is interviewed often for documentaries.

J. Allen Hynek

Now deceased, Dr. Hynek was formerly an astronomer at Ohio State University who became an Air Force UFO investigator who worked with Project Blue Book in 1948. He developed the categories of close encounters of the first through fifth kinds. Dr. Hynek eventually became dissenchanted with Blue Book because of its decietful intent, and he ultimately revealed his belief in the reality of both UFO's and the military cover-up.

Philip Imbrogno

UFO researcher Philip Imbrogno investigated the Hudson Valley sightings from 1983 through 1988. J. Allen Hynek and Imbrogno published a book covering the events.

George Knapp

A UFO researcher and a TV reporter for KLAS-TV, Las Vegas, Mr. Knapp became very active in UFO investigations in the 1980s with an ongoing probe into Area 51 that climaxed with the 1987 interview of Robert Lazar, who allegedly reverse-engineered alien discs at S-4. Knapp also investigated the Height 611 crash in Siberia. He is often interviewed for documentaries.

Dr. William C. Levengood

A biophysicist, Dr. Levengood has worked as a serologist on crop circles worldwide. His theory of crop circle formation centers on a plasma vortex that originates in the ionosphere and is formed by superheated ions that are a form of highly active swirling microwave energy. Evidence of this effect is found in the plant nodes of crop circle wheat, which is blown out from being superheated on the inside. Dr. Levengood's field research methodology is being implemented by other researchers around the world.

Michael Lindeman

Editor of CNI News and a UFO researcher, Michael Lindeman is often interviewed for television documentaries.

Dr. Bruce Maccabee

Dr. Bruce Maccabee is an optical physicist and an expert in photo analysis. He is a research physicist under contract with the United States Navy and is director of the Maryland Chapter of MUFON. Dr. Maccabee has authenticated most of the Gulf Breeze UFO photography and is highly regarded as a video analyst. He believes UFOs are real, and that Earth is being visited.

John E. Mack

Dr. Mack is a Harvard psychiatrist, a Pulitzer Prize recipient, and the founder of The Program for Extraordinary Experience and Research (PEER). John Mack is one of the most highly respected alien abduction researchers in the world. He believes it is a genuine phenomenon and is producing a documentary on the 1994 event in Ruwa, Zimbabwe at the Arial School. He also co-chaired the MIT Conference on the abduction phenomenon. John's book *Abduction* was a best-seller.

Jaime Mausson

A UFO researcher and a TV journalist in Mexico City, Mexico, Mr. Mausson anchors his own weekly television program, the Mexican version of *60 Minutes*. He has documented what many regard as the largest UFO mass sighting in history, which began with the last solar eclipse of the century in 1991. Thousands of videos have poured into him over the years. Most have been authenticated by experts.

Dr. Thomas R. McDonough

He is the SETI coordinator of the Planetary Society, a quintessential skeptic who constantly points out natural, earthly, or human explanations for extraterrestrial visitation.

Christopher O'Brien

Mr. O'Brien leads UFO research in the very active, very mysterious San Luis Valley region of Colorado. He is particularly knowledgeable reguarding the twelve thousand documented cattle mutilation cases.

Robert Oechsler

A NASA mission specialist from 1974 to 1977 and a UFO researcher, Robert Oechsler is a meticulous investigator who understands the importance of details, such as those regarding Robert Lazar's employment at Area 51. Oechsler has been interviewed numerous times for television documentaries.

Vitario Paccaccini

The leading investigator of the 1996 UFO crash in Varginha, Brazil, Paccaccini mapped out the series of events that included recovered live aliens, numerous eyewitness accounts, and a Brazilian military cover-up complete with United States intelligence participation.

Nick Pope

Nick Pope was a British Ministry of Defense investigator from 1985 to 1988 and is a UFO researcher. Once a die-hard skeptic, Nick Pope quickly became a believer during his three-year career with the Ministry of Defense where he had access to all of the UFO case files. Pope has appeared on several documentaries.

Professor Michael Persinger

A neural psychologist at Laurentian University, Sudbury, Ontario, Canada, Dr. Persinger is well known for his human-based approach to the unexplained. For example, he attributes sightings of "Earth lights" and "luminous phenomena" to natural Earth-based occurrences. He attributes alien abductions to neural activity.

Dr. Yulii Platov

He is the chairman of the Commission on UFOs of the Academy of Sciences in Russia.

David E. Pritchard

An MIT, prize-winning physicist, Dr Pritchard co-chaired the MIT conference on the alien abduction phenomenon. Dr. Pritchard is one of the most highly esteemed minds in the world regarding the laws of physics. He bases his theories regarding extraterrestrial life on the current Earth-known laws of physics.

Kevin Randle

A former air force captain currently in the air force reserve, Kevin Randle is one of the most energetic UFO investigators in the world. He spent six years investigating the Roswell incident and is absolutely certain it involved the crash of an alien spacecraft. He believes that the government is not only concealing UFO evidence, but is propagating disinformation. Randle is one of the most frequently interviewed UFO experts on TV documentaries.

Malcolm Robinson

Malcolm Robinson is the founder of Strange Phenomena Investigations, Scotland. Robinson investigated the UFO abduction case of Garry Wood and Colin Wright.

Mark Rodeghier

He is a Twenty-two-year veteran UFO researcher and is head of The Center for UFO Studies (CUFOS). Based on overwhelming evidence Rodeghier believes the hard-core scientific community is neglecting UFOs as a genuine phenomenon.

Jeff Sainio

A professional video and photo analyst for MUFON, he performs international video and photo analysis for MUFON and other clientele. Mr. Sainio has authenticated many Gulf Breeze, Florida videos and still photographs He has worked extensively with *Sightings*.

John Saliba, Ph.D.

A professor of comparative religion at the University of Detroit, Dr. Saliba is an authority on the religious implications of the extraterrestrial phenomenon.

Derrell Sims and Dr. Roger Leir

Derrell Sims and Dr. Roger Leir are alien abduction researchers specializing in implants research. Sims and Leir have retrieved several suspected alien implants from abductees. Derrell Sims possesses many implants and continues to work with science labs around the world in testing the objects for extraterrestrial origin.

Clifford Stone

A UFO historian in Peru, Stone has researched UFO events around the world, but is an authority on the relationship of the Nazca lines to ufology.

Chris Styles

A UFO investigator in Shag Harbor, Nova Scotia, Chris Styles thoroughly investigated the UFO crash into Shag Harbor. He has uncovered hundreds of pages of Canadian military documents through the Canadian version of the Freedom of Information Act, that indicate a genuine UFO encounter.

Professor Michael Swords

He is a professor of natural sciences at Western Michigan University and is the editor of *The Journal of UFO Studies*.

Franklin Wilks

Franklin Wilks is a hypnotherapist and UFO Researcher in Australia.

Recommended Television Programs and Networks

Please consult the Directory of Television Networks in the back of the book for scheduling information and availability of home videos:

A Star is Born, Solar Empire, 1997, 60 minutes
on The Learning Channel
air dates: 12/12/97

"Alien Abduction, A Skeptical Inquiry," 1997, 60 minutes
on The Discovery Channel
air dates: 11/28/97

"Alien Abductions", *The Unexplained,* 1997, 60 minutes
on The Arts & Entertainment Network
air dates: 09/06/98

Alien Abductions/Implants, *Hard Copy,* 1998, 3 minutes
air dates: 07/17/98

Alien Encounter, 1997, 60 minutes
on The Learning Channel
air dates: 01/23/98, 03/26/98, 07/30/98, 08/02/98

"Alien Secrets: Area 51," 1996 120 minutes
on The Learning Channel
air dates: 12/08/97, 12/08/97, 01/19/98, 04/28/98, 05/03/98, 07/16/98

"Aliens, Are We Alone?" 120 minutes
on The Learning Channel
air dates: 07/19/98

Aliens, Future Fantastic, 1996, 60 minutes
on The Learning Channel
air dates: 03/24/97, 01/23/98, 07/19/98

Aliens Invade Hollywood, 60 minutes
on The Learning Channel
air dates: 03/24/97, 01/22/98

Alien Neighbors, Solar Empire, 1997, 60 minutes
on The Learning Channel
air dates: 12/12/97

"Aliens: Where Are They?", Science of the Impossible, 60 minutes
on The Discovery Channel
air dates: 07/13/98

Allagash, *Unsolved Mysteries,* 1994, 23 minutes
on Lifetime
air dates: 12/04/97

Anatomy of an Alien, 60 minutes
on The Discovery Channel
air dates: 02/06/98

"Ancient Aliens," *In Search of History,* 1997, 60 minutes
on The History Channel
air dates: 03/03/98, 06/17/98

"Are Aliens Trying to Contact Us?," *Arthur C. Clarke's Mysterious Universe,* 1994, 30 minutes
on The Discovery Channel
air dates: 10/24/98, 07/26/98, 01/17/98

"Area 51: The Real Story," 1997, 60 minutes
on The Discovery Channel
air dates: 08/12/98

Belgium UFO Sightings, *Unsolved Mysteries*, 21 minutes
on Lifetime
air dates: 06/17/98

"Black Holes: the Ultimate Abyss," 60 minutes
on The Discovery Channel
air dates: 03/29/98

Case of the U.F.O.s, 1982, 60 minutes
on The Learning Channel
air dates: 03/25/98, 01/24/98, 05/01/98

Close Encounters, *The Unexplained,* 1998, 60 minutes
on The Arts & Entertainment Network
air dates: 07/09/98

Close Encounters of the Fifth Kind, 60 minutes
on The Learning Channel
air dates: 03/27/97, 01/24/98

Crop Circles, *Arthur C. Clarke's Mysterious Universe,* 1994, 30 minutes
on The Discovery Channel
air dates: 03/14/98, 07/12/98

Crop Circles, *Unsolved Mysteries,* 1990, 15 minutes
on Lifetime
air dates: 02/03/98

Discover Magazine, 1996, 60 minutes
on The Discovery Channel
air dates: 12/27/97

E.T. Please Phone Earth, 1992, 60 minutes
on The Learning Channel
air dates: 03/26/98, 01/24/98

Extraterrestrials, *A&E Classroom,* 1997, 40 minutes
on The Arts & Entertainment Network
air dates: 04/09/98

Extraterrestrial Exorcism, *Strange Universe,* 12 minutes
on UPN
air dates: 02/26/98

Extraterrestrial Life, *The Unexplained*, 1997, 60 minutes
on The Arts & Entertainment Network
air dates: 02/01/98, 10/04/98

Flight 19, *Unsolved Mysteries*, 1990, 25 minutes
on Lifetime
air dates: 07/30/98

"Flightpaths to the Gods," *The Unexplained*, 1997, 60 minutes
on Arts & Entertainment Network
air dates: 06/11/98

Guardian, *Unsolved Mysteries*, 15 minutes
on Lifetime
air dates: 06/22/98

Healing Aliens, *Unsolved Mysteries*, 3 minutes
on Lifetime
air dates: 03/26/98

"Hubble: *Secrets from Space*," 1997, 60 minutes
on The Discovery Channel
air dates: 05/01/98, 05/02/98

Hudson Valley UFO, *Unsolved Mysteries*, 17 minutes
on Lifetime
air dates: 10/01/98

Incredible Shrinking Planet, Future Fantastic, 1996, 60 minutes
on The Learning Channel
air dates: 12/16/97, 07/19/98

Inside Area 51, 1997, 60 minutes
on The Discovery Channel
air dates: 12/21/97

Men in Black, *Unsolved Mysteries*, 1996, 8 minutes
on Lifetime
air dates: 05/26/98, 03/25/98

Mexico UFO's, *Unsolved Mysteries*, 1995, 8 minutes
on Lifetime
air dates: 09/15/98

Missing Time, *Unsolved Mysteries,* 20 minutes
on Lifetime
air dates: 10/07/98

Mysterious Forces Beyond, 1994, 30 minutes
on The Learning Channel
air dates: 03/28/97

Mysteries of Alien Beings, *Unsolved Mysteries,* 1994, 16 minutes
on Lifetime
air dates: 12/03/97, 12/04/97, 07/24/98

"Mysteries of Alien Beings," *Unsolved Mysteries,* 1994, 60 minutes
on Lifetime
air dates: 08/11/98

"Mystery of the Crop Circles," *Science Mysteries* 1996, 60 minutes
on The Discovery Channel
air dates: 07/12/98

"Mysteries of the Universe," A Science Odyssey, 120 minutes
on The Public Broadcasting System
air dates: 01/12/98

New Aircraft, *Unsolved Mysteries,* 7 minutes
on Lifetime
air dates: 06/27/98

"On Jupiter...," *Science Mysteries,* 1996, 60 minutes
on The Discovery Channel
air dates: 03/15/98

Overlords of the UFO, 1976, 120 minutes
on Turner Network Television
air dates: 09/13/98

"*Oz Encounters,* UFOs in Australia" 60 minutes
on The Discovery Channel
air dates: 09/27/98

"Phantom Lights," *Strange but True?* 1996, 30 minutes
on The Discovery Channel
air dates: 05/24/98

"RAF Woodbridge," *Strange but True?* 1997, 30 minutes
on The Discovery Channel
air dates: 01/11/98, 11/05/98

"Roswell," *History Undercover*, 1997, 60 minutes
on The History Channel
air dates: 06/04/98

Roswell, *Unsolved Mysteries*, 26 minutes
on Lifetime
air dates: 08/11/98

Sightings, Series First Aired 1991, Went Into Syndication 1994
on The Sci-Fi Channel
air dates: 1991 through 1998

Space Planes and The Future of Space Travel, 1997, 60 minutes
on The Learning Channel
air dates: 03/23/98

Space Trek, Solar Empire, 1997, 60 minutes
on The Learning Channel
air date; 12/12/97

Spaceships and Aliens, The Sci-Fi Files, 1997, 60 minutes
on The Learning Channel
air dates: 04/26/98, 05/02/98

"Stargazers," *Assignment Discovery*, 1994, 30 minutes
on The Discovery Channel
air dates: 10/21/98

Strange Beings & UFO's, Mysteries of the Unexplained, 1995, 60
minutes
on The Discovery Channel
air dates: 06/18/98

Supernatural Beings, *Unsolved Mysteries*, 8 minutes
on Lifetime
air dates; 04/29/98

The Edges of Darkness, Solar Empire, 1997, 60 minutes
on The Learning Channel
air dates: 02/27/98

"The Giants of Easter Island," *Arthur C. Clarke's Mysterious Universe,*
1994, 30 minutes
on The Discovery Channel
air dates: 10/31/98

"The Quest: Is Anyone Out There?," 1996, 30 minutes
on The Learning Channel
air dates: 03/28/97

The Roswell Incident, 1995, 60 minutes
on The Learning Channel
air dates: 12/08/97, 01/18/98, 04/30/98

The Secret KGB UFO Files, 1998, 90 minutes
on Turner Network Television
air dates: 09/13/98

"The UFO Cover-Up?, Live from Area 51," A TNT Larry King Special,
1994, 120 minutes
on Turner Network Television
air dates: 09/13/98

"UFO Cover Up? Live," 1988, 120 minutes
on WGN-TV Chicago
air dates: Fall 1988

"UFO Cults," *The Unexplained,* 1997, 60 minutes
on The Arts & Entertainment Network
air dates: 08/23/98

"UFO Deep Secrets," 1966, 60 minutes
on The Discovery Channel
air dates: 01/04/98, 02/28/98, 07/03/98, 08/02/98

UFO Encounter, *Unsolved Mysteries,* 1992, 13 minutes
on Lifetime
air dates: 08/19/98

UFO Experience, *Unsolved Mysteries,* 7 minutes
on Lifetime
air dates: 05/27/98

UFO Footage/Implants, *Beyond Bizarre,* 1998, 20 minutes
on The Discovery Channel
air dates: 06/02/98

"UFO Great Balls of Light," 1996, 60 minutes
on The Discovery Channel
air dates: 01/23/98, 02/28/98

"UFO Reason To Believe," 1996, 60 minutes
on The Discovery Channel
air dates: 12/08/97, 01/04/98, 05/09/98

"UFOs II: Have We Been Visited?," 1997, 120 minutes
on The Arts & Entertainment Network
air dates: 02/22/98, 07/19/98

UFOs Above and Beyond, 1996, 60 minutes
on The Learning Channel
air dates: 01/21/98, 07/16/98

UFOs & Alien Encounters, 1996, 60 minutes
on The Learning Channel
air dates: 03/25/97, 05/27/98, 01/21/98, 08/12/98

UFOs and Close Encounters, 1995, 60 minutes
on The Learning Channel
air dates: 03/28/97, 01/24/98, 05/01/98

"UFO's and Pilots," *Strange but True?,* 1997, 30 minutes
on The Discovery Channel
air dates: 03/26/98

"U.F.O.s," *Arthur C. Clarke's Mysterious World,* 1980, 30 minutes
on The Discovery Channel
air dates: 05/24/98

"UFO," *Science Frontiers,* 1994, 60 minutes
on The Learning Channel
air dates: 03/25/97, 01/22/98, 07/31/98, 08/02/98

UFO Sightings, *Unsolved Mysteries,* 8 minutes
on Lifetime
air dates: 09/21/98

"UFO's Over Phoenix, Anatomy of a Sighting," 1997, 60 minutes
on The Discovery Channel
air dates: 03/29/98

UFO Photographs, *Unsolved Mysteries,* 10 minutes
on Lifetime
air dates: 06/22/98

"*UFO's,* Stories of Abductions," 1996, 120 minutes
on The Learning Channel
air dates: 07/26/98, 10/23/98

"*UFOs:* The First Encounters," 1996, 60 minutes
on The Arts & Entertainment Network
air dates: 07/19/98

"*UFO* Uncovering The Evidence," 1996, 60 minutes
on The Discovery Channel
air dates: 12/30/97, 01/04/98, 06/27/98

Unidentified Flying Objects, 1956, 120 minutes
on Turner Network Television
air dates: 09/13/98

Universe, 3 minutes
on CNN Headline News
air dates: 01/11/98

Universe Dust, 2 minutes
on CNN Headline News
air dates: 01/09/98

We are Not Alone, *Alien Hunters,* 1997, 60 minutes
on The Learning Channel
air dates: 01/19/98, 04/29/98, 05/03/98, 07/19/98, 07/28/98,
08/02/98

We are Not Alone, *Sky Watchers,* 1997, 60 minutes
on The Learning Channel
air dates: 01/18/98, 04/29/98, 05/03/98, 07/19/98, 07/29/98,
08/02/98

We are Not Alone, *Space Voyagers,* 1998, 60 minutes
on The Learning Channel
air dates: 01/19/98, 04/30/98, 05/03/98, 07/27/98, 08/02/98

Where Are All the UFO's?, 1996, 120 minutes
on The Arts & Entertainment Network
air dates: 02/22/98

Wytheville, VA, *Unsolved Mysteries*, 1992, 20 minutes
on Lifetime
air dates: 06/30/98

Recommended Books

This list has been compiled to give the reader a comprehensive perspective of the entire extraterrestrial phenomenon.

Abduction
by John E. Mack

Above Top-Secret
by Timothy Good

A History of UFO Crashes
by Kevin Randle

Alien Agenda
by Jim Marrs

Alien Identities
by Richard C. Thompson

The Allagash Abductions: Undeniable Evidence of Alien Interventions
by Raymond E. Fowler

Area 51: The Dreamland Chronicles
by David Darlington

Breakthrough
by Whitley Strieber

The Cash-Landrum Incident
by John F. Schuessler

Chariots of the Gods
by Erich Von Daniken

Close Encounters of the Fourth Kind: Alien Abductions, UFOs, and the Conference at MIT
by C.D.B. Bryan

Communion: A True Story
by Whitley Strieber

Conspiracy of Silence
by Kevin Randle

The Encyclopedia of UFO
by Ronald D. Story

Fingerprints of the Gods
by Graham Hancock

Groom Lake Map Set
by Peter Merlin (available through Ufomind Bookstore on the Internet)

The Hudson Valley UFO Sightings
by Dr. J. Allen Hynek and Phillip J. Imbrogno

The Interrupted Journey: Two Lost Hours Aboard a Flying Saucer
by John G. Fuller

Intruders: The Incredible Visitations at Copley Woods
by Budd Hopkins

Missing Time
by Budd Hopkins

The Mysterious Valley
by Chris O'Brien

Open Skies, Closed Minds
by Nick Pope

Sightings
by Susan Michaels

Top-Secret/Majic
by Stanton Friedman

Travis Walton, Fire in the Sky: The Walton Experience
by Travis Walton

The Truth About the UFO Crash at Roswell
by Kevin Randle and Don Schmitt

The UFO Controversy in America
by David Jacobs

The UFO Coverup
by Barry Greenwood and Lawrence Fawcett

The UFO Encyclopedia, (3 vols.)
by Jerome Clark

The UFO Evidence
by Richard Hall

The UFO Experience: A Scientific Inquiry
by Dr. J. Allen Hynek

UFO Phenomena and the Behavioral Scientist
by Richard Haines

Visitors From Time
by Marc Davenport

Recommended Videotapes, Audio Tapes, and CD-ROMS

The Monuments of Mars (video)
The Terrestrial Connection: 800-641-7575

The UFO Report (video)
from *Sightings* or wherever videos are sold

Sightings: The UFO Encyclopedia (CD-ROM)
from Simon and Schuster Interactive
Obtain this CD-ROM from your bookstore or by inquiring at:
http://www.scifi.com/sightings

The Edwards Air Force Base Encounter (audio cassettes)
by Producer Sam Sherman
Obtain this audio tape series from your bookstore or by inquiring at:
http://www.scifi.com/sightings

The UFO Anthology (CD-ROM)
by Dreamland Interactive
http://4dreamland.com

UFOs: Down to Earth (video)
from The Discovery Channel: 800-615-4949

UFOs: The Best Evidence (video)
by George Knapp: Obtain this video by calling 702-227-1818 or at:
http://www.ufomind.com/catalog/subject/area51/doc

Recommended Internet Sites

Camelot Productions
The site of *The Magic of Our Universe*
http://www.camelotpublishing.com

CUFON (The Computer UFO Network)
http://www.cufon.org

Hubble Space Telescope Photographs of the Universe
http://antwrp.gsfc.nasa.gov/apod

Paranormal Phenomena Archive
Information reguarding extraterrestrial life
http://www.in-search-of.com

The Arts and Entertainment Network
http://www.AandE.com

The Black Vault
Created by eighteen-year-old John Greenewald, Jr., this site
includes over 6,000 pages of government documents obtained
through the Freedom of Information Act.
http://www.blackvault.com

The CNI News
A bi-monthly newsletter by UFO reseracher Michael Lindemann
http://www.cninews.com

The Discovery Channel
http://www.discovery.com

The History Channel
http://www.HistoryChannel.com

The Karinya Site
Information on crop circles and UFOs
http//www.kariyna.com

The Learning Channel
http://www.tlc.com

The McCoy-Goode case article and photographs, *The Houston
Chronicle*
http://www.houstonchronicle.com/voyager/ufo/encounter
good-mccoy.html

The S-4 Database
A comprehensive UFO data archive
http://area51.icom.net

The Sci-Fi Channel
Sightings available through the Dominion site, which can further
access all major paranormal links
http://www.scifi.com/sightings

The Ufomind Paranormal Index and Bookstore
A comprehensive source of books, videos, and CD Roms
http://www.ufomind.com/catalog

Unsolved Mysteries
http://www.unsolved.com

Your Public Broadcasting Station
http://www.pbs.org

Organizations Worldwide

There are currently over one hundred research organizations. The
following list includes many of those that are national and international
in scope, serious in purpose, and wide-ranging in their regard of UFO-
related subject matter. For the complete list refer to this site: http://
www.ufoinfo.com/organizations/org_usa.shtml

Abductees Anonymous
266 W. El Paso Avenue
Clovis, CA 93611-7119
http://www.cybergate.com/~ufonline

CAUS (Citizens Against UFO Secrecy)
P. O. Box 20351
Sedona, AZ 86341-0351
Phone: 612-431-2426
http://www.caus.org

CCCS (Centre for Crop Circle Studies)
P. O. Box 146
Guildford, Surrey
England GU25JY

CNACCS (Center for North American Crop Circle Studies)
P. O. Box 4766
Lutherville, MD 21094
Phone: 410-628-1522
FAX: 410-628-1524

CPR-USA
Colin Andrews
P. O. Box 3378
Branford, CT 06405
Phone: 203-483-0822

CSETI (The Center for the Study of Extraterrestrial Intelligence)
P. O. Box 15401
Asheville, NC 28813
Phone: 704-274-5671
FAX: 704-274-6766
http://www.cseti.org

CUFOS (J. Allen Hynek Center for UFO Studies)
2457 W. Peterson Avenue
Chicago, IL 60659
Phone: 312-271-3611
FAX: 312-465-1898
http://www.cufos.org/indcx.html

FUFOR (Fund for UFO Research)
P. O. Box 277
Mount Rainier, MD 20712
Phone/FAX: 703-684-6032
http://www.fufor.org

ISUR (International Society for UFO Research)
P. O. Box 52491
Atlanta, GA 30355
http://www.isur.com

Intruders Foundation
P. O. Box 30233
New York, NY 10011
FAX: 212-352-1778
http://www.if.aic.com

MUFON (Mutual UFO Network)
103 Oldtowne Road
Segwin, TX 78155-4099
Phone: 512-379-9216
http://www.rutgers.edu/-mcgrew/MUFON

NAICCR (North American Institute for Crop Circle Research)
649 Silverstone Avenue
Winnipeg, Manitoba
Canada R3T 2V8

NSRC (National Sighting Research Center)
Bob Sylvester (Co-Director)
P. O. Box 76
Emerson, NJ 07630

National UFO Reporting Center
P. O. Box 45623
University Station
Seattle, WA 98145
UFO hotline: 206-722-3000
Contact Person: Peter Davenport
http://www.ufocenter.com

Project SIGN Research Center
P.O. Box 8552
Albuqerque, NM 87198
http://www.projectsign.com

Ufology Research of Manitoba
Box 1918
Winnipeg, Manitoba
Canada R3C3R2
Contact: Chris Rutkowski

UFO Reporting and Information
P. O. Box 832
Mercer Island, WA 98040, USA
Voice Line: 206-721-5035

Endnotes

1 "*UFOs*: The First Encounters," prod. Lionel Friedberg, The Arts & Entertainment Network, 19 July 1998.

2 "*UFO's*: Above and Beyond," narr. James Doohan, writ. Chris Wyatt, prod. John Goodwin, The Learning Channel, 16 July 1998.

3 "The UFO Report," *Sightings*, narr. Tim White, writ. Susan Michaels, prod. Henry Winkler and Ann Daniel, The Sci-Fi Channel, 4 Jan. 1998.

4 "*UFOs*: The First Encounters," 19 July 1998.

5 "*UFOs*: The First Encounters," 19 July 1998.

6 "UFOs: Japan," *Sightings*, nar. Tim White, writ. Susan Michaels, prod Henry Winkler and Ann Daniel, The Sci-Fi Channel, 19 March 1998.

7 "*UFOs*: The First Encounters," 19 July 1998.

8 "*UFOs*: The First Encounters," 19 July 1998.

9 "*UFOs*: The First Encounters," 19 July 1998.

10 "*UFOs*: The First Encounters," 19 July 1998.

11 "UFOs: Japan," *Sightings*, 19 March 1998.

12 "*UFO's*: Above and Beyond," 16 July 1998.

13 "The UFO Report," *Sightings*, 4 Jan. 1998.

14 "*UFOs*: The First Encounters," 19 July 1998.

15 "UFOs: Japan," *Sightings*, 19 March 1998.

16 "*UFOs*: The First Encounters," 19 July 1998.

17 "*UFO's*: Above and Beyond," 16 July 1998.

18 "*UFOs*: The First Encounters," 19 July 1998.

19 "Mysteries of Alien Beings," *Unsolved Mysteries*, narr. Robert Stack, writ. Raymond Bridgers and Terry Dunn Muerer, prod. Terry Dunn Muerer and John Cosgrove, Lifetime, 4 Dec. 1997.

20 "*UFOs*: The 100 Year Cover-up," *Sightings*, In Depth and Beyond, narr. Tim White, writ. Susan Michaels, prod. Henry Winkler and Ann Daniel, 1 Jan. 1998.

21 "*UFOs*: The 100 Year Cover-up," *Sightings*, 1 Jan. 1998.

22 "Tunguska," *Sightings*, narr. Tim White, writ. Susan Michaels, prod. Henry Winkler and Ann Daniel, The Sci-Fi Channel, 17 May 1998.

23 "*UFOs*: The 100 Year Cover-up," *Sightings*, 1 Jan. 1998.

24 "*UFOs*: The 100 Year Cover-up," *Sightings*, 1 Jan. 1998.

25 "*UFO's*: Above and Beyond," 16 July 1998.

26 Z., Ryan, *Atomic Bomb*, <http://darter.ocps.k12.fl.us/classroom/who/ darter1/ atomic.htm>, 22 Nov. 1998.

27 "*Trinity and Beyond*: The Atom Bomb Movie," narr. William Shatner, prod. Peter Kuran and Alan Munro, The Learning Channel, 29 March 1998.

[28] Luck, Steve, ed. *Oxford Family Encyclopedia*, 1st edition, New York, New York: Oxford University Press, Inc. 1997. (320)

[29] Luck, Steve, ed. *Oxford Family Encyclopedia*, 1997. (467)

[30] *Webster's Encyclopedic Unabridged Dictionary of the English Language*, Deluxe ed. rev. New York, New York: Gramercy Books, a Division of Random House Publications, Inc. 1996. (206)

[31] Luck, Steve, ed. *Oxford Family Encyclopedia*, 1997. (84)

[32] "*UFO's II* Have We Been Visited?" narr. Michael Dorn, prod. Lisa Bourgoujian, The Arts & Entertainment Network, 22 Feb. 1998.

[33] "*UFO's*: Above and Beyond," 16 July 1998.

[34] "*UFO's*: Above and Beyond," 16 July 1998.

[35] "*UFO* Reason to Believe," narr. Paul Anthony, prod. Jeremy Evans, The Discovery Channel, 8 Dec. 1997.

[36] "*UFO's*: Above and Beyond," 16 July 1998.

[37] *Sightings*, narr. Tim White, writ. Susan Michaels, prod. Henry Winkler and Ann Daniel, The Sci-Fi Channel, 10 March 1998.

[38] "Mantell Re-Examined," *Sightings*, narr. Tim White, writ. Susan Michaels, prod. Philip Davis, The Sci-Fi Channel, 30 March 1998.

[39] "*UFO's II* Have We Been Visited?" 22 Feb. 1998.

[40] "*UFO's II* Have We Been Visited?" 22 Feb. 1998.

[41] *Atomic Archive*, AJ Software & Multimedia, <http://www.atomicarchive.com/Timeline/Time1940.html>, 22 Nov. 1998.

[42] "*UFO's*: Above and Beyond," 16 July 1998.

[43] "*UFO's II* Have We Been Visited?" 22 Feb. 1998.

[44] "Mysteries of Alien Beings," *Unsolved Mysteries*, 4 Dec. 1998.

[45] "*UFO's II* Have We Been Visited?" 22 Feb. 1998.

[46] "*The UFO Cover-Up?* Live from Area 51", A TNT Larry King Special, narr. Larry King, writ. Tom Farmer, prod. Carrie Stevenson, TNT, 13 Sept. 1998.

[47] "Mysteries of Alien Beings," *Unsolved Mysteries*, 4 Dec. 1997.

[48] "UFOs: Japan," *Sightings*, 19 March 1998.

[49] "UFOs: Japan," *Sightings*, 19 March 1998.

[50] "*UFO's*: Above and Beyond," 16 July 1998.

[51] "UFOs: Japan," *Sightings*, 19 March 1998.

[52] "UFOs: Japan," *Sightings*, 19 March 1998.

[53] Luck, Steve, ed. *Oxford Family Encyclopedia*, 1997. (332)

[54] "UFOs Over FDR," *Sightings*, narr. Tim White, writ. Susan Michaels, prod. Henry Winkler and Ann Daniel, The Sci-Fi Channel, 3 June 1998.

[55] "*UFO's*: Above and Beyond," 16 July 1998.

[56] "*UFO's II* Have We Been Visited?" 22 Feb. 1998.

[57] "*The UFO Cover-Up?* Live from Area 51", A TNT Larry King Special, 13 Sept. 1998.

[58] "*UFO* Reason to Believe," 8 Dec. 1997.

[59] "Trapped in Time," *Sightings*, narr. Tim White, writ. Susan Michaels, prod. Lindsey Paddor, The Sci-Fi Channel, 15 March 1998.

[60] "*UFO's II* Have We Been Visited?" 22 Feb. 1998.

[61] "UFOs: Japan," *Sightings*, 19 March 1998.

[62] "Socorro, New Mexico, UFO Investigation," *Sightings*, In the News, narr. Tim White, writ. Susan Michaels, prod. Rob Morhaim, The Sci-Fi Channel, 25 March 1998.

[63] "Deliberate Deception," *Sightings*, narr. Tim White, writ. Susan Michaels, prod. Philip Davis, The Sci-Fi Channel, 25 March 1998.

[64] "UFOs: Japan," *Sightings*, 19 March 1998.

[65] "The UFO Report," *Sightings*, 4 Jan. 1998.

[66] "UFOs: Japan," *Sightings*, 19 March 1998.

[67] "UFOs: Japan," *Sightings*, 19 March 1998.

[68] "UFOs: Japan," *Sightings*, 19 March 1998.

[69] "The UFO Report," *Sightings*, 4 Jan. 1998.

[70] "Top Secret Projects," *Sightings*, narr. Tim White, writ. Susan Michaels, prod. Henry Winkler and Ann Daniels, The Sci-Fi Channel, 3 Feb. 1998.

[71] *Unsolved Mysteries*, The Unexplained, narr. Robert Stack, writ. Raymond Bridgers and Terry Dunn Muerer, prod. Terry Dunn Muerer and John Cosgrove, Lifetime, 19 Aug. 1998.

[72] "*UFO's II* Have We Been Visited?" 22 Feb. 1998.

[73] "Shag Harbor Investigation," *Sightings*, narr. Tim White, writ. Susan Michaels, prod. Philip Davis, The Sci-Fi Channel, 3 March 1998.

[74] *Sightings*, narr. Tim White, writ. Susan Michaels, prod. Henry Winkler and Ann Daniel, The Sci-Fi Channel, 8 Feb. 1998.

[75] "*UFO's II* Have We Been Visited?" 22 Feb. 1998.

[76] "Silent Intruder," *Sightings*, narr. Tim White, writ. Susan Michaels, prod. Philip Davis, The Sci-Fi Channel, 25 March 1998.

[77] "UFO Confrontation: Mansfield," *Sightings*, narr. Tim White, writ. Susan Michaels, prod. Philip Davis, The Sci-Fi Channel, 14 Jan. 1998.

[78] *Unsolved Mysteries*, The Unexplained, narr. Robert Stack, writ. Raymond Bridgers and Terry Dunn Muerer, prod. Terry Dunn Muerer and John Cosgrove, Lifetime, 19 June 1998.

[79] "The UFO Report," *Sightings*, 4 Jan. 1998.

[80] "*UFO's*: Above and Beyond," 16 July 1998.

[81] "Clear Intent," *Sightings*, narr. Tim White, writ. Susan Michaels, prod. Philip Davis, The Sci-Fi Channel, 5 Feb. 1998.

[82] "*UFO* Great Balls of Light," prod. Jeremy Evans, The Discovery Channel, 23 Jan. 1998.

[83] "*UFO's*: Above and Beyond," 16 July 1998.

[84] "The Secrets of Alien Abduction," *Sightings*, In Depth and Beyond, narr. Tim White, writ. Susan Michaels, prod. Henry Winkler and Ann Daniel, The Sci-Fi Channel, 14 March 1998.

[85] "*UFO's II* Have We Been Visited?" 22 Feb. 1998.

[86] "The Secrets of Alien Abduction," *Sightings*, 14 March 1998.

[87] "UFO Confrontation: Iran," *Sightings*, narr. Tim White, writ. Susan Michaels, prod. Philip Davis, The Sci-Fi Channel, 19 Feb. 1998.

[88] "*UFO* Reason to Believe," 8 Dec. 1997.

[89] "Photography: The Technology of photography: SPECIAL PHOTOSENSI-TIVE SYSTEMS: Electronic photography." *Britannica Online*. <http://www.eb.com:180/cgi-bin/g? DocF=macro/5005/2/61.html>Accessed 07 October 1998.

[90] "*UFO's:* Above and Beyond," 16 July 1998.

[91] "Without a Trace," *Sightings*, narr. Tim White, writ. Susan Michaels, prod. John Bayliss and Ruth Rafidi, The Sci-Fi Channel, 8 March 1998.

[92] "*Oz Encounters*, UFOs in Australia," narr. Martin Sacks, writ. Debbie Byrne, prod. Debbie Byrne, The Discovery Channel, 27 Sept. 1998.

[93] "UFO Confrontation: Mansfield," *Sightings*, 14 Jan. 1998.

[94] "*UFO* Great Balls of Light," 23 Jan. 1998.

[95] "*UFO's II* Have We Been Visited?" 22 Feb. 1998.

[96] *Discovery News*, ABC News, 3 July 1998.

[97] "Mysteries of Alien Beings," *Unsolved Mysteries*, 4 Dec. 1997.

[98] "Extraterrestrial Life," *The Unexplained*, narr. Norm Woodel, writ. Jamie Ceaser and Rollie Hudson, prod. Jamie Ceaser, The Arts & Entertainment Network, 9 March, 1998.

[99] "Hudson Valley UFO Sighting," *Unsolved Mysteries*, The Unexplained, narr. Robert Stack, writ. Raymond Bridgers and Terry Dunn Muerer, prod. Terry Dunn Muerer and John Cosgrove, Lifetime, 1 Oct. 1998.

[100] *Alien Hunters*, We Are Not Alone, narr. Colin Stinton, prod. Sara Woodford, The Learning Channel, 3 May 1998.

[101] "*UFO* Deep Secrets," narr. Paul Anthony, prod. Jeremy Evans, The Discovery Channel, 4 Jan. 1998.

[102] "Whitley Strieber's Breakthrough," *Sightings*, narr. Tim White, writ. Susan Michael, The Sci-Fi Channel, 4 March 1998.

[103] "*UFO* Uncovering the Evidence," narr. Paul Anthony, prod. Jeremy Evans, The Discovery Channel, 4 Jan. 1998.

[104] "UFO Encounter: Shikmona," *Sightings*, narr. Tim White, writ. Susan Michaels, prod. Ruth Rafidi and Phillip Lapkin, The Sci-Fi Channel, 18 Feb. 1998.

[105] *Unsolved Mysteries*, The Unexplained, narr. Robert Stack, writ. Raymond Bridgers and Terry Dunn Muerer, prod. Terry Dunn Muerer and John Cosgrove, Lifetime, 3 June 1998.

[106] "*UFO* Reason to Believe," 8 Dec. 1997.

[107] *Sky Watchers*, We Are Not Alone, narr. Colin Stinton, prod. Sara Woodford, The Learning Channel, 3 May 1998.

[108] "*UFO* Deep Secrets," 4 Jan. 1998.

[109] "*UFO's*: Above and Beyond," 16 July 1998.

[110] *Unsolved Mysteries*, The Unexplained, narr. Robert Stack, writ. Raymond Bridgers and Terry Dunn Muerer, prod. Terry Dunn Muerer and John Cosgrove, Lifetime, 17 June 1998.

[111] <http://popularmechanics.com/popmech/sci/9706stmim.html>(Access date: 28 Aug. 1998).

[112] "Whitley Strieber's Breakthrough," *Sightings*, 4 March 1998.

[113] "Montreal Mass Sighting," *Sightings*, narr. Tim White, writ. Susan Michaels, prod. Henry Winkler and Ann Daniel, The Sci-Fi Channel, 15 Jan. 1998.

[114] "Avebury Mystery Lights," *Sightings*, narr. Tim White, writ. Susan Michaels, prod. Henry Winkler and Ann Daniel, The Sci-Fi Channel, 20 Jan. 1998.

[115] "*UFO's*: Above and Beyond," 16 July 1998.

[116] *Unsolved Mysteries*, The Unexplained, narr. Robert Stack, writ. Raymond Bridgers, prod. Cosgrove Meurer Productions, Lifetime, 15 Sept. 1998.

[117] "UFOs: Japan," *Sightings*, 19 March 1998.

[118] "Close Encounters of the Fourth Kind," *Sightings*, In the News, narr. Tim White, writ. Susan Michaels, prod. Rob Morhaim, The Sci-Fi Channel, 5 March 1998.

[119] "Mexico Mass Sightings," *Sightings*, Update, narr. Tim White, writ. Susan Michaels, prod. Henry Winkler and Ann Daniel, The Sci-Fi Channel, 2 Feb. 1998.

[120] *Unsolved Mysteries*, The Unexplained, 15 Sept. 1998.

[121] "Cluster UFO," *Sightings*, narr. Tim White, writ. Susan Michaels, prod. Philip Davis and Rob Sharkey, The Sci-Fi Channel, 17 March 1998.

[122] "S.E.T.I. Resurrected," *Sightings*, narr. Tim White, writ. Susan Michaels, prod. Henry Winkler and Ann Daniel, The Sci-Fi Channel, 18 May 1998.

[123] "Sightings On Line," *Sightings*, narr. Tim White, writ. Susan Michaels, prod. Henry Winkler and Ann Daniel, The Sci-Fi Channel, 2 March 1998.

[124] "UFO Contact: The Holyland," *Sightings*, narr. Tim White, writ. Susan Michaels, prod. Henry Winkler and Ann Daniel, The Sci-Fi Channel, 6 Feb. 1998.

[125] "*Oz Encounters*, UFOs in Australia," 27 Sept. 1998.

[126] *Unsolved Mysteries*, The Unexplained, 15 Sept. 1998.

[127] "Area 51, Nevada," *Sightings*, In The News, narr. Tim White, writ. Susan Michaels, prod. Henry Winkler and Ann Daniel, The Sci-Fi Channel, 18 Feb. 1998.

[128] "Gulf Breeze Encounters," *Sightings*, narr. Tim White, writ. Susan Michaels, prod. Henry Winkler and Ann Daniel, The Sci-Fi Channel, 10 May 1998.

[129] "Shag Harbor Investigation," *Sightings*, 3 March 1998.

[130] "Idaho UFO Flap," *Sightings*, 2 Feb. 1998.

[131] "New Mexico UFO Mystery," *Sightings*, narr. Tim White, writ. Susan Michaels, prod. Henry Winkler and Ann Daniel, The Sci-Fi Channel, 1 June 1998.

[132] "UFO Investigation," *Sightings*, narr. Tim White, writ. Susan Michaels, prod. Henry Winkler and Ann Daniel, The Sci-Fi Channel, 8 March 1998.

[133] "UFO Investigation," *Sightings*, 8 March 1998.

[134] "Ruwa Re-Examined," *Sightings*, narr. Tim White, writ. Susan Michaels, prod. Henry Winkler and Ann Daniel, The Sci-Fi Channel, 22 March 1998.

[135] *"The UFO Cover-Up?* Live from Area 51," A TNT Larry King Special, 13 Sept. 1998.

[136] *Sightings*, narr. Tim White, writ. Susan Michaels, prod. Henry Winkler and Ann Daniel, The Sci-Fi Channel, 15 March 1998.

[137] "Contact Israel," *Sightings*, In The News, narr. Tim White, writ. Susan Michaels, prod. Henry Winkler, The Sci-Fi Channel, 11 March 1998.

[138] "UFO Encounters: Shikmona," *Sightings*, narr. Tim White, writ. Susan Michaels, prod. Ruth Rafidi and Phillip Lapkin, The Sci-Fi Channel, 18 Feb. 1998.

[139] "UFO Encounter at 30,000 Feet," *Sightings*, narr. Tim White, writ. Susan Michaels, prod. Ann Daniel, The Sci-Fi Channel, 14 July 1998.

[140] "Winchester, England, Crop Circles," *Sightings*, In the News, narr. Tim White, writ. Susan Michaels, prod. Kim Steer, The Sci-Fi Channel, 4 March 1998.

[141] "The Watchers," *Sightings*, narr. Tim White, writ. Susan Michaels, prod. Kim Steer, The Sci-Fi Channel, 13 April 1998.

[142] "Colorado Cattle Mutations," *Sightings*, narr. Tim White, writ. Susan Michaels, prod. Kim Steer, The Sci-Fi Channel, 30 Dec. 1997.

[143] "Rachel, Nevada, Area 51," *Sightings*, In the News, narr. Tim White, writ. Susan Michaels, prod. Henry Winkler and Ann Daniel, The Sci-Fi Channel, 3 March 1998.

[144] "Cluster UFO," *Sightings*, 17 March 1998.

[145] "Rachel, Nevada, Area 51," *Sightings*, In The News, narr. Tim White, writ. Susan Michaels, prod. Henry Winkler and Ann Daniel, The Sci-Fi Channel, 4 March 1998.

[146] *"Oz Encounters,* UFOs in Australia," 27 Sept. 1998.

[147] "The Brazilian E.T. Case," *Sightings,* narr. Tim White, writ. Susan Michaels, prod. Philip Davis and Adam Stepan, The Sci-Fi Channel, 26 March 1998.

[148] "Men in Black," *Unsolved Mysteries,* The Unexplained, narr. Robert Stack, writ. Raymond Bridgers and Terry Dunn Muerer, prod. Terry Dunn Muerer and John Cosgrove, Lifetime, 25 March 1998.

[149] "Crop Circles," *Sightings,* Update, narr. Tim White, writ. Susan Michaels, prod. Henry Winkler and Ann Daniels, The Sci-Fi Channel, 29 March 1998.

[150] "Houston, Texas, UFOs," *Sightings,* In the News, narr. Tim White, writ. Susan Michael, prod. Henry Winkler and Ann Daniel, The Sci-Fi Channel, 28 April 1998.

[151] "New York, Marketing UFO," *Sightings,* In The News, narr. Tim White, writ. Susan Michael, prod. Henry Winkler and Ann Daniel, The Sci-Fi Channel, 11 March 1998.

[152] "UFOs: Japan," *Sightings,* 19 March 1998.

[153] *Oz Encounters,* 27 Sept. 1998.

[154] *"UFOs:* The 100 Year Cover-up," *Sightings,* 1 Jan. 1998.

[155] "Case Closed," *Sightings,* narr. Tim White, writ. Susan Michael, prod. Joyce Goldstein, The Sci-Fi Channel, 28 April 1998.

[156] *"UFOs:* The 100 Year Cover-up," *Sightings,* 1 Jan. 1998.

[157] *Discovery News,* ABC News, 3 July 1998.

[158] *"UFO*-Above Top Secret," dir. Yin Gazda, prod. Yin Gazda, Coriolis Films, 1991.

The Philadelphia
Experiment

The Philadelphia Experiment

Definition

The Philadelphia Experiment was an experiment allegedly conducted by the United States Navy in Philadelphia Naval Ship Yard on August 12, 1943. The purpose of the experiment was to render the *U.S.S. Eldridge*, a ship with full crew, radar invisible by manipulating the electric and magnetic fields surrounding the ship. Reportedly, the ship not only became radar invisible, but completely vanished for four hours. It reappeared in its previous physical position, but the physical effect on the crew members was devastating.

Statistics

- As of 1998 there were four books in print on the subject of The Philadelphia Experiment. One author is listed only as "Commander X" and the first books were published in the 1980s. This clandestine authorship along with the fact that the first books appeared forty years after an event of such significance may be an indication of intense deliberate government concealment. For a complete book list see resource section in this chapter (Numbers obtained from *R. R. Bowker's Books in Print*, the 1998 list).

- In 1997 there was around one half hour of combined documentary segments aired on the subject of The Philadelphia Experiment. In 1998 there were around one and one half hours of documentaries aired on the subject (Numbers derived from Gissen, Jay, ed. *The Cable Guide*, 1997, 1998).

- "Instead of merely becoming invisible from radar or even the naked eye, legend has it the *Eldridge* was actually transported through space and time" (*New Visions of the Future*, Ancient Prophecies III, 28 June 1998).

- "They have the technology today to move back and forth through the time continuum — both past and future. Yes, we can time travel today" (Strom, Andrew, International Lecturer and Author, Interview, *New Visions of the Future*, Ancient Prophecies III, 28 June 1998).

- "They do not want the public to know they've had access to time travel for over forty years" (Bielek, Al, Author, Interview, *New Visions of the Future*, Ancient Prophecies III, 28 June 1998).

Case History

So you thought time travel was impossible. Well, think again! The United States navy not only rendered a ship invisible to radar, they unintentionally made it vanish completely. Legend has it that on a clear, late summer day in 1943, navy officials looked on from two observer ships as the *U.S.S. Eldridge* began its ill-fated four-hour journey somewhere in time.

An Atlantic shipping lane was not a very healthy place to be during World War II. In the early 1940s, German U-boats were picking off merchant and supply ships faster than the navy could count. To the navy, a desperate situation required a desperate solution. They needed a way to make ships invisible to German radar. They had heard of promising new technology being developed at Princeton University and so turned for answers to the brilliant minds of Albert Einstein and Nikola Tesla who were working with that group.[1]

In the late 1930s, the Princeton scientists were successful in making small objects invisible by altering the electrical and magnetic energy fields surrounding the objects. Tesla's forte was electrical engineering. As pressure mounted with continued German victories in the Atlantic, the navy allegedly outfitted the *U.S.S. Eldridge* for a full-scale test.

The first test was conducted using dogs, cats, and other domestic animals. They were variously placed in metal cages throughout the ship, on and below deck. The switch was thrown and the electric and magnetic field generators were engaged, creating a massive surge of energy.

After the power was turned off, sailors began their inspection of the ship and its furry occupants. It is said they discovered a few problems. Some animals had radiation burns, while others had disappeared entirely. The navy reportedly proceeded forward with phase II regardless of the first run results. On August 12, 1943, the *U.S.S. Eldridge*, fully staffed, was plunged into the same experiment, known today as the Philadelphia Experiment or the Montauk Experiment.[2]

Initial results looked normal and favorable. The ship immediately became radar invisible. Then suddenly, in a great flash of light, the *U.S.S. Eldridge* with full complement vanished from Philadelphia Harbor. The ship was missing for four hours. It is said the ship was actually transported through time and space to its original position in the harbor. An inspection crew boarded the ship after it reappeared to document results. What they found was horrible beyond their wildest imaginations.

Crew members were wandering aimlessly in a hazy green mist. Many were very abnormal both mentally and physically. Most horribly, some men were actually fused with the bulkhead. Their bodies were sticking out of walls and steel decks. Some sailors reportedly walked into thin air and vanished forever.

The U. S. Navy officially denied the entire event, it is believed, for two reasons. First, it was impossible to even begin to explain what happened to family members of the crew, or to anyone else for that matter. Even today in 1998, most people can't conceive of such an event. Second, the experiment actually worked. Humans had actually conquered the boundaries of time and space. Testimonial evidence suggests that in 1943 the navy built the technology and proved that travel through time was possible. It occurred before many eyes aboard two observer ships, an aircraft carrier, and a commercial ship, the *S.S. Freoseth*.[3]

To this day, the navy continues to deny the possibility of time travel or that this event ever took place.

Prevailing Theories Regarding the Philadelphia Experiment are:

1. The *U.S.S. Eldridge* was shot through the space–time continuum and either went backward or forward in time.

2. The *U.S.S. Eldridge* appeared in Norfolk Harbor 275 miles away, then reappeared in Philadelphia Naval Ship Yard, which also indicates a space–time jump.

Beyond the Facts

Many implications come to mind with the possibility of travel through time and space. If in fact the Philadelphia Experiment did occur as evidence suggests, it becomes more acceptable for us to imagine how extraterrestrial beings have mastered electromagnetic or gravitational field manipulation for instantaneous transportation through time and space. This would solve problems of astronauts having to cope with G-forces and age deviation when traveling light-years from Earth. In fact, the term "light-year" would lose its importance because light speed would no longer be a barrier to space travel.

The green haze reportedly encountered on deck just after the *U.S.S. Eldridge* reappeared is reminiscent of other green hazes. Some UFO sightings, such as the Valentich case of 1978, as well as some Bermuda Triangle cases, such as the disappearance of Flight 19, have reported a similar green haze around the craft. Some UFOs have been seen enveloped in multicolored haze or clouds. Could there be a connection? If electromagnetic field manipulation is a common link in these cases, could this haze be a clue to some form of alien propulsion technology?

If, as the evidence suggests, the U.S. government possessed knowledge of time travel back in 1943, we can only imagine how they might have developed and refined this technology some fifty-five years later, perhaps somewhere in the Nevada desert. After all, this was the U.S. Navy's first stab at stealth technology.

To supplement television documentary research for this segment, the author attempted to locate the only book available on the subject in a large university library. The book was listed as "missing." The author then checked the library of his alma mater, which houses seven million volumes. The book was again listed as "missing."

Certain Area 51 employer tax forms indicate that "MAJIC" or MJ-12, the purported covert agency currently researching UFO technology is housed in the Department Of Naval Intelligence. The Philadelphia Experiment was allegedly conducted by the Department of Naval Intelligence. Coincidence? Could the Philadelphia Experiment have laid the groundwork for research at Area 51, or S-4?

Resources for Further Investigation
Recommended Television Progams and Networks

Please consult the Directory of Television Networks in the back of the book for scheduling information and availability of home videos:

"Flight 19:" *Sightings*, 5 minutes
on The Sci-Fi Channel
air dates: 08/02/98, 09/27/98

"Strange Disappearances," *The Unexplained*, 1998, 60 minutes
on The Arts & Entertainment Network
air dates: 08/20/98

New Visions of the Future, Ancient Prophecies III, 1995, 120 minutes
on The Learning Channel
air dates: 06/28/98

The Bermuda Triangle, 1979, 125 minutes
on TBS
air dates: 12/13/98

Recommended Books

How to Construct the Philadelphia Experiment: Time Travel is Real
by Steven Gibbs

The Montauk Project: Experiments in Time
by Preston B. Nichols

The Philadelphia Experiment
by William Moore

The Philadelphia Experiment Chronicles; Exploring the Strange Case of Alfred Bielek and Dr. M. K. Jessup (available in the year 2000) by Commander X

Recommended Internet Sites

Camelot Productions
The site of *The Magic of our Universe*
http://www.camelotpublishing.com

The Arts and Entertainment Network
http://www.AandE.com

The Discovery Channel
http://www.discovery.com

The History Channel
http://www.HistoryChannel.com

The Learning Channel
http://www.tlc.com

The Philadelphia Experiment
http://www.angelfire.com/tx/phillyexp

The Philadelphia Experiment and UFT
http://www.all-natural.com/twa-phil.html

The Philadelphia Experiment from A-Z
http://www.wincom.net/softarts/philexp.html

The Philadelphia Experiment (Project Rainbow)
http://www.in-search-of.com

The Philadelphia Experiment: U.S. Navy FAQ
http://www.history.navy.mil/faqs

The Sci-Fi Channel
Sightings available through the Dominion site, which can further access all major paranormal links
http://www.scifi.com/sightings

Unsolved Mysteries
http://www.unsolved.com

Endnotes

[1] *New Visions of the Future,* Ancient Prophecies III, narr. David McCallum, prod. Paul Klein, The Learning Channel, 28 June 1998.

[2] *New Visions of the Future,* Ancient Prophecies III, 28 June 1998.

[3] *New Visions of the Future,* Ancient Prophecies III, 28 June 1998.

Crystal Skulls

Crystal Skulls

Definition

Crystal Skull. A carving usually from one solid block of genuine pure quartz crystal in the shape of the human skull. Some crystal skulls are said to possess great spiritual powers.

Statistics

• As of 1998 there were no books in print on the subject of crystal skulls (Numbers obtained from from *R. R. Bowker's Books in Print.*, the 1998 list). (*However, see Recommended Books.*)

• In 1997 there were approximately one and one half hours aired on the subject of crystal skulls, with around two hours of documentaries aired on the subject in 1998 (Numbers derived from Gissen, Jay, ed. *The Cable Guide*, 1997, 1998).

• "The legend of the crystal skulls handed down by generations of Native American Indians foretells that one day thirteen skulls will return to the land of their origin. There they will reveal the mysteries of the Universe and save mankind" ("The Mystery of the Crystal Skulls," *The Unexplained*, 4 June 1998).

• The Mayan word for crystal is "limbal" meaning "light knowledge" ("The Mystery of the Crystal Skulls," *The Unexplained*, 4 June 1998).

• "In natural form, quartz crystals are hexagonal and have positive and negative charges on each face. This electrical characteristic called piezoelectricity *(See the Glossary)* is used to power instruments from watches to telephones" (Kusters, Jack, Hewlett Packard, Interview, "The

Mystery of the Crystal Skulls," *The Unexplained*, 4 June 1998).

- "Some legends say the crystal skulls come from a more advanced civilization, from a continent now believed to be submerged beneath the waves — the lost continent of Atlantis" ("The Mystery of the Crystal Skulls," *The Unexplained*, 4 June 1998).

- "The idea that the skulls have a celestial origin is common to many of the legends" ("The Mystery of the Crystal Skulls," *The Unexplained*, 4 June 1998).

History

Throughout the world there are only a handful of people and museums blessed with the good fortune of possessing one of the world's most unusual gemstone carvings. Crystal skulls carved from pure quartz crystal are not only rare, but to this day remain mysterious. They range in size from those held in your palm to complete life-size specimens that are elaborate and perfect in every anatomical detail.

Crystal skulls first began appearing in the modern world toward the end of the nineteenth century. Some were purchased by museums at auction, while others were acquired by individuals in fascinating ways. Little is known about the origins of the skulls, partly because they cannot be carbon-dated and partly because one has never been unearthed in an official archeological dig. They are shrouded in legends of mystical, psychic, and supernatural powers. Using the power of the skulls, some psychics claim they can channel back tens of thousands of years and see the history of the skull and the history of the Earth and the entire Universe.

Mythology of crystal skulls played a significant role in Mayan culture. The skull, the symbol of death, was also the symbol of rebirth. The Maya believed that death was simply another phase of life. Mayan architecture and land planning mimicked the stars and the planets. They believed their ancestors came from the heavens and the crystal skulls were gifts from their sky gods. After death, the Mayans believed they would be joined with their celestial ancestors.[1]

Other ancient Central American civilizations such as the Aztecs and Mixtecs also viewed death, the afterlife, and the skull as integral cultural components. The Aztecs in particular may have been responsible for carving crystal skulls because they had extensive lapidary accomplishments. The skull was a featured motif in these cultures and was incorporated into costumes, jewelry, and even architecture. The Aztecs, in a continuous effort to satiate their numerous gods, sacrificed one of their own on a daily basis. The heads of these victims were dried and kept on racks by the thousands. The Spaniards were fascinated by this ritual and the human skull was introduced by Franciscan Monks into the European Catholic Church.[2]

To this day, whether some crystal skulls are authentic pre-Columbian relics or contemporary replicas remains in abeyance. Quartz crystal is carved, engraved, or polished in one of two ways, either by hand or with mechanized engraving wheels. Since the Middle Ages, the village of Eider Oberstien in East Germany has retained the reputation as Europe's major stone carving center. Large quantities of rock crystal of exceptional size and quality were imported from South America to Germany in the nineteenth century. Crystal skulls began showing up in America in the late 1800s. Recently, the British Museum laboratory examined five of the best-known crystal skulls and determined that two of them had been machine-tooled and therefore were probably carved in the late 1800s. The other three and others remain a mystery.[3]

The prevailing theories regarding crystal skulls are:

1. Some crystal skulls are "genuine," meaning they were carved using hand tools, probably by pre-Columbian tribes of Mexico, and Central and South America. They are genuine quartz crystal. Their

mystical powers or other-worldly origins cannot be proved or disproved.

2. Some crystal skulls are "fake." They are carved from genuine quartz crystal, but probably during the nineteenth century. They remain magnificent *objets d'art,* but are not ancient.

Documented Cases

Following are the best-known crystal skulls, their current owners, and their fascinating stories:

The Skull of Doom

Currently owned by Anna Mitchell-Hedges of Ontario, Canada, the Skull of Doom is unquestionably one of the best-crafted skulls ever found. Carved from one solid block of pure quartz crystal, the piece consists of two separate interlocking parts — the skull and jaw. The clarity of the crystal and the quality of carving and polishing are exceptional. Anna Mitchell-Hedges discovered the skull in 1924 while exploring the lost city of Lubaantun with her father in British Honduras. The skull was examined by gemologist Allan Jobbins of the British Museum of Mankind in London. Weighed in both air and water, the skull was found to be genuine pure quartz crystal. No engraving or carving flaws were found on its surface that might indicate whether it was carved by hand or machine. Therefore, its age could not be determined. The raw quartz crystal probably came from Brazil. The source of the artwork has not been determined. Anna Mitchell-Hedges believes her skull is 3,600 years old, in accordance with the beliefs of the Mayan people in the vicinity of the discovery.[4]

Jack Kuster, a Hewlett-Packard authority on crystals and computers, examined the skull in the 1970s. He also determined it was carved from one single block of genuine quartz crystal, but could not determine its place or date of origin. He suggested that only three places, Brazil, Madagascar, or the former Soviet Union, could have been sources for raw crystal of such exceptional quality. Kuster estimated that it would take about one year to carve and polish the skull using modern high-speed, diamond-tipped grinding wheels. Traditional methods probably using beach sand and water would have taken Aztec, Mayan, or Mixtec artisans sixty to seventy years — or about three generations.[5]

Psychics have also inspected the Mitchell–Hedges skull and believe spirits live within it and communicate information about the origins of the Universe to them. Carol Wilson, a psychic who has used her powers to help the Toronto Police Department solve a difficult murder case, channeled with the spirits of the skull. Carol received messages that revealed the skull's origin and ancient history, suggesting the skull may be over 100,000 years old. Forensic artist Richard Neave unmasked a female South American Indian when he sketched flesh, facial features, and hair over the skull.[6]

Max

This skull is currently owned by JoAnn Parks of suburban Houston, Texas. It was gifted to her by a mystical healer who died in 1980. The healer's work with JoAnn's cancer-stricken daughter helped the girl live another three years. JoAnn kept the skull in a box in her closet where it remained untouched for seven years until she began dreaming about it. Mayans and other Native Americans that have visited JoAnn claim her skull is from the city of Atlantis. Originally, it came from the Pleiades, a group of seven stars in the constellation Taurus. Many Native Americans also believe it is encoded with the history of Earth and of mankind.[7]

Sha-Na-Ra

This skull belongs to parapsychologist Nick Nocerino. Using psychometry he located this skull in the Guerrero Province of southern Mexico. It was found in a terra cotta basket. Nick claims he can read a record of the skull's history in the skull itself, and that it has given him the power to heal.[8]

The British Museum Skull

Currently owned by the British Museum in London, England, this skull was acquired from Tiffany's in New York around 1898. Its clarity is exceptional. A microscopic examination revealed even parallel groves consistent with modern emery or diamond-tipped grinding wheels. Although this skull is quartz crystal, it was probably made in the nineteenth century.[9]

The Smithsonian Skull

This skull is currently owned by the Smithsonian Institution in Washington, DC, where it was mailed to the curator, Dr. Jane Walsh. The skull was examined at the same time as the British Museum skull and was also found to have been carved with modern tools, probably in the late nineteenth century.[10]

Beyond the Facts

The crystal skull is a powerful symbolic representation of the afterlife of ancient cultures such as the Maya. Perhaps a few people from these ancient cultures had near-death experiences (NDE) and these positive events had some bearing on their fearless view, indeed their celebration, of death? The Maya, like the Egyptians on the other side of the world and millennia before them, practically worshiped death as a passage into the great afterlife. The NDE theory may be less glamorous than a celestial connection between crystal skulls and Mayan afterlife, but it is quite worthy of further investigation (*see the chapter "Life After Death"*).

Contemporary psychics can channel through crystal skulls, and they can confirm ancient legends that state that the skulls contain the history of the Earth and the entire Universe. What might this tell us about the psychic powers of ancient tribes? Also recent discoveries in psi research may lend further credibility to contemporary psychics' claims of channeling ability (*see the chapter "Extrasensory Perception"*).

In crystal skulls we note the appearance, yet again, of an electric force, this time occuring naturally in a quartz crystal rather than as an electromagnetic field, as with UFOs and the *USS Eldridge*. Piezoelectricity can be derived from quartz found in the ground. When ordinary quartz is squeezed hard enough, it will make your watch run with no wasted energy. What other electric marvels may be unearthed in the rain forests, and in what other forms? Imagine the wealth of natural power that is hidden elsewhere in our Universe.

Resources for Further Investigation
Leading Research Scientists and Investigators

Dr. Ian Freestone
Working at the British Museum Research Lab in London, England, Dr. Freestone investigates the origin and composition of antiquities and was instrumental in examining the crystal skulls.

Paula Gunn-Allen
A professor at the University of California Department of Psychology, she is also a psychic. As a result of her channeling through crystal skulls, she believes that they are transceivers for intergalactic communication with other quadrants of universal consciousness.

Allan Jobbins
A gemologist at the British Museum of Mankind Research Laboratory in London, England, Mr. Jobbins examined the Mitchell–Hedges crystal skull and was unable to determine its origin or the carving date of the skull.

Han Jurgen-Henn
He is a master carver of crystal from Eider Oberstein, Germany and knows a great deal about the crystal trade of the late nineteenth century.

Jack Kusters
Dr. Kusters, a scientist and authority on quartz crystal at Hewlett-Packard labs, examined the Mitchell–Hedges crystal skull and was unable to

determine its origin or the carving date of the skull. He determined that both the skull and jaw were carved from one block of genuine quartz crystal. He also figured that it would take one year minimum to carve the skull using modern tooling techniques and approximately seventy years using primitive hand tooling. He is an authority on piezoelectricity.

F.R. Nick Nocerino
Nick Nocerino used psychometry to locate a crystal skull, "Sha-Na-Ra," in central Mexico. Nocerino believes this skull has given him the power to heal.

Ea Orgo
A gemologist, Mr. Orgo is an authority on quartz crystal.

Dr. David Pendergast
David Pendergast of the Royal Ontario Museum is an authority on pre-Columbian culture and artifacts.

Dr. John Pohl
Dr. John Pohl of University of California is an authority on pre-Columbian art and culture.

Jamie Sams
Jamie Sams is a Native American author and an authority on Native American culture and mysticism.

Linda Schele
Linda Schele is a professor at the Texas Archeology Department. She deciphered the hieroglyphics in the Mayan ruins at Palenque and discovered the history of the sky god Pakava. She learned that Pakava was referred to as "an astronaut from another world who had come to help the Maya learn how to create a Stone Age civilization."

Margaret Sax
Margaret Sax, of the the British Museum Research Laboratory in London, England, investigates the origins and composition of antiquities and was instrumental in comparative examination of crystal skulls at the British Museum. She determined that the British Museum skull and the Smithsonian skull were "fakes" carved in the late nineteenth century.

Dr. Karl Taub

Dr. Karl Taub of the University of California is an authority on pre-Columbian lapidary art, including crystal.

Dr. Jane Walsh

Dr. Walsh is the curator of the Smithsonian Institution. She is an authority on crystal skulls and the keeper of the Smithsonian skull, which was determined to be of contemporary origin, probably from the late nineteenth century.

Recommended Television Programs and Networks

Please consult the Directory of Television Networks in the back of the book for scheduling information and availability of home videos:

"Ancient Wisdom," *Arthur C. Clarke's Mysterious World*, 1980, 12 minutes on The Discovery Channel
air date: 05/31/98

"The Mystery of the Crystal Skulls," *The Unexplained*, 1996, 60 minutes on The Arts & Entertainment Network
air date: 06/04/98

Recommended Books

Mysteries of the Crystal Skulls Revealed
by Sandra Bowen, F. R. "Nick" Nocerino, and Joshua Shapiro
http://www.amazon.com

Recommended Internet Sites

Camelot Productions
The site of *The Magic of Our Universe*
http://www.camelotpublishing.com

Crystal Skulls: Skeletons of a Mysterious Past
http://www.parascope.com/articles/0197/skull_03.htm

Paranormal Phenomena Archive
http://www.in-search-of.com

The Arts and Entertainment Channel
http://www.AandE.com

The Discovery Channel
http://www.discovery.com

The Society of Crystal Skulls International
http://www.crystalskullsociety.org

The Ufomind Paranormal Index and Bookstore
http://www.ufomind.com

Organizations
The Society of Crystal Skulls International
http://www.crystalskullsociety.org
Founder: F.R. "Nick" Nocerino

Endnotes

[1] Pendergast, Dr. David with The Royal Ontario Museum, Interview, "The Mystery of the Crystal Skulls," *The Unexplained*, narr. Norm Woodel, writ. Peter Minns, prod. The BBC A&E Network, Co-Producers, The Arts & Entertainment Network, 4 June 1998.

[2] "The Mystery of the Crystal Skulls," *The Unexplained*, 4 June 1998.

[3] "The Mystery of the Crystal Skulls," *The Unexplained*, 4 June 1998.

[4] "Ancient Wisdom," *Arthur C. Clark's Mysterious World*, narr. Stanley Anderson, prod. John Fairley, The Discovery Channel, 31 May 1998.

[5] "The Mystery of the Crystal Skulls," *The Unexplained*, 4 June 1998.

[6] "The Mystery of the Crystal Skulls," *The Unexplained*, 4 June 1998.

[7] "The Mystery of the Crystal Skulls," *The Unexplained*, 4 June 1998.

[8] "The Mystery of the Crystal Skulls," *The Unexplained*, 4 June 1998.

[9] "The Mystery of the Crystal Skulls," *The Unexplained*, 4 June 1998.

[10] "The Mystery of the Crystal Skulls," *The Unexplained*, 4 June 1998.

The Phenomenon
of Falling Stuff

The Phenomenon of Falling Stuff

Definition

The Phenomenon of Falling Stuff. Fish, frogs, fruit, nuts, and other objects fall from the sky with no apparent reason or explanation.

Statistics

- As of 1998 there were no books in print on the subject of the phenomenon of falling stuff (Numbers obtained from from *R. R. Bowker's Books in Print*, the 1998 list).

- In both 1997 and 1998 only one hour of combined documentary segments aired on the subject of the phenomenon of falling stuff (Numbers derived from Gissen, Jay. ed. *The Cable Guide*, 1997, 1998).

- For decades, perhaps centuries, fish, frogs, fruit, and nuts have fallen from the sky in various parts of the world with little or no explanation. These events occur very rarely and are documented primarily in England and in the northeastern United States.

History

Very little is known about the rare anomaly of living and inanimate objects falling from the sky for no apparent reason. Even more scarce are those who research and document these events. Arthur C. Clarke is the leading investigator scientifically exploring this strange anomaly.

Although they are sketchy and unproven, a few theories attempt to explain how fish and frogs appear to fall from the sky, yet some events of fish falling hundreds of miles from the nearest body of water and of apples and hazelnuts falling from a still, clear sky remain a complete mystery.

As far as falling fish go, tornadoes or waterspouts could possibly be responsible for sucking the contents of entire ponds into the air only to release them in showers upon unsuspecting citizens. There may be a different explanation for raining frogs. Dr. Richard Griffiths of the University of Canterbury in Kent, England believes that in some instances reports of frogs falling from the sky, are more likely instantaneous masses due to explosive breeding and migration from ponds, which was activated by the wet weather. Most events of live fish and frogs, hazelnuts, or fresh apples of several varieties falling from the sky for no apparent reason remain unexplained.[1]

Documented Cases

Derek and Adrienne Haythornwhite

One stormless night in Acrington, a little town in northern England, the Haythornwhites were rudely awakened by a thudding noise on their roof. Adrienne donned her robe and proceeded downstairs to investigate. Looking out from her front door, Adrienne found nothing, no sound, nothing. At her back door she discovered something completely different.

Apples were raining down from a clear night sky. Some were bouncing off the tool shed, while others penetrated the ground like small meteorites, making craters in the lawn. The apple storm continued for two hours and neatly dumped several varieties ankle deep into the fenced back yard of Derek and Adrienne's townhouse. Oddly, not one apple fell in the neighbors' yard on one side and only a few bounced over the fence on the other. A neighbor across the street, Joan Corke, heard the early morning commotion and ran to investigate the next day. She remains as perplexed as the Haythornwhites.

There had been no rain or wind that evening. Searching for any conceivable explanation to this bizarre event, the Haythornwhites phoned the local airport to see if any aircraft had passed overhead during the night. None were logged.[2]

Ron Newton and Ivey Crouch

Ron Newton and Ivey Crouch were enjoying a romantic stroll down the chase in the quaint English village of Finchingfield when an ominous dark cloud rolled out of nowhere and began descending over them. It fell lower and lower until the couple sought refuge under the canopy of a large old tree beside a cottage. The next sound they heard resembled the natural sound of hail, but the next thing they saw startled them into an agitated state of disbelief.

Live, shimmering fish one to three inches long were falling in the branches overhead. After pelting the cottage roof, they started sliding and flopping down on the path around Ron and Ivey. Ivey, only 16, began crying at the spectacle of live fish out of their natural habitat. In a feeble attempt to save the creatures, the couple found an old shoe box and started to gather the fish. As fish continued to fall by the thousands, the couple realized their efforts were in vain, and they gave up. Ron and Ivey along with other witnesses on the chase were shocked and frightened by the incident.[3]

Hard Evidence

The most compelling evidence suggesting the reality of this phenomenon is the falling objects themselves, coupled with documented, reliable, multiple eyewitness accounts of the events. The exemplary Haythornwhite case remains unexplained.

Beyond the Facts

Truly one of the most bizarre of all universal anomalies, the phenomenon of apples, fish, nuts, and frogs falling from the sky with no apparent reason stretches the human imagination to its limits. In fact, it has been included here among more familiar anomalies because of its outlandish degree of strangeness. We never know what may lie beneath such stones until we turn them over.

One highly rewarding aspect of this investigation, I suggest, is the investigation itself. The process of the process, if you will. This phenomenon tests the boundaries of our imaginative reasoning. It really makes us think!

Consider the Haythornwhites where hundreds of perfectly good apples of several varieties fell neatly, mind you, precisely within the fenced confines of their back yard, and nowhere else. The event is witnessed by at least three seemingly normal individuals, and all possible explanations are ruled out such as atmospheric or weather conditions, or the apples falling from an aircraft. This is not an isolated incident either, as other such cases, though rare, have been documented elsewhere in the world.

What could possibly be going on here? This phenomenon leaves us with barely any reasonable explanation. Dr. Griffith's suggestion that frogs and toads "rain" down due to an overactive need to breed is plausible, but it doesn't explain the falling apples, fish, or hazelnuts. The waterspout theory might fit only in those events occurring near bodies of water. But what about the landlocked Haythornwhites?

I believe one clue might lie in the type of falling objects we are dealing with. In all known cases, the objects are found in nature, such as apples, fish, frogs, and nuts. Knives and tires don't rain from the sky. Furthermore, these natural items are oddly of a culinary variety. To determine exactly what bearing this astonishing revelation may have on solving this puzzle — your guess is as good as mine. The thought process or expansion of our intellectual parameters that leads us to a reasonable theory may prove to be as valuable as the theory itself.

One other possible explanation as yet unconsidered is that the phenomenon of falling stuff is in some way associated with poltergeist activity (*see chapter on Hauntings*).

Resources for Further Investigation

Leading Research Scientists and Investigators

Arthur C. Clarke

He is a world-rcnowned scientist and a best-selling author who investigates the paranormal, the supernatural, and the unexplained. He is also the host and creator of the following television programs: *Arthur C. Clarke's World of Strange Powers, Arthur C. Clarke's Mysterious World,* and *Arthur C. Clarke's Mysterious Universe.* He researched and chronicled the phenomenon of mysterious falling objects in 1980 and again in 1995, producing two episodes on the subject.

Dr. Richard Griffiths

Dr. Griffiths, is a biologist, from the University of Canterbury, in Kent, England who travels the world investigating frog and toad behavior and habitats. He has followed reports of falling frogs and toads and believes these events can be explained in terms of conventional science and biology, primarily cross migration from breeding ponds triggered by the weather. In his opinion, frogs and toads do not really fall from the sky but give this impression because of the incredible numbers that develop and leave the breeding pond at the same time.

Recommended Television Programs and Networks

Please consult the Directory of Television Networks in the back of the book for scheduling information and availability of home videos:

"Falling Phenomena," *Arthur C. Clarke's Mysterious Universe,* 1995,
30 minutes
on The Discovery Channel
air dates: 05/31/98

Recommended Internet Sites

The Discovery Channel
http://www.discovery.com

Endnotes

[1] "Falling Phenomena," *Arthur C. Clarke's Mysterious Universe*, narr. Ed Green, writ. Cathryn Garland, prod. Simon Westcott, The Discovery Channel, 31 May 1998.

[2] "Falling Phenomena," *Arthur C. Clarke's Mysterious Universe*, 31 May 1998.

[3] "Falling Phenomena," *Arthur C. Clarke's Mysterious Universe*, 31 May 1998.

Vampires

Vampires

Definitions

Vampire. In fiction: A reanimated dead person characterized by unnatural pale skin and long incisors that are used to suck blood from persons during the night.

Vampire. In Eastern European folklore: A vampire is a dead person who is brought back to life usually by a restless undeparted human spirit. Occasionally during hours of darkness, it rises from the grave to feed upon or raise havoc with living humans who are usually former family members or villagers. The word *Vampire* was first used in English around 1790 and was derived from the hungarian word *vampir* which is further derived from a Slavic mythical creature called an *Upir* which lived by eating the living.

Statistics

- As of 1998 there were sixty books in print on the subject of vampires. The oldest dates back to 1973 with only five still in print from the 1970s, and eleven from the 1980s. There was a dramatic increase during the 1990s with 1 in 1990, 2 in 1992, 3 in 1993, 6 in 1994, 10 in 1995, 8 in 1996, and 7 in 1997 (Numbers obtained from from *R. R. Bowker's Books in Print*, the 1998 list).

- In 1997 there were approximately four hours of documentaries aired on the subject of vampires, and in 1998 there were around eight hours of vampire documentaries (Numbers derived from Gissen, Jay. ed. *The Cable Guide*, 1997, 1998).

• "The first Dracula movie was the 1922 German film *Nosferatu.* Adapted without permission of Bram Stoker's estate, all copies were ordered destroyed" ("The Real Dracula," *In Search of History,* 18 May 1998).

• During her lifetime in the sixteenth century, Countess Elizabeth Bathery strung from the rafters, skewered, and drained 650 servant girls, then bathed in and drank their blood believing it made her look younger ("Vampires," *Unnatural History,* 26 Jan. 1998).

• "Garlic, reputed to be a cure-all, was also apprized to be a vampire repellent. But its real value lay in masking the odor of decaying flesh as vampire hunters dug up a corpse" ("Vampires," *Unnatural History,* 26 Jan. 1998).

• "Some vampires were buried in Germany with a net of thousands of knots because they love to untie knots and would be busy in the grave for eternity" ("The Search for Dracula," *Science Mysteries,* 11 Jan. 1998).

• "In the second quarter of the nineteenth century, a vampire kit was available for purchase in Eastern Europe. It contained a pistol and silver balls, garlic, a stake and sword" ("Vampires," *Unnatural History,* 26 Jan. 1998).

• After researching vampires for seven years, the Irish writer Bram Stoker created the perfect vampire, Dracula, a bloodthirsty, nocturnal, sexual creature who spawned some two hundred films.

History

The legend of blood-sucking entities dates back to a winged, clawed creature of Hebrew mythology named "Lillith," who, incidently, was Adam's first wife.[1] Evicted from the Garden of Eden for acting against his will, she roamed the Earth and cursed its early inhabitants by haunting them and indulging in the blood of their first born. This could very well have been the first vampire, although not called such at that time because the word "vampire" comes from the Hungarian word *vampir,* which is further derived from Slavic mythology and an apparition called an *Upir* — who lived by eating the flesh of the living. The Hungarians also had a name for a restless corpse, Nosferatu, which in 1443 meant "the undead."[2]

Egyptian history tells of a vampire spirit who like Lillith feasted on children's blood. The winged Ekimu was a Babalonian creature who hunted humans for eternity, according to legend. The "Lamia," disguised as a beautiful woman, would stalk young Greek men to drink their blood,[3] and the ancient Romans feared a bloodthirsty demon called a Strager.[4]

By the fifteenth century the bubonic plague, also called the Black Death, spread profusely throughout Europe killing twenty-five percent of the population. The disease was called the Black Death because it left victims discolored with black-and-blue faces. Many villagers who were only in a comatose state were pronounced dead, and unbelievably, were buried alive. Their hands and faces became drenched in their own blood as they frantically attempted to claw their way out of their coffins. Unable to explain the plague, much less find a cure for it, villagers blamed the "undead," and in so doing, fueled the fire of the vampire myth.[5]

In 1897, the Irish writer Bram Stoker molded perhaps the most notorious beast of all time from the real life facts of a fifteenth-century Romanian prince named Vladislavs Dracula. Dracula literally means "son of Dracule," and the word *Dracule*, also his father's name, means either "dragon" or "devil." Later, Vlad Dracula became "Vlad the Impaler" when he impaled twenty thousand Turkish prisoners on stakes in a field in the path of his advancing enemies, the Ottoman Turks. Stoker blended the nocturnal versatility of the fanged bat with Vlad Dracula's incessant thirst for his enemies' blood and added for the first time the undeniable magnet of human attention — sex — to nineteenth-century vampire stories. Neck-biting became synonymous with sexual intercourse. Stoker's Dracula inspired some two hundred films, and the fictitious "long-in-the-tooth" Don Juan of the undead propelled a host of real bloodsuckers through history and into our recent past and present.[6]

Vampires fall into five categories:

1. Those created in the folklore of Eastern Europe and the Americas. If there is a real vampire, he belongs in this category. This creature bites victims in the chest, usually just above the heart, not in the neck. Ironically, one Eastern European tradition to ward off a vampires was to drink *his* blood before he could drink yours.

2. Vampires born from a misinterpretation of medical and forensic conditions during the Middle Ages. This poor "undead" soul nearly expired from the bubonic plague, awakened in his coffin in a shallow grave, and frantically clawed his way to freedom only to find his friends and family chasing after him with a mallet and a stake.

3. Fictional vampires are based partly on legends and partly on the real history of Romanian king Vladislavs Dracula. This is the Bram Stoker, Bella Logossi vampire of movie fame who sleeps in a coffin by day and occasionally stalks the necks of victims by night in the form of a bat.

4. The barbaric psycho–serial killers such as Countess Elizabeth Bathery or Geoffrey Daumer. These social non sequiturs all seem to "get off" on drinking and sometimes bathing in the blood of others. They are compulsive blood drinkers sick from a condition known as Renfield's Syndrome.

5. Contemporary younger vampires are harmless, perhaps discontent with society and a member of a vampire club out to have a good time. They voluntarily give their blood to one another and dress in sensual, slinky Victorian clothes, thus carrying forward the Stoker vampire sex tradition.

Documented Cases
Vlad Dracula, the Impaler

The historical Dracula, Vladislavs Walachia Weywoden, upon whom Bram Stoker based his master creature, was born in 1451 in Segvashwara, Transylvania. His father, king of Walachia, belonged to the Order of the Dragon and was sworn to protect the church from the Ottoman Turks. In the Romanian tongue, *dracule* means "the dragon" or also "the devil." Vlad Dracula was named after his father Vlad Dracule. Therefore "Dracula" translates as "Son of the Dragon" or "Son of the Devil." Vlad Dracula was not a vampire, but rather a ruler who would boil people, skin them alive, or cut off their ears. Occasionally he would nail their hats to their heads, but his favorite method of dispatching humans was by impaling them on a stake. Hence his nickname, Vlad the Impaler.

Walachia was racked by civil war in the fifteenth century. Throughout his childhood, Vlad Dracula was periodically held hostage by the sultan of neighboring Turkey to keep Vlad's father from invading. At age 17, Vlad Dracula was released from prison and gained the throne of Walachia after his father and brother had been killed by the Turks. In a well-documented event, the young Vlad built a banquet hall, invited the nobles who betrayed and killed his father to a large banquet. After a sumptuous feast and entertainment, Vlad locked everyone in the hall and set it ablaze from the outside. I guess you might say he had "roast Turkey."

From that time forward, Vlad really lived up to his name as the Son of the Devil. Monks spread the news of his horrors. He decapitated people and cut off noses, ears, and genitals. He supposedly ate human flesh, drank human blood, and insisted his guests join him when he dined in a field of writhing, moaning, impaled prisoners. One time as the Turks were advancing, they came upon twenty thousand Turkish prisoners impaled on stakes. At this sight the Turkish troops dismounted, bowed down on the ground at the carnage, and proclaimed Vlad — "Lord Impaler." Eventually Vlad's debauchery caught up with him and he was assassinated in 1476. His head was brought to the sultan as proof that he was dead. He was buried in a monastery on Snagoff Lake. Even after his death, Vlad was still full of surprises. Archeologists opened the grave in front of the alter in the 1930s and reported it empty. The Romanian view of Vlad the Impaler is that of a man who loved his country, a protector of the church and its ideals. He justly impaled those who betrayed church and country.[7]

Countess Elizabeth Bathery

Born in 1560 into a powerful Hungarian family with a history of madness, Elizabeth Bathery would eventually epitomize the family profile. She married a young nobleman Forenz Nessadi. Early on, Elizabeth's thirst for blood became evident as young peasant girls began disappearing at night. She acquired the habit of imprisoning, torturing, and killing the girls whenever her gallant husband would venture off to war. He vanished mysteriously in 1604. During her "experiments," Elizabeth would hoist a young girl to the rafters, pierce her body, and drink as blood ran down. Believing that she would attain eternal life from this young blood, she began bathing in it as well. Soon the castle grounds were filled with graves of the dead girls. The servants then began filling the forest with bodies. Villagers discovered blood-drenched corpses and of course immediately cried, "Vampire!" Finally in 1610, the countess's cousin learned of the charades and executed the servants and sealed Elizabeth in her room, where all had transpired.[8] Elizabeth withered away in 1614, but in her own diary she admitted consuming the blood of 650 girls during her reign of terror.[9]

Arnold Powell

Early in the 1730s, Austrian medical officers witnessed a vampire execution in the Serbian village of Medvegia. This is the case of Arnold Powell. A series of mysterious deaths were then blamed on him, so the villagers decided to dig him up. The medical officers witnessing the procedure described the body as undecayed. Fresh blood flowed from nose, mouth, and ears. New nails had replaced old ones. The villagers smelled vampire and drove a stake through Powell's heart. Whereby a groan emanated from his mouth. This case is typical of many from eighteenth-century Eastern Europe: Normal corpse characteristics were misinterpreted as evidence that a vampire had just returned from a kill.[10]

Mercy Lena Brown

In the late eighteenth and early nineteenth centuries, doctors of the Brown family in England could not explain why several Brown family members were dying. As a last resort they dug up all the bodies to discover only one that remained undecayed — that of Mercy Lena Brown. Her heart held fresh blood, so they cut it out, burned it, mixed the blood with ashes and water, and drank it, thinking that this would prevent further attacks. In fact there is far more evidence that people drank the blood of the dead, than that the dead drank the blood of the living. The practices were most common Eastern Europe.[11]

J.B.

"J.B.," as he is known from the initials inscribed on a brass plaque on his coffin, was originally from Connecticut. He now rests in the National Museum of Health and Medicine in Washington, D.C. A forensic anthropologist discovered that someone had jumbled J.B.'s bones into a skull and crossbones pattern, a practice known to identify a vampire. J.B. was later found to have had tuberculosis — a disease that ties many vampire cases together as a result of the characteristics of death.[12]

Fritz Harmon

In the early 1920s, a German butcher named Fritz Harmon lured twenty-seven young boys to his home where he killed them with a bite to the neck, then drank their blood and sometimes dined on their flesh. He finally put his skills as a butcher to good use when he ground up the remaining bodies and parts and sold it as sausage in his shop.[13]

Beyond the Facts

The study of vampires presents a good example of how humans throughout history have drawn conclusions from their limited knowledge of the Universe, in this case from normal corpse characteristics resulting from bubonic plague in medieval Europe and tuberculosis in eighteenth- and nineteenth-century New England. Vampires were created as the only possible explanations for the deaths based on then current knowledge. The cases of Arnold Powell, Mercy Lena Brown, and "J.B." illustrate perfectly how the living explained away that which they did not understand by using their historical frame of reference, or their "comfort zone," if you will.

The New England witches of Salem are another historical anomaly similar to the vampire in that humans perceive of demonic evil instead of some more likely physical or mental illness, or just plain childhood pranks. Limited knowledge of human physiology or psychology played a role in the harsh and often fatal treatment of suspected witches which was also fueled by strict religious doctrine.

Much can be learned from exploring the universal anomalies of our past. The vampire has been thoroughly inspected and has revealed most if its secrets. As enchanting as the vampires of Eastern European folklore and Bram Stoker are, greater value is derived from understanding how humans of those times perceived and dealt with the unknown. Armed with little, if any, scientific knowledge of disease and death, they juggled ignorance, fear, and imagination to find an answer. Perhaps they had not evolved enough to contemplate other possibilities, possibilities such as the characteristics of dying that today we know to be fact and truth.

Today, don't humans limit the understanding of contemporary anomalies in the same narrow way our ancestors did? For some humans today, aren't extraterrestrials equivalent to the vampires of medieval Eastern Europe. Forensic science beyond the scope of humans at that time eventually evolved to provide answers. Knowing this, should we be considering every conceivable approach to understanding our exponentially larger Universe?

Resources for Further Investigation
Leading Research Scientists and Investigators
Paul Barber

Folklorist and author Paul Barber is a leading authority on the history of vampires, both fictitious and folkloric. He points out that the vampires of Eastern European folklore were usually swollen, dark-skinned peasants or farmers rather than thin, pale aristocrats with long canines. Paul is well versed on the history of Vlad Dracula as the real life inspiration for Bram Stoker's *Dracula*, as well as the medieval perception of death and dying with respect to vampirism.

Michael Bell

He is a Rhode Island folklorist and a colleague of Paul Sledzik. Through his research into the undead, Bell has become an American vampire hunter. Working with courthouse, library, and cemetery records throughout New England, Michael Bell has uncovered over a dozen vampire accounts from the late eighteenth and early nineteenth centuries. Details of these stories, such as villagers and family members digging up and mutilating suspected corpses of their own, strongly resemble traditional vampire cases of Eastern Europe. Bell's most startling discovery was the case of Sarah Tillinghast, the purported vampire daughter of New England farmer Stutley Tillinghast.

Dr. William Cone

Dr. Cone is a clinical psychologist interested in the impact on humans of the vampire's seductive power and control. This control and the subsequent gift of eternal life given to the victims is the give-and-take force that Cone believes propels the vampire myth through time and continues to captivate human interest.

Norine Dresser

Norine Dresser is a historian and author often interviewed for her views on the sexuality and romanticism woven into the vampire mystique.

Dr. Leonard George

Psychiatrist Leonard George has researched in Great depth the sociophysiological meaning of blood, the human life-force, as it pertains to vampire behavior. He contends that the magnetism of blood may have been psychologically programmed into humans over the challenging course of human evolution. Blood shed during human conflict for instance arouses the fear response and usually indicates danger, according to Dr. George. As an authority on Renfield's Syndrome, the four-stage medical condition of craving blood, Leonard George also describes how some humans can develop from getting a simple scratch to becoming vampire-like serial killers.

Benjamin LeBlanc

He is a Canadian student of vampire folklore and an authority on the history of Dracula.

Dr. Raymond McNally

A Fulbright Fellowship recipient, a professor of history, and an author, Dr. McNally is often interviewed on television documentaries for his broad knowledge of Vladislavs Dracula. In 1972, after leaving Romania, he discovered the link between Vlad Dracula and Bram Stoker's fictional character.

Dr. J. Gorton Melton

Known and respected for his insightful interpretations of vampire folklore and the life-force of blood, Dr. Melton is often interviewed for television documentaries.

Leslie Shepard

Founder of the Bram Stoker Society in Dublin, Ireland, Shepard is an authority on the writer's life and times.

Paul Sledzik

A forensic anthropologist, Sledzik is an authority on New England vampirism, the case of J. B. in particular, and on the physiological characteristics of dying as related to vampire folklore.

Recommended Television Programs and Networks

Please consult the Directory of Television Networks in the back of the book for scheduling information and availability of home videos:

"Joan of Arc, Soul on Fire,*"* *In Search of History,* 1998, 60 minutes
on The History Channel
air dates: 03/18/98

Modern Day Vampires, *Unsolved Mysteries,* 7 minutes
on Lifetime
air dates: 03/19/98

Salem Witch, *Unsolved Mysteries,* 5 minutes
on Lifetime
air dates: 03/05/98

Sightings, Series First Aired 1991, Went Into Syndication 1994
on The Sci-Fi Channel
air dates: 1991 through 1998

"The Real Dracula," *In Search of History,* 1998, 60 minutes
on The History Channel
air dates: 05/18/98, 07/23/98, 10/27/98

"The Search for Dracula", *Science Mysteries,* 60 minutes
on The Discovery Channel
air dates: 01/11/98

"Vampires," *The Unexplained,* 1998, 60 minutes
on The Arts & Entertainment Network
air dates: 05/07/98

"Vampires," *Unnatural History,* 1997, 30 minutes
on The Learning Channel
air dates: 01/26/98, 05/28/98

"Vampires, Witches, Werewolves & Vampires,*"* 25 minutes
on The Learning Channel
air dates: 08/13/98

"Witchcraft," *In Search of History,* 1997, 60 minutes
on The History Channel
air dates: 08/12/98, 10/28/98

"Witches," *Unnatural History,* 1997, 30 minutes
on The Learning Channel
air dates: 01/26/98, 05/28/98

"Witches, Witches, Werewolves & Vampires," 25 minutes
on The Learning Channel
air dates: 08/13/98

Recommended Books
The Vampire Book
by Dr. J. Gorton Melton

Vampires, Burial, and Death
by Paul Barber

American Vampires
by Norine Dresser

In Search of Dracula
by Raymond T. McNally and Radu R. Florescu

Hollywood Gothic: The Tangled Web of Dracula
by David J. Skal

Dracula
by Bram Stoker

The Vampire © 1819 (if you can find it)
by John Polidari

Recommended Internet Sites
Camelot Productions
The site of *The Magic of Our Universe*
http://www.camelotpublishing.com

Paranormal Phenomena Archive
http://www.in-search-of.com

The Arts and Entertainment Channel
http://www.AandE.com

The Discovery Channel
http://www.discovery.com

The History Channel
http://www.HistoryChannel.com

The Learning Channel
http://www.tlc.com

The Sci-Fi Channel
Sightings available through the Dominion site, which can further access
all major paranormal links
http://www.scifi.com/sightings

The Ufomind Paranormal Index and Bookstore
http://www.ufomind.com

Unsolved Mysteries
http://www.unsolved.com

Organizations
Temple of The Vampire
P. O. Box 3582
Lacey, WA   98509
http://pw1.netcom.com/?temple/home.html

Endnotes

[1] LeBlanc, Benjamin, Interview, "The Search for Dracula," *Science Mysteries,* narr. Eli Wallach, writ. Eleanor Grant, prod. Nicola Valcor and Tom Naughton, The Discovery Channel, 11 Jan. 1998.

[2] "Vampires," *Unnatural History,* narr. Mark Hamill, writ. Anne McGrail, prod. Michael Tetrick, The Learning Channel, 26 Jan. 1998.

[3] "Vampires," *Unnatural History,* 26 Jan. 1998.

[4] "The Search for Dracula," *Science Mysteries,* narr. Eli Wallach, writ. Eleanor Grant, prod. Nicola Valcor and Tom Naughton, The Discovery Channel, 11 Jan. 1998.

[5] "Vampires," *Unnatural History,* 26 Jan. 1998.

[6] "The Search for Dracula," *Science Mysteries,* 11 Jan. 1998.

[7] "The Search for Dracula," *Science Mysteries,* 11 Jan. 1998.

[8] "Vampires," *Unnatural History,* 26 Jan. 1998.

[9] "The Real Dracula," *In Search of History,* narr. David Ackroyd, writ. Charles Ryan, prod. Charles Ryan, The History Channel, 18 May 1998.

[10] "The Search for Dracula," *Science Mysteries,* 11 Jan. 1998.

[11] "The Search for Dracula," *Science Mysteries,* 11 Jan. 1998.

[12] "The Search for Dracula," *Science Mysteries,* 11 Jan. 1998.

[13] "Vampires," *Unnatural History,* 26 Jan. 1998.

Unidentified Lake Creatures

Nessie
Champ
Elsie
Memphry
Ogopogo
Ishii

Unidentified Lake Creatures

Definition

Unidentified Lake Creatures. An unknown animal believed to inhabit several of the hundreds of deep freshwater lakes primarily in the Earth's northern hemisphere. Typically, eyewitness testimony describes those creatures as twenty to sixty feet long, six to eight feet in width, and usually featuring a long neck and small head, with one or two humps on the back, and dark gray in color.

Statistics

* As of 1998 there were sixty books in print on the subject of unidentified lake creatures, including all categories listed on the title page (Numbers obtained from *R. R. Bowker's Books in Print*, the 1998 list).

* In 1997 there were around three and one half hours of documentaries covering the subject of unidentified lake creatures, which includes all categories listed on the title page. In 1998 there were around seven hours and forty-five minutes of documentaries (Numbers derived from Gissen, Jay. ed. *The Cable Guide*, 1997, 1998).

* Loch Ness is one of the deepest lakes in the world; it is 900 feet deep, 22 miles long, and 1.5 miles wide ("Monsters of the Lakes," *Arthur C. Clarke's Mysterious World*, 7 June 1998).

* Lake Okanagan in Kelowna, British Columbia in western Canada is 130 miles long and 800 feet deep, and is believed to be home to Ogopogo ("Monsters of the Lakes," *Arthur C. Clarke's Mysterious World*, 7 June 1998).

• Over the past 1,500 years there have been ten thousand reported sightings of the lake creature in Loch Ness ("The Loch Ness Secret," *Paleo World*, 6 May 1998).

• Celtic scholars claim that Loch Ness was christened after a water goddess named "Nessa" ("The Loch Ness Monster," *In Search of History*, 27 July 1998).

• Loch Ness, Britain's largest freshwater lake, lies between Fort Augustus to the southwest and Inverness to the northeast. Seeing anything below fifty feet deep is impossible due to peat, which over centuries has drained into the lake from surrounding hills ("Loch Ness," *Great Mysteries and Myths of the Twentieth Century*," 30 January 1998).

• "Documented sightings of mysterious sea creatures suggest that small populations of unknown animals may inhabit as many as ninety lakes in Canada and the United States" ("In the Shadows," *Animal X*, 30 Aug. 1998).

Geographical Identification by Name:

Unidentified Lake Creatures have been named according to their geographical location. Eyewitness evidence suggests these names likely refer to water-dwelling animals that resemble either a plesiosaur or an ichthyosaur.

Nessie

This name was coined in the 1930s by eyewitnesses to describe creatures purported to be dwelling in Loch Ness of northwest Scotland. "Nessie" is short for The Loch Ness Monster.

Champ

In the 1970s the name "Champ" was given by eyewitnesses to a creature that dwells in Lake Champlain, which forms the north-south basin between the Adirondack Mountain range and the Green

Mountain range in the northeastern United States.

Elsie

A name likely coined by eyewitnesses to describe a creature that dwells in Lake Champlain.

Memphry

Eyewitnesses named a creature "Memphry" that dwells in Lake Memphremagog, a lake that straddles the U.S. and Canadian border between Vermont and Quebec.

Ogopogo

This name was given to a creature that dwells in Lake Okanagan, which lies north to south between Vernon and Penticton, in the Canadian province of British Columbia.

Ishii

The name coined by an eyewitness to describe a creature that dwells in lake Akida on the southern Japanese island of Kyushu.

History

Between two million and 10,000 years ago, nearly all of the world's high elevation lakes were carved by glaciers during the Earth's most recent ice age called the Pleistocene era. Some zoologists consider these deep, dark, cold, and murky habitats to be quite suitable for Jurassic period water-dwelling creatures such as the plesiosaurs and the ichthyosaurs. Though video documentation of bizarre lake animals continues to pile up around the world, little hard evidence exists that could prove they survived extinction over sixty-five million years ago.

High mountain lakes were once a part of the oceans. Abundant fish stocks likely found their way into these deep troughs and over time may have become the primary food source that lured large, ancient, aquatic predators into the lakes. Over countless millennia, these saltwater connectors closed off at the ends forming the freshwater lakes of today. It is highly possible that some large sea creatures became trapped, with no choice but to adjust with time to their new confined freshwater surroundings.

Worldwide, deepwater lakes may number in the thousands, with close to ninety straddling the United States and Canadian border alone.[1] All are potentially suitable homes for small populations of plesiosaur or ichythyosaur type creatures.

Both Lake Champlain in upstate New York and Lake Memphremagog just to the east and over the border in Quebec are home to creatures affectionately named "Champ" and "Memphry," respectively. French explorer and founder of New France (now known as Canada), Samuel de Champlain, may have glimpsed Champ as early as 1609. As many as three hundred sightings have been reported since, and researcher Jacques Boisuert has amassed more than two hundred eyewitness accounts of Memphry in Lake Memphremagog.[2]

Other known harbors of freshwater monsters are Lake Okanagan in British Columbia, home of Ogopogo, Lake Akida, home to Ishii on the Japanese island of Kyushu, and Sweden's Lake Storsjon, home to an as-yet-unnamed creature. But unquestionably the most famous among the world's deepest freshwater lakes is Loch Ness, which slices off the Northwest Highlands of Scotland.

For millennia, Loch Ness has remained shrouded in mystery as thick as its looming fog. Documented Scottish legend from A.D. 565 tells of the Christian Saint, Columba, who yanked a swimmer from the jaws of a loch creature called a "kelpie" or water horse.[3]

Mysterious reports survive from the eighteenth century, including one where military road builders disturbed two massive creatures while blasting rock along the Glen Mor,[4] and others documented by Scottish historians who described strange occurrences such as windless waves, finless fish, or floating islands.[5] Other nineteenth-century eyewitnesses described giant salamanders.[6]

In 1933, the modern era of Nessie was ushered in with newspapers clamoring to publish stories such as the one that occurred April 14 of that year. John and Aldie Mackay were driving back home from a trip to the loch's northern point when Mrs. Mackay spotted a tremendous black, rounded torso with two humps that undulated up and down through the water. A flurry of similar sightings continued through the summer culminating in a November photograph taken by Mr. Hugh Grey, which was plastered on the front page of the local newspaper, the *Daily Sketch*.[7]

Then came the hoaxes. First, Nessie's footprints were allegedly discovered by big game hunter Marmaduke Weatheral; they were later confirmed by British Museum zoologists to be authentic hippopotamus footprints complete with trophy markings, very likely from Weatherall's trophy room. Then there was the famous "surgeon's photo" of Nessie's head and neck, snapped by London gynecologist Kenneth Wilson — the picture was later thought to be that of a handcrafted wooden head atop a toy submarine. This photo remains controversial.

Legitimate sightings continued, however, with a dozen or so documented by troops stationed along the loch during World War II, another by the Makintosh family in 1952,[8] and one by Peter McNabb that became the popular photograph of Nessie squirming through the lake beside the ruins of Urquhart Castle.[9]

The hunt for Nessie finally entered the scientific realm on April 23, 1960 when British aerospace engineer Tim Dinsdale filmed a huge hump trailing through the surface of Loch Ness. The 16 mm footage was authenticated as an animate object by the Joint Air Reconnaissance Intelligence Centre, the photo analysis division of the Royal Air Force.[10]

The British Parliament stepped into the picture when respected member David James, along with other dedicated monster hunters, assembled The Loch Ness Investigation Bureau, armed with boats and submarines. In 1967, Dr. Roy Mackal, a retired professor from the University of Chicago, took the helm of LNI, seeking scientific results through comprehensive investigation of the entire Loch Ness ecosystem, including the food chain, water conditions, and physical descriptions of the animal.

As the LNI search was winding down in 1971, The Academy of Applied Sciences, headquartered in Boston, Massachusetts, was just cranking up under the direction of an MIT graduate named Robert Rines. Armed with an arsenal of sonar arrays and stroboscopic cameras, Rines prepared to attack Nessie head on underwater. He and his team set up base camp in Urquhart Bay,[11] and for two years they monitored their ingenious sonar-triggered "camera trap." In 1972 their patience was rewarded with one photo delineating a flipper and another revealing a purported Nessie head, nostrils and all. Both photos, though digitally analyzed at California's Jet Propulsion Laboratory in Pasadena, eventually drew criticism from former LNI chief Roy Mackal as well as from other scientists, and today they remain controversial. Still, other sightings continued.

Operation Deep Scan was launched in 1987 with a flotilla of nineteen powerboats lined up across the entire width of Loch Ness. They tracked its twenty-three-mile length, probing to the bottom with echo sounding equipment. Led by researcher Adrian Shine, the team ultimately detected three large unidentified animate objects.

Though no conclusive evidence of Nessie has ever been uncovered, sightings of the elusive creature and her worldwide cousins continue. Significant theories of exactly what these beings may be vary somewhat but most cite the Jurassic realm of possibilities including a plesiosaur, an ichthyosaur, a mosasaur, or the zugladon. But of course, every now and then, a hand-carved horse head strapped on top of a toy submarine is liable to show its phony head.

Beyond the Facts

What is it about humans that makes us so curious about life, so hungry for the truth, so eager to catch the monster in the lake? The mere fact that something as mysterious as Loch Ness exists, in Scotland — the land of mysticism, is intriguing. Our gravitation toward the mysterious is such an interesting human tendency. It keeps us excited about life. It keeps us looking.

What is so different between our investigation of the elusive Nessie or Champ or Ishii and the extraterrestrial survey of our planet Earth? Are they not both peaceful scientific endeavors to quench curiosity? What is the difference between a research vessel floating on the surface of Loch Ness — probing for Nessie, and an extraterrestrial research vessel floating in space — learning more about the inhabitants of planet Earth? Perhaps the only difference lies within the human ability to adjust to the complex reality of our universal living space. Perhaps it is time for us to consider ourselves as Earthlings living in a Universe of possibilities rather than the Universe existing around human possibilities.

What is it about humans that drenches our pursuit of truth in the cut and dried, in the black and white, in the proof positive? I suppose by definition truth must be whole; it must be proven. Truth cannot be simply believed; something must be proven either black or white to be truth. But perhaps it is belief itself — belief in the faithfully supported hypothesis, in the notion, if you will, that "Nessie exists!," that Champ is just around the next bend of the lake — perhaps belief is the dangling carrot of hope that drives the very engine of science. Belief is what keeps people coming to Loch Ness in search of their dragon. Belief is what drives the scientist; it is what propels the hypothesis through the scientific method to the holy grail of proof, to truth itself. Belief leads us to truth. Every now and then a coelacanth washes up in some fisherman's net off the coast of Madagascar and hammers home the importance of belief. It makes us reopen our minds to all possibilities, however unlikely they may be.

One effective mind-expanding exercise is to look up Loch Ness in Scotland in a good world atlas.[12] Study it's long fingerlike shape. Then flip through other countries of the world to see for yourself just how many other similar lakes might be suitable for creatures like Nessie. Look at Canada for example.

Resources for Further Investigation
Leading Research Scientists and Investigators

The following leading researchers partially represent the worldwide scientific interest in unidentified lake creatures. Though all could be considered dracontologists which literally means "those who study dragons", in this case unknown deepwater lake dragons, each researcher has pursued these creatures in his own unique way.

Mike Benton

A paleontologist from Bristol University in England, Mike Benton believes the Loch Ness creature may be one of either an ichthyosaur, a mosasaur, or a plesiosaur.

Jacques Boisuert

Leading investigator at Lake Memphremagog, Boisuert is the authority on Memphry. He has amassed over two hundred eyewitness accounts of the creature and is well versed on the Iroquois legends dating back hundreds of years.

Dr. Jose Bonaparte

A paleontologist living in Argentina. Dr. Bonaparte is studying the lake creature sighted numerous times in a high elevation lake in Argentina.

Alastair Boyd

Alastair Boyd is a Loch Ness historian from the Scottish Highlands. He knows the legends of Loch Ness as well as he knows the terrain. Boyd is a knowledgeable source for historic details of Loch Ness sightings from A.D. 565 to the present.

Tim Dinsdale

On April 23, 1960, Tim Dinsdale, a British space engineer and Loch Ness explorer, filmed a large dark hump and its wake as it swam across Loch Ness. The 16 mm footage was authenticated in 1960 as an animate object by the film analysis division of the Royal Air Force.

Akihike Ikemizu

Mr. Ikemizu formed the Ishii Investigation Group and leads the photographic search for the creature, Ishii, dwelling in Lake Akida, Japan.

Paul LeBland, Ph.D.

Paul LeBland is a professor at the University of British Columbia. Ogopogo, the purported creature of Lake Okanogan has been Paul's primary focus of research. He believes cumulative evidence suggests the existence of some large unknown lake-dwelling animal.

Dr. Roy Mackal

A retired professor in biochemistry from the University of Chicago, Dr. Mackal became involved in the search for Nessie in the 1960s and assumed the directorship of the Loch Ness Investigation Bureau in 1967. For four years Mackal applied his knowledge of biochemistry and the scientific method to his search for Nessie. Conservative in his approach, Dr. Mackal found Loch Ness to be a suitable habitat for a large freshwater mammal, but also that some sightings may be due to the bizarre lake surface atmospheric conditions.

Roger Parker

Researcher of the Loch Ness creature, Roger Parker and his team took a high-tech approach to revealing the mysteries of Nessie. Parker's boat equipped with hydrophones, cameras, underwater microphones, sonar, and monitors for detecting lake-bottom disturbances picked up the signatures of two large underwater animals.

Robert Rines

Robert Rines is President of the Academy of Applied Sciences in Boston, Massachusetts. He is also a Boston attorney and MIT graduate, and in the early 1970s he tackled the Nessie mystery from under the water. Rines outfitted two boats with sonar-triggered stroboscopic cameras and eventually obtained several photographs of Nessie's upper torso and flipper. His famous flipper shot of 1972 was authenticated by Pasadena's Jet Propulsion Laboratory, but mainstream science remains undecided.

Adrian Shine

Director of The Loch Ness Project, Adrian Shine launched Operation Deep Scan in 1987 to locate Nessie and to collect data on the unique Loch Ness ecosystem. He probed eighty percent of the loch end to end with a lineup of nineteen sonar-equipped powerboats. Shine never found Nessie but learned much about Loch Ness.

Richard Smith

Richard Smith is the leading researcher at Lake Champlain focusing his efforts on the creature named Champ thought to be living in the lake. He initiated a sophisticated investigation to expose Champ using sonar and underwater cameras, his knowledge of deep lake formation, and the related underwater food chain. Smith has also closely re-examined the controversial "surgeon's photograph" of Nessie, and believes the photo may be genuine.

Dr. Felipé Valverde

An evolutionary biologist living in Argentina, Dr. Valverde is pursuing an interest in the unknown lake creature of Lake Nowiwapi in Argentina.

Recommended Television Programs and Networks

Please consult the Directory of Television Networks in the back of the book for scheduling information and availability of home videos:

"In the Shadows," *Animal X,* 1997, 30 minutes
on The Discovery Channel
airdates: 8/30/98

Lake Champlain Serpent, *Unsolved Mysteries,* 1992, 10 minutes
on Lifetime
air dates: 07/13/98

Lizard Man, *Extremely Weird*, 1995, 2 minutes
on The Learning Channel
air dates: 01/03/98, 01/31/98

"Loch Ness," *Great Mysteries and Myths of the Twentieth Century*,
30 minutes
on The Learning Channel
air dates: 01/30/98

"Monsters of the Deep," *Arthur C. Clarke's Mysterious World*, 1980,
30 minutes
on The Discovery Channel
air dates: 05/03/98

"Monsters of the Lakes," *Arthur C. Clarke's Mysterious World*, 1980,
30 minutes
on The Discovery Channel
air dates: 06/07/98

"Mysteries of the Sea," *Arthur C. Clarke's Mysterious Universe*,
30 minutes
on The Discovery Channel
air dates: 05/24/98

"Mythical Beasts & Monsters," *Unnatural History*, 1997, 60 minutes
on The Learning Channel
air dates: 01/27/98, 05/29/98

Sea Monsters, *Extremely Weird*, 1995, 7 minutes
on The Learning Channel
air dates: 01/03/98, 01/31/98

Sightings, Series First Aired 1991, Went Into Syndication 1994
on The Sci-Fi Channel
air dates: 1991 through 1998

Strange Beings and UFO's, Mysteries of the Unexplained, 1995,
60 minutes
on The Discovery Channel
air dates: 06/18/98

The Loch Ness Monster, 1998, 60 minutes
on The History Channel
air dates: 07/27/98, 10/08/98

"Turkish Lake Monster," *Animal X,* 1997/1998, 7 minutes
on The Discovery Channel
air dates: 05/17/98

"Unidentified Sea Creatures," *Strange but True?,* 1997, 30 minutes
on The Discovery Channel
air dates: 03/05/98, 10/15/98

Recommended Books
Loch Ness Monster
by Tim Dinsdale

Monsters of the Sea
by Richard Ellis

The Loch Ness Monster. The Evidence
by Steuart Campbell

Recommended Internet Sites
Camelot Productions
The site of *The Majic of Our Universe*
http://www.camelotpublishing.com

Paranormal Phenomena Archive
http://www.in-search-of.com

The Arts and Entertainment Network
http://www.AandE.com

The Discovery Channel
http://www.discovery.com

The History Channel
http://www.HistoryChannel.com

The Learning Channel
http://www.tlc.com

The Sci-Fi Channel
Sightings available through the Dominion site, which can further access
all major paranormal links
http://www.scifi.com/sightings

The Ufomind Paranormal Index and Bookstore
http://www.ufomind.com/catalog/l/lochness

Unsolved Mysteries
http://www.unsolved.com

Organizations

AAS (Academy of Applied Science)
Boston, Massachusetts
President, Robert Rines

Champ Quest
An operation mounted to search for the creature of Lake Champlain
Richard Devel

The Ishii Investigation Group
Akihike Ikemizu, Founder
Through observation they seek photographic evidence of Ishii.

LNI (The Loch Ness Investigation Bureau)
Formed in 1961 by David James, a member of Parliament. Roy Mackal
became Director in 1967. Closed in 1971.

LNP (The Loch Ness Project)
Home of Operation Deep Scan launched in 1987
Director, Adrian Shine

Endnotes

[1] "In the Shadows," *Animal X*, narr. Betsy Aidem, writ. Wendy Wilson and Cathryn Garland. prod. Melanie Ambrose and Max Jacobson-Gonzalez, The Discovery Channel, 30 Aug. 1998.

[2] "In the Shadows," *Animal X*, 30 Aug. 1998.

[3] "The Loch Ness Monster," *In Search of History*, narr. David Ackroyd, writ. Steve Muscarella and Melissa Jo Peltier, prod. Melissa Jo Peltier, The History Channel, 27 July 1998.

[4] "Loch Ness," *Great Mysteries and Myths of the Twentieth Century*, narr. Michael Carroll, writ. Wendy Wilson, prod. Sharon Gillooly, The Learning Channel, 30 Jan. 1998.

[5] "The Loch Ness Monster," *In Search of History*, 27 July 1998.

[6] "Loch Ness," *Great Mysteries and Myths of the Twentieth Century*, 30 Jan. 1998.

[7] "Loch Ness," *Great Mysteries and Myths of the Twentieth Century*, 30 Jan. 1998.

[8] "The Loch Ness Monster," *In Search of History*, 27 July 1998.

[9] "Loch Ness," *Great Mysteries and Myths of the Twentieth Century*, 30 Jan. 1998.

[10] "The Loch Ness Monster," *In Search of History*, 27 July 1998.

[11] "Loch Ness," *Great Mysteries and Myths of the Twentieth Century*, 30 Jan. 1998.

[12] *Oxford Atlas of the World*, 5th edition, New York, New York: Oxford University Press, Inc. 1997, (18, 130-131).

Unidentified Wilderness Creatures

Bigfoot
Sasquatch
Oma
Yeti
Abominable Snowman
Yeren
Skunk Ape
Mologrande
Almas

General Definition

The author has taken the liberty to group all subjects in this segment under one general definition as they all seem to share similar physical characteristics and live in remote wilderness areas of the world. More formal definitions available on individual subjects follow.

Unidentified Wilderness Creatures. They comprise a variety of very large, hairy, smelly, bipedal humanoids purported to inhabit the remote wilderness areas of the world. Many share similar physical characteristics. The creatures' names vary with geographical habitat.

Statistics

• As of 1998, there were thirty-four books in print regarding Bigfoot, Sasquatch, Yeti, or the Abominable Snowman. Eight were published before 1990, with a consistent output of three to four books per year during the 1990s (Numbers obtained from *R. R. Bowker's Books in Print*, the 1998 list).

• In 1997 there were around four hours and fifteen minutes of documentaries aired on the subject of Bigfoot, Sasquatch, Yeti, or the Abominable Snowman. 1998 produced a little over ten hours (Numbers derived from Gissen, Jay. ed. *The Cable Guide*, 1997, 1998).

• "Either the most complex and sophisticated hoax in the history of anthropology has continued for centuries without being exposed, or the most man-like and largest non-human primate on Earth has managed to survive in parts of North America and remains undiscovered by modern science" (Gill, G. W., President, The American Board of Anthropology, Interview, "Bigfoot," *Ancient Mysteries,* 29 March 1998).

- "There have been 1,500 U.S. sightings of Bigfoot. Estimated height is between six and eight feet. Estimated weight is between 280 pounds and 700 pounds. Indians of the Northwest call it "Sasquatch." Americans of the Northwest call it "Bigfoot" (*Strange Beings and UFOs,* Mysteries of the Unexplained, 5 April 1998).

- "They are tall, have huge shoulders, and a short neck. They have a very human face, a straight nose, and small lips. It is not an ape's face or a gorilla's face. We think we are looking at a very primitive human" (Byrne, Peter, Director, Bigfoot Research Project, "Bigfoot," *Ancient Mysteries,* 29 March 1998).

- "All fifty U.S. states and all ten Canadian provinces have reported sightings or found tracks of this mysterious animal" ("Bigfoot," *Ancient Mysteries,* 29 March 1998).

- Current estimates suggest 450,000 U.S. citizens are involved in the search for Bigfoot (In the News, *Sightings,* 23 Feb. 1998).

- "Several tracks with dermal ridges are the most definitive evidence of the existence of Bigfoot" (Krantz, Dr. Grover, Interview, "Bigfoot," *Ancient Mysteries,* 29 March 1998).

- Sasquatch live in small groups of one male and three, four, or five females. This is the breeding community. There are approximately two thousand Sasquatch living in the Pacific Northwest and adjacent Canadian provinces (Krantz, Dr. Grover, Interview, "Bigfoot," *Ancient Mysteries,* 29 March 1998).

Cultural and Geographical Identification by Name

All names refer to a very large hairy humanoid:

Bigfoot

This name was coined by a roadwork crew in 1958 when they discovered large footprints at their worksite in northwestern California.

Geographically, it refers to creature living primarily in the U.S. Pacific Northwest, but "Bigfoot" is probably the name most widely used to describe this creature throughout the world.

Sasquatch

This name originated within the Native American tribes of British Columbia, predates the name "Bigfoot," and is currently used widely in the U.S. and Canada. The name means "wild man of the woods," and geographically refers to a creature primarily of British Columbia and the U.S. Pacific Northwest.

Oma

This name was first used by the Native American Hoopa living in the Hoopa Valley of Northern California. The name means "boss of the woods" and predates "Bigfoot." It refers to a person that takes care of the mountains and is primarily used by the Hoopas of Northern California.

Yeti

This name was formed by the Sherpas of Tibet and Nepal in the Himalayan Mountain range of southern Asia. This term greatly predates the name "Bigfoot." The word means "man-bear" or "snow-field man," and geographically refers to a creature of the Himalayan Mountains of Tibet and Nepal. The name is becoming more common worldwide.

Abominable Snowman

This name first appeared in a 1921 British press article about British explorer Colonel Howard Berry and the strange, large, human-like footprints he discovered 21,000 feet up Mt. Everest. The papers first called the creature "the abominably smelling man," then "the abominable man," then finally, "the abominable snowman." This Western terminology is synonymous in all respects with the Yeti. This name predates the name "Bigfoot."

Yeren

This name was coined by the people along the China-Vietnam border areas. The name predates the name "Bigfoot" and geographically refers to a creature of China and Vietnam. It is used primarily in those areas.

Skunk Ape

This name was given to an unknown biped by the people of southern Florida. It is fairly recent and does not predate "Bigfoot." Geographically, the name refers to a creature of Florida, primarily of the Everglades. The name is most familiar in Florida, but is becoming better known worldwide.

Molograndé

This name was formed by the people of the Amazon basin in South America. The name means "enormous ape-like creature," and geographically refers to a creature of the Amazon rain forests. It is used primarily in that area.

Almas

This name was established by the nomadic herdsmen of Siberia in northern Russia. Geographically, it refers to a creature of Siberia and is used primarily in that region.

History

Sightings of large, hairy, elusive humanoids, usually sporting an extremely undesirable odor, have persisted in remote parts of the world throughout history. The Bible, with the story of Esau, and the Babylonian epic of Gilgamesh, 2000 B.C., both refer to a hairy, wild, man-like creature. The wild man of the woods is prevalent throughout the Middle Ages in illustrations, engravings, and stonework.[1]

Of the nine or so known names given to this hairy man of the wilderness (*see Statistics*), the two best known are Bigfoot in the U.S. Pacific Northwest and Canada, and Yeti in the Himalayan Mountain range of Nepal and Tibet. Bigfoot is called Sasquatch by Native Americans, and Yeti is called the Abominable Snowman by some people of the Western world.

Legends of Sasquatch, the wild man of the woods, run deep with the Native Americans of British Columbia. The Hoopa tribes of the Northern California mountains describe their own version of Bigfoot called Oma, the boss of the woods. Other Native Americans along the Columbia River carved ape-like faces into stones and painted unexplained hairy giant men with broad shoulders on baskets. Explorer Leif Eriksson with his fellow Norsemen recorded the oldest known encounter with Bigfoot in A.D. 986. On their first journey to the new world, they wrote about hairy, swarthy, ugly monsters with great black eyes.[2]

As white men pushed west in the 1800s, Bigfoot sightings became more prevalent. President Teddy Roosevelt described a very strange creature in his book *The Wilderness Hunter* that walked upright and uttered harsh, ominous howls. In 1958 Bigfoot got its name from workmen on a road in Northern California. News of a cast made of one of several large footprints was eventually picked up by the Associated Press news line. The most astonishing evidence to hit the world, however, came in a 1967 Super-8 mm film by Bigfoot enthusiast Roger Patterson.

For centuries the Yeti has been known to the Asian Sherpas living in the Himalayas. Tales of this elusive creature appear in eleventh-century Hindu poetry. An eighteenth-century Tibetan dictionary of disease lists the curative properties of the flesh of a creature it refers to as a wild man–animal of the mountains. A hairy figure of the snowman drawn on one of the journal pages may very well be the oldest surviving illustration of the Yeti.

Buddhist monks at the Pangboché monastery in Nepal carry on the Yeti folklore. The purported hand of a Yeti, called the "Pangboché hand," is housed there along with other coveted relics. Although Sherpas sometimes intermix the physical and metaphysical worlds, other evidence was uncovered when Americans and Europeans first explored the high Himalayan elevations in the 1920s. Three expeditions were launched in the second half of the twentieth century to bring back hard evidence of the Yeti. The first was mounted by the British *Daily Mail* in 1953 and consisted of three hundred Sherpa guides and scientists who returned with only photos of footprints. The Slick expedition, the most successful, set off in 1957. A highly publicized rival trip to debunk the Yeti myth was carried out in 1960 by Sir Edmond Hillary and Marlin Perkins. Strong evidence brought back by Tom Slick eventually thwarted Hillary and Perkins.[3]

Today, sightings of very large hairy humanoids come in from all remote parts of the world (*see Statistics*). Most recent are reports from Israel and Indonesia. A handful of scientists and scholars devote their lives to in-depth sophisticated Bigfoot and Yeti research (*see Resources for Further Investigation*). Evidence of several types is collected, analyzed, and filed on computer: footprint casts, unusual hair samples from sighting areas, fecal material, photographs, videos or films shot at sightings, recording of Bigfoot screams, analysis of possible nests, and evidence of eating and migration patterns.

The prevailing theories regarding Bigfoot, Yeti, and other unidentified hominids:

1. This creature is an evolved form of Gigantopithicus, the largest and most mild-mannered of the ancient apes, who stood ten feet tall and roamed Southeast Asia 800,000 years ago. *Homo erectus* migrated out of Africa one million years ago, hunting Gigantopithicus into extinction 300,000 years ago.

2. This creature is some large hominid form of unclassified, unknown primate — an extremely primitive form of human being.

3. This creature is, as Peter Byrne humorously puts it, "a man in a fur suit that's been doing it for two hundred years, perhaps he is part of some secret society and they jump out on the road and go 'boo!' to people in the dark."[4]

Hard Evidence

For Bigfoot:

Of the hundreds of footprint casts made of Bigfoot, several actually show dermal ridges. These casts have withstood forensic scrutiny and are considered to be some of the most definitive evidence for the existence of Bigfoot (Krantz, Dr. Grover, Interview, "Bigfoot," *Ancient Mysteries,* 29 March 1998).

Unusual hair samples are typically found in areas of sightings throughout the Northwestern U.S. DNA testing of these and other strikingly similar strands found in other states confirms these animals to be of an unknown species (*Strange Beings and UFOs,* Mysteries of the Unexplained," 5 April 1998).

For the Yeti:

Boxes of evidence and information were brought back from the Slick expedition in the Himalayas. They remained untouched on the Slick estate for years after Tom Slick's death. Eventually discovered by investigator Loren Coleman, they included at least two types of hard evidence: many different types of hair samples and fecal material. The fecal material was analyzed in laboratories both in the United States and in Paris, and was found to contain parasites of an unknown primate.

Two bones taken from the Pangboché hand of a purported Yeti by Peter Byrne were given to W. C. Osmond Hill, a London University primatologist, who found them to be from an unknown primate (Coleman, Loren, Investigator and Author of *Tom Slick and the Search for the Yeti,* Interview, "The Abominable Snowman," *In Search of History,* 30 April 1998).

For the Yeren:

Hair samples from areas of Yeren sightings on the Greenwell expedition in China were taken to the nuclear physics lab at the University of Shanghai. There, they examined the amount of iron and copper present in the strands. Every primate species has a certain ratio of iron and copper in their hair specific to that species. The physicists determined the ratio in the test hairs to be that of a species as yet undiscovered (Greenwell, Richard, Secretary, International Society of Cryptozoologists, Interview, "The Abominable Snowman," *In Search of History*, 30 April 1998).

Documented Cases

Roger Patterson

Bigfoot enthusiast and author, Roger Patterson, and companion, Robert Gimlin, literally stumbled upon what remains to this day, perhaps the most convincing evidence of the existence of Bigfoot.

On the crisp, clear morning of October 20, 1967, Patterson and Gimlin were rounding a bend at Bluff Creek in northwestern California when their horses were suddenly startled by another larger animal squatting along the opposite bank of the creek. Patterson's horse nearly threw him to the ground and Gimlin quickly restrained his from doing the same. Free from his mount, Roger Patterson grabbed his Super-8 mm movie camera and filmed a large, hairy bipedal hominid bounding away from them along the creek and back into the woods. The 952 color frames have to this day passed exhaustive scrutiny. Both the film itself and the creature in the film appear to be genuine.

Scientists worldwide have examined this footage. Among them are cryptozoologist Dr. Grover Krantz and primate anatomist Jeff Meldrum. Both agree that the locomotion of the creature in the film is very reminiscent of the great apes, yet it walks on two legs. The upright manner of walking is similar to *Homo sapiens* with the exception of a slight slouch and the ape-like way it turns its head and chest at the same time.[5]

Jeff Meldrum pointed out details that only an expert in primatology would be able to duplicate: "The subject of the Patterson film walked with a very bent-kneed gate. She's walking very flat-footed. There is a lot of overlap in support between the two limbs and the creature swivels its entire upper body. It's the same way great apes with their thick upper necks have to move when looking back in mid stride."[6]

Six years earlier in the same area of Bluff Creek, investigator Peter Byrne had photographed a fourteen and one half inch long footprint on a road. In collaboration with Dr. Grover Krantz, a professor of anthropology, Bryne recently compared his photograph with casts taken from the Patterson film creature in 1967. Both men agree it is very likely that the two footprints are one and the same.[7]

Beyond the Facts

Around the world and with greater frequency, unknown or previously thought extinct animals and plant life are discovered. To better understand the incredible diversity of our Universe, it helps to become more aware of earthly diversity. Knowledge about unusual discoveries makes it easier for some to accept the reality of a creature like Bigfoot. Following is a brief account of how time and time again nature has diasppointed the skeptics.

In the 1870s several giant squid up to sixty-five feet in length washed up on the shores of Newfoundland.[8] Another fifty-seven-foot specimen was found on the New Zealand coast in 1948.[9] Prior to these discoveries, the giant squid or Kraken was known only from tales of eighteenth- and nineteenth-century sailors. Then, there is the coelacanth — a true living fossil first fished up from the deep waters of southern Africa in 1938,[10] and again in 1952 off the nearby island of Madagascar.[11] Prior to 1938 scientists thought the coelacanth had been extinct since the end of the Cretaceous period some sixty-five million years ago.

Another bizarre sea creature, the oarfish, first washed up on a Bermuda beach in 1860, and one was recently captured on video while still alive along the California coast.[12] Prior to these encounters, the magnificent thirty-foot-long silver oarfish with its long red mane was merely a sea serpent, embedded deep within the human imagination.

While surveying the mid-ocean ridge four miles down in the Pacific, scientists were stunned to find an entire ecosystem thriving not on photosynthesis but on chemosynthesis. A food chain of bacteria, sea anemonies, crabs, tubeworms, and thousands upon thousands of shrimp were living around huge geothermal vents called black smokers that spewed 700°F water laden with minerals and toxic hydrogen sulfide.[13] Since 1977 when this discovery was made, the notion of similar ecosystems on other planets has become more scientifically plausible.

In 1996 scientists announced to the world that a Mars meteor found in Antarctica contained imprints of microscopic extraterrestrial life.[14]

Considering all of these astonishing encounters is it not possible that a large unknown hominid is perhaps living in the wilderness areas of our own world? If this is possible as hard evidence suggests, try to imagine the endless myriad of life-forms awaiting discovery among the hundreds of billions of other stars within our own galaxy, the Milky Way.

Resources for Further Investigation
Leading Research Scientists and Investigators

PeterByrne
Peter Byrne is the director of the Bigfoot Research Project in Mt. Hood, Oregon. The Bigfoot Research Project receives grant funding from the Academy of Applied Science in Concord, New Hampshire. Peter Byrne is conducting perhaps the largest and most sophisticated in-depth investigation of Bigfoot ever launched. The project is similar in approach to studies of whales and dolphins. Project personnel collect and assimilate all available Bigfoot information both historical and current. The first objective is to learn about the creature, its eating, family, and migration habits. Then Byrne hopes to make contact and eventually to communicate with it. Initial results are promising in that behavioral patterns are forming. Peter Byrne has been trying to prove the existence of Bigfoot for thirty years and has investigated thousands of sightings. He joined the Slick group on a ten-year expedition in the

Himalayas searching for the Yeti.

Loren Coleman

An investigator and the author of *Tom Slick and the Search for the Yeti*, Loren Coleman is an authority on the Slick expeditions in search of the Yeti in the Himalayas and is also responsible for uncovering hard evidence from the Slick expeditions.

Jeff Glickman

Jeff Glickman is a Board Certified Forensic Examiner and the executive director of the North American Science Institute. The NASI web site (*see Recommended Internet Sites*) is a must for the novice or professional researcher.

Dr. Richard Greenwell

A cryptozoologist and the secretary for the International Society of Cryptozoology, Tucson, Arizona, Greenwell investigates sightings of unverified animals. His objective is identification of unknown, unclassified animals. He conducted his own expedition into the remote wilderness bordering Vietnam and China in search of the Yeren,[15] from which he produced hard evidence through analysis of hair samples. Greenwell has studied the unknown hairy humanoids in all parts of the world, including Florida,[16] the Pacific Northwest, and China. He believes there is enough strong evidence to warrant continued investigation.

Dr. Grover Krantz

Dr. Grover Krantz is a cryptozoologist and a professor of anthropology at Washington State University. Dr. Krantz studied Bigfoot for over twenty years and is a world authority on cryptozoology — the study of hidden animals. He believes that Sasquatch are descendants of *Gigantopithicus blacky*, a long extinct Southeast Asian gorilla that likely migrated to North America via the Bering Strait land bridge.

Jeff Meldrum

An associate professor of anthropology and anatomy at Idaho State University, Pocatello, Idaho, Jeff Meldrum is an authority on primate locomotion and footprints. He believes hairy humanoids in both the Patterson film and the "Snow Walker" video are not hoaxes because of the locomotion and the primate-like behavior.

Matt Moneymaker

Mr. Moneymaker heads up the Bigfoot Field Researchers' Organization, which maintains a database of all Bigfoot and Sasquatch eyewitness reports and related observations.

Eugene Scott

Eugene Scott, the executive director of the National Center for Science Education, believes there is not enough evidence for the existence of Bigfoot or Yeti.

Recommended Television Programs and Networks

Please consult the Directory of Television Networks in the back of the book for scheduling information and availability of home videos:

"Bigfoot," *Ancient Mysteries*, 60 minutes
on Arts & Entertainment Network
air dates: 03/29/98

"Bigfoot, Skunk Ape, Sasquatch, Salawa" *Animal X*, 1997/1998,
19 minutes
on The Discovery Channel
air dates: 05/17/98

Colorado Bigfoot, *Unsolved Mysteries*,1989, 7 minutes
on Lifetime
air dates: 07/08/98

"Mysteries of the North," *Arthur C. Clarke's Mysterious Universe*, 30 minutes
on The Discovery Channel
air dates: 01/31/98

"Mythical Beasts & Monsters," *Unnatural History*, 1997, 60 minutes
on The Learning Channel
air dates: 01/27/98, 05/29/98

Sightings, Series First Aired 1991, Went Into Syndication 1994
on The Sci-Fi Channel
air dates: 1991 through 1998

Strange Beings and UFO's, Mysteries of the Unexplained, 1995,
60 minutes
on The Discovery Channel
air dates: 04/05/98, 06/18/98

"The Abominable Snowman," *In Search of History,* 1997, 60 minutes
on The History Channel
air dates: 01/15/98, 04/30/98

"The Cavemen," *In Search of History,* 1997, 60 minutes
on The History Channel
air dates: 06/04/98

"The Last Neandertal?," *In Search of History,*60 minutes
on The Discovery Channel
air dates: 10/02/98

"The Missing Apeman," *Arthur C. Clarke's Mysterious World,* 1980,
30 minutes
on The Discovery Channel
air dates: 05/17/98

Yeti, *Unsolved Mysteries,* 1992, 18 minutes
on Lifetime
air dates: 06/29/98

Recommended Books
Big Footprints
by Grove Krantz

Sasquatch
by Roland Smith

Tom Slick and the Search for the Yeti
by Loren Coleman

Yeti, Abominable Snowman
by Elaine Landau

Recommended Internet Sites
Camelot Productions
The site of *The Magic of Our Universe*
http://www.camelotpublishing.com

Bigfoot/Sasquatch Database
http://www.moneymaker.org

Paranormal Phenomena Archive
http://www.in-search-of.com

The Arts and Entertainment Network
http://www.AandE.com

The Discovery Channel
http://www.discovery.com

The History Channel
http://www.HistoryChannel.com

The Learning Channel
http://www.tlc.com

The Sci-Fi Channel
Sightings available through the Dominion site, which can further access
all major paranormal links
http://www.scifi.com/sightings

The Ufomind Paranormal Index and Bookstore
http://www.ufomind.com

Unsolved Mysteries
http://www.unsolved.com

Organizations

BFRO (Bigfoot Field Researchers' Organization)
http://www.moneymaker.org
curators@moneymakers.org
mmkr@bigfoot.com
note: BFRO, NASI, and BRP conduct research collectively

BIGFOOT Co-op (Newsletter)
14602 Montevideo Drive
Whittier, CA   90605

BRP (Bigfoot Research Project)
P. O. Box 126
Mt. Hood, Oregon 97041
800-BIG-FOOT (not available from all areas)
541-352-7000
541-352-7535 (FAX)
TBRP@teleport.com
Peter Byrne, Director
note: BFRO, NASI, and BRP conduct research collectively

CBS (Center for Bigfoot Studies)
10926 Milano Avenue
Norwalk, CA 90650-1638
909-351-9034
Danny Perez, Director

NASI (The North American Science Institute)
209 Oake Avenue, Suite 202
Hood River, Oregon 97031
541-387-4300
541-387-4301 FAX
http://www.nasinet.org
E-mail: NASI@gorge.net
Executive Director: Jeff Glickman
note: BFRO, NASI, and BRP conduct research collectively

The International Society for Cryptozoology
Tucson, Arizona
520-884-8369

Endnotes

[1] "The Abominable Snowman," *In Search of History*, narr. David Ackroyd, prod. Tim Evans, The History Channel, 30 April 1998.

[2] "Bigfoot," *Ancient Mysteries*, narr. Leonard Nemoy, writ. Rob Englehardt, prod. James P. Taylor, Sr., The Arts & Entertainment Network, 29 March 1998.

[3] "The Abominable Snowman," *In Search of History*, 30 April 1998.

[4] "Bigfoot," *Ancient Mysteries*, 29 March 1998.

[5] Krantz, Dr. Grover, Interview, "Bigfoot," *Ancient Mysteries*, 29 March 1998.

[6] Meldrum, Jeff, Primate Anatomist, Interview, *Strange Beings and UFOs*, Mysteries of the Unexplained, narr. James Coburn, writ. Shamus Culhane, prod. Joel Westbrook, The Discovery Channel, 5 April 1998.

[7] *Strange Beings and UFOs*, Mysteries of the Unexplained, 5 April 1998.

[8] "The Loch Ness Monster," *In Search of History*, narr. David Ackroyd, writ. Steve Muscarella and Melissa Jo Peltier, prod. Melissa Jo Peltier, The History Channel, 27 July 1998.

[9] Ellis, Richard, Interview, *Strange Beings and UFOs*, Mysteries of the Unexplained, 5 April 1998.

[10] Luck, Steve, ed., *Oxford Family Encyclopedia*, 1st edition, New York, New York: Oxford University Press, Inc., 1997 (167).

[11] "The Loch Ness Monster," *In Search of History*, 27 July 1998.

[12] "Creatures of the Abyss," *Sci Trek*, narr. Will Lyman, ed. David Hope, prod. Nicolas Kent and Vanessa Phillips, The Discovery Channel, 8 August 1998.

[13] "Creatures of the Abyss," *Sci Trek*, 8 August 1998.

[14] *Strange Beings and UFOs*, Mysteries of the Unexplained, 5 April 1998.

[15] "The Abominable Snowman," *In Search of History*, 30 April 1998.

[16] "Bigfoot, Skunk Ape, Sasquatch, Salawa," *Animal X*, narr. Betsy Aidem, writ. Wendy Wilson, Cathryn Garland, prod. Shauna Stafford, Julie Mapleston, and Melenie Ambrose, The Discovery Channel, 17 May 1998.

Spontaneous Human Combustion

Spontaneous Human Combustion

Definition

Spontaneous Human Combustion. The ignition of a human body part from within the body for no apparent reason and with no external source of fire. The English phrase was first documented around 1805.

Statistics

• As of 1998 there were four books in print on the subject of spontaneous human combustion (Numbers obtained from *R. R. Bowker's Books in Print*, the 1998 list).

• In 1997 there was close to one hour of combined documentaries aired on the subject of spontaneous human combustion. In 1998 there were three hours and forty-five minutes of documentaries aired on the subject (Numbers derived from Gissen, Jay, ed. *The Cable Guide*, 1997, 1998).

• The historical profile of a typical SHC victim is an overweight, alcoholic, older woman possibly alone at the time of the event ("Spontaneous Human Combustion," *The Unexplained*, 19 Feb. 1998).

• "On the outskirts of Vienna, a minister preaching fire and brimstone was said to have exploded into flames witnessed by a stunned congregation of sixty" ("Spontaneous Human Combustion," *Extremely Weird*, 31 Jan. 1998).

• Scientific research has determined that human cadavers will burn completely to powder only if subjected to fire in excess of 2,000°F for a consistent period of twelve hours (Arnold, Larry, Interview, "Spontaneous Human Combustion," *Beyond Bizarre*, 2 June 1998). Yet a

Pennsylvania woman burned completely to ash in only twenty minutes leaving her left hand and legs untouched ("Spontaneous Human Combustion," *The Unexplained*, 19 Feb. 1998).

- "In classic, quintessential spontaneous human combustion cases, the point of origin of the energy that consumes the victim appears to originate in the torso, in the center part of the body, and radiates outward, much like a human fireball" (Arnold, Larry, Leading SHC Researcher, Interview, "Spontaneous Human Combustion," *The Unexplained*, 19 Feb. 1998).

- "England, 1938: a new bride was dancing without her husband, when, before you could say: Got a match?, she was one" ("Spontaneous Human Combustion," *Extremely Weird*, 31 Jan. 1998).

History

The true mystery of spontaneous human combustion exists in combustion temperature comparisons. A house burns at $1,500°F$.[1] A human body burns for several hours, as many as twelve, at 2,200 to $2,600°F$ in a cremation oven called a retort, and even then bone fragments remain with the ash and must be mechanically pulverized. During the SHC phenomenon a living, breathing human is reduced to ash and powder in as little as twenty minutes leaving only parts of limbs. In stark contrast, a house fire victim is usually found intact with the smaller extremities such as fingertips, toes, the nose, or earlobes nearly always obliterated.[2]

Spontaneous human combustion received its name around the turn of the nineteenth century, but its history may date back to the Middle Ages. The medieval notion that everything in existence was made up of earth, wind, fire, and water was widely accepted and villagers thought that fire could erupt unpredictably from the human form. Biblical reference to SHC may have been made in the book of Leviticus, which depicts the sons of Aaron being consumed by a strange flame.[3]

Victorian preoccupation with the phenomenon surfaced in Charles

Dickens's 1852 classic series *Bleak House* where the author dispatches the drunkard Mr. Crooks with a violent episode of spontaneous human combustion.[4] Bizarre deaths from fire continued to show up in reports through the nineteenth and twentieth centuries, but serious scientific research has only recently evolved. Leading researcher and author Larry Arnold has logged over four hundred cases and claims that the general public has little knowledge of SHC and that the medical profession in particular denies its existence.[5]

The prevailing but unproven theories regarding spontaneous human combustion are as follows:

1. One theory is called the "candle effect" which occurs when human body fat becomes fuel for its own fire. But this theory doesn't account for the ignition source.

2. The "human Hiroshima effect" is another concept put forth by researcher Larry Arnold. A chain reaction begins with ignition at the subatomic level of the body and progresses outward to the atomic level, then very rapidly to the physical human structure. This process releases tremendous energy and vaporizes the body's water content.[6]

3. A third theory suggests that a high level of either anger or depression triggers a malfunction of the hypothalamus, an organ in the brain that controls body temperature, which then starts a chain reaction igniting the inner torso with tremendous outward superheated energy.[7]

Documented Cases
Mary Reeser

Two painters from a house across the street and landlady Mrs. Panzy Carpenter experienced the shock of a lifetime on July 3, 1951. That morning they entered Mary Reeser's room on the second floor of her boarding house in St. Petersburg, Florida. Earlier, while attempting to deliver a telegram, Mrs. Carpenter scorched her hand on the doorknob. Mary Reeser's remains occupied a pile in the center of the room and included an adult human skull reduced to the size of a grapefruit, a few vertebrae fused completely together, the heel of her left foot and a little ash, all of which collectively weighed only ten pounds.

Though what remained of Mary clearly showed signs of intense heat around 2,000°F, all other objects in the room were nearly untouched by the flames. An electric clock had stopped, indicating the time of the fire had been around 4:20 A.M., candles on the dresser were barely melted, the mirror was cracked, yet no other furniture, bed linens, draperies, or carpet were burned. This conflicting evidence completely baffled all investigators including police, firemen, and insurance and medical personnel. The officials concluded and the coroner's report stated that Mary Reeser died as a result of fire, the origin of which remains unknown.[8]

Jack Angel

Some spontaneous human combustion victims have lived to tell about their incredible ordeal. Jack Angel is one such person.

On the evening of November 11, 1924, clothing representative Jack Angel pulled into a motel in Savannah, Georgia for the night, only to find his room rented to another party. He returned to his motor home in the parking lot to get a good night's rest before a meeting with a clothing buyer the following morning. Jack never made it to that appointment.

Four days later, Mr. Angel awoke to find his right hand incinerated from the inside out. He was also badly burned on his right chest, his groin and the nape of his neck. A few of his vertebrae had also fused together. Physicians determined that Jack's burns originated from within the body and were caused by some high energy electrical type source. Evidence of any electrical malfunction in his motor home or anywhere else near him could not be found. Most significantly, Jack's pajamas, bed linens, and bed were all untouched by fire. This case is well documented with photographs and physicians reports.[9]

Hard Evidence

The most convincing evidence confirming the reality of spontaneous human combustion lies with the victims, their medically documented wounds, and their firsthand accounts of the fires as they transpired. These testimonials, coupled with even a simple understanding of combustion temperatures as outlined in the history section, provide strong evidence suggesting that something very unusual is taking place in the body during these events. The ignition source of SHC remains theoretical.

Beyond the Facts

Why is mainstream science, in this case the medical profession, so afraid to investigate the unexplained? What harm is there in following human curiosity to the cutting edge of discovery, and why does mainstream science seem to shun scientists who do so? Why are some humans so afraid to crawl out of their shell and have a good look around?

Spontaneous human combustion is not unlike the phenomenon of falling stuff in its top-notch rating on the meter of the bizarre. But what is the difference in the clinical investigation of SHC and some strange unknown virus? Both affect the human organism. What is the difference between the scientific investigation of say the Ebola virus, spontaneous human combustion, or extraterrestrial life? They are all legitimate human problems seeking solutions. The scientific method can be applied to one as well as it can to the others. Then why is mainstream science eager to pursue viruses and reluctant to take a good hard look at all the evidence supporting the reality of anomalies such as extraterrestrial life or SHC?

The problem may lie in the gap between the burgeoning complexity of new scientific challenges such as understanding extraterrestrial life and the slower evolution of the human scientific mentality. The problem lies with the historical inflexibility of the human scientific comfort zone to consider all possibilities. Mainstream science accepts challenges such as viruses that fall within this zone and rejects issues such as SHC or extraterrestrial visitation that fall outside the zone. A perfect example is listening for extraterrestrial radio waves from deep space instead of applying the scientific method to the overwhelming evidence indicating that E.T. has already come and gone.

As with other anomalies it is very interesting to observe the reasoning process of the researchers involved. Consider Joe Nickell.

Mr. Nickell and others with similar views try to explain unusual phenomena in terms of known concepts even when these concepts are not supported by the facts and all the evidence. In documentary interviews regarding SHC, Mr. Nickell points to cigarette or pipe smoking accidents as the cause for human combustion, even though countless fire investigation reports of cigarette burn victims seem to contradict his reasoning:[10] SHC victims are reduced almost completely and very quickly to ash by intense heat whereas cigarette burn victims are not.

Research is often limited by what is already known about the Universe rather than being inspired by the actual Universe, which is far more complex and far more fascinating. The pursuit of real truth demands careful scrutiny of all evidence regardless of how unfamiliar it may seem. The most comfortable hypothesis may not be the best hypothesis. It is not a matter of skepticism versus belief, it is a matter of thoroughness. Being thorough is good science. Ignoring significant evidence is not.

In the fascinating SHC cases of Jack Angel and Mary Reeser, could it be possible for some dormant mechanism in the brain to periodically rear its head, altering human physiology enough to cause spontaneous human combustion? Could some hidden power of the mind become energized under physical, spiritual, or emotional stress, as Arthur C.

Clarke suggests may be happening in cases of stigmata (*see the chapter on Miracles and Angels*). A recent medical study confirmed that depression can increase the likelihood of cancer through release of a substance in the body that reduces the effectiveness of the immune system.[11] Could humans possess a built-in self-destruct mechanism activated by depression that could help trigger a deadly disease such as cancer, or a case of spontaneous human combustion, to end an unhappy physical existence?

Resources for Further Investigation
Leading Research Scientists and Investigators

Larry Arnold

He is the leading investigator of spontaneous human combustion and has written a book on the four hundred cases he has researched over the past twenty years. He has been interviewed for documentaries more than any other researcher. He believes that people with type A hot-tempered personalities are good candidates for SHC. Larry has investigated those who died from SHC and those who survived the experience.

Arthur C. Clarke

Veteran researcher, author, and host of his own television documentary, Arthur Clarke has researched the better-known cases such as Mary Reeser and George Mott as well as those of British surgeon Jonathan Earnshaw, which involved exploding stomach operations.

Joe Nickell

The editor of the *Skeptical Inquirer*, Mr. Nickell seeks to attach conventional, historical causes or explanations to unexplained phenomena. He does not explain evidence that could refute his conventional reasoning, preferring to explain the Universe by what is known rather than by what could be known with more study.

Recommended Television Programs and Networks

Please consult the Directory of Television Networks in the back of the book for scheduling, information, and availability of home videos:

Sightings, Series First Aired 1991, Went Into Syndication 1994
on The Sci-Fi Channel
air dates: 1991 through 1998

"Spontaneous Human Combustion," *Arthur C. Clarke's Mysterious Universe*, 30 minutes
on The Discovery Channel
air dates: 05/17/98, 10/17/98, 05/17/98

"Spontaneous Human Combustion," *Beyond Bizarre*, 12 minutes
on The Discovery Channel
air dates: 06/02/98

"Spontaneous Human Combustion," *Extremely Weird*, 1995,
8 minutes
on The Learning Channel
air dates: 01/03/98, 01/31/98

"Spontaneous Human Combustion," *The Unexplained*, 1997,
60 minutes
on The Arts & Entertainment Network
air dates: 02/19/98

Recommended Books

Ablaze!
by Larry Arnold

Bleak House
by Charles Dickens

Spontaneous Human Combustion
by Jenny Randles and Peter Hough

Recommended Internet Sites

Camelot Productions
The site of *The Magic of Our Universe*
http://www.camelotpublishing.com

Paranormal Phenomena Archive
http://www.in-search-of.com

The Arts and Entertainment Network
http://www.AandE.com

The Discovery Channel
http://www.discovery.com

The Learning Channel
http://www.tlc.com

The Sci-Fi Channel
Sightings available through the Dominion site, which can further access
all major paranormal links
http://www.scifi.com/sightings

The Ufomind Paranormal Index and Bookstore
http://www.ufomind.com

Unsolved Mysteries
http://www.unsolved.com

Organizations

Parascience International
Director Larry Arnold

Endnotes

[1] Purdy, Robert, retired Emergency Services Coordinator for Essex County, New York, Interview, "S.H.C.," *Sightings*, Update, narr. Tim White, writ. Susan Michaels, prod. Henry Winkler and Ann Daniel, The Sci-Fi Channel, 7 June 1998.

[2] Natale, Carl, President, UBA Fire Investigators, Interview, "Spontaneous Human Combustion," *The Unexplained*, narr. Norm Woodel, writ. Gaylon Emerzian, prod. Gaylon Emerzian, The Arts & Entertainment Network, 19 Feb. 1998.

[3] "Spontaneous Human Combustion," *The Unexplained*, 19 Feb. 1998.

[4] "Spontaneous Human Combustion," *The Unexplained*, 19 Feb. 1998.

[5] "Spontaneous Human Combustion," *Extremely Weird*, narr. Jay Thomas, ed. Tony Black, prod. Alexander Enright, The Learning Channel, 31 Jan. 1998.

[6] Arnold, Larry, Interview, "Spontaneous Human Combustion," *The Unexplained*, narr. Norm Woodel, writ. Gaylon Emerzian, prod. Gaylon Emerzian, The Arts & Entertainment Network, 19 Feb. 1998.

[7] Arnold, Larry, Interview, "Spontaneous Human Combustion," *The Unexplained*, narr. Norm Woodel, writ. Gaylon Emerzian, prod. Gaylon Emerzian, The Arts & Entertainment Network, 19 Feb. 1998.

[8] "Spontaneous Human Combustion," *Extremely Weird*, 31 Jan. 1998.

[9] "Spontaneous Human Combustion," *Extremely Weird*, 31 Jan. 1998.

[10] Haggerty, Chief Paul, Retired, Upper Darby Fire Dept., Interview, "Spontaneous Human Combustion," *The Unexplained*, narr. Norm Woodel, writ. Gaylon Emerzian, prod. Gaylon Emerzian, The Arts & Entertainment Network, 19 Feb. 1998.

[11] *CNN Headline News*, 15 Dec. 1998.

Miracles
and
Angels

Miracles and Angels

Definitions

Miracle. An event wherein the occurrence and cause of which are not governed by the human laws of nature or physics, and where a supernatural or divine power is perceived as the cause of the event. Most major world religions incorporate the concept of miracles in their belief systems. The word was first documented in English around 1150 and is derived from the Middle English Language.

Angel. A spiritual being inferior to God but superior to man, the purpose of which is to act as an attendant or messenger of God. The concept of the angel is used in Judaic, Islamic and Christian religions. The Christian hierarchy of angels consists of nine orders with Seraphim at the top, Cherubim, Thrones, Dominations, Virtues, Power, Principalities, and Archangels in descending order, and with Angels at the lowest position before man. The word originated in English around A.D. 950 and has evolved from the Greek word *angelos* meaning "messenger of God."

Statistics

- As of 1998, there were 540 books in print on the subjects of "miracles" and "angels." The numbers of books remaining in print has increased from 1 in 1949 to 96 in 1997 with dramatic increases through the 1990s. This activity suggests an equally dramatic increase in interest in the phenomena of miracles and angels (Numbers obtained from *R. R. Bowker's Books in Print*, the 1998 list).

- In 1997 there were approximately five hours and forty minutes of documentaries aired regarding miracles and angels. In 1998 there were fifteen hours and fifteen minutes of documentaries aired on the subjects (Numbers derived from Gissen, Jay. ed. *The Cable Guide*, 1997, 1998).

• Eighty-two percent of Americans believe in the healing power of personal prayer. Seventy-three percent believe praying for someone else can help cure their illness. Seventy-seven percent believe God sometimes intervenes to cure people with a serious illness, and sixty-four percent believe doctors should join their patients in prayer when patients request it (*CNN Time Poll*, 1996).

• Research at Harvard, Duke, Tufts, and Stanford suggests a link may exist between the power of the mind and the power to heal (*Sightings*, 18 May 1998).

• "Nowhere in the miraculous book of miracles, the Hebrew Bible, does the word 'miracle' occur" ("Magic and Miracles in the Old Testament," *Mysteries of the Bible*, 7 June 1998).

• Cases of alleged miracles are rigorously reviewed by Vatican theologians and medical experts and must be proven beyond all doubt prior to being proclaimed a miracle. Cases with any questionable aspects whatsoever are immediately rendered unworthy of being authenticated ("Miracles and Sainthood," *Strange But True?*, 12 March 1998).

• "The Vatican archives house accounts and details of authenticated miracles dating back to the sixteenth century" ("Miracles and Sainthood," *Strange But True?*, 12 March 1998).

• "The Books of Saints contains all persons beatified as saints by the Pope. To be canonized, a candidate must prove one or two miracles that have been attributed to their power of intercession" ("Miracles and Sainthood," *Strange But True?*, 12 March 1998).

• "To date, the Roman Catholic Church has documented sixty-five miracles of Bernadette's Spring in Lourdes, France. Eighteen of these people are still living today. Many thousands of others believe they have been cured while at Lourdes though their miracles were not authenticated by the church" (*Unsolved Mysteries,* 10 July 1998).

- *The Oxford Family Encyclopedia* claims that as many as five million people make the pilgrimage to Lourdes every year (*Oxford Family Encyclopedia,* 1997, p. 408).

- Stigmata are wounds that mimic those sustained by Jesus during his crucifixion. Founder of the Franciscan order, Saint Francis of Assisi, also allegedly received the wounds of Christ in a miracle of A.D. 1224, and it is believed 330 other people have received stigmata over the past six hundred years (*Oxford Family Encyclopedia,* 1997, p. 639).

- At least 150 studies have been conducted on the healing power of prayer in hospitals, clinics, and laboratories. These studies indicate significant physiological changes such as reduced blood pressure, lowered heart rate, reduced cholesterol levels, and improved immune system changes (Dossey, Dr. Larry, Interview, "Miracles and Sainthood," *Strange But True,* 12 March 1998).

History

The Bible refers to many extraordinary events that surpass all known human laws of nature and were caused by supernatural forces. Yet these events are not once referred to as miracles in the Old Testament text. Attempts have been made by some scholars to explain away some early Biblical miracles as natural events. Even these skeptics, however, find no argument with the historical timing between natural events and Biblical events. Miraculous in itself, this precise timing between these two sets of events is found throughout the Bible. One example of a Biblical timing miracle is the concurrence of the ten plagues implemented by God in Exodus to release the Israelites from bondage with ten natural events that occurred in sequence at precisely the same points in history.

Another example of concurrent timing, was the parting and release of the Red Sea by Moses to drown the Egyptians pursuing the Israelites, and a tidal wave caused by a volcano in the Mediterranean.[1]

Apparently, however, not all "the magic of our universe" is available for human use. In the Bible, God makes a terse distinction between his divine miracles and forbidden human magic. Moses was reprimanded fiercely by God when he did not follow his divine instructions of miracle fulfillment and attempted to achieve the same results by providing drinking water from a rock near the end of Exodus (20:12). Moses, briefly and unintentionally, had switched from acting as the conduit between God and the Israelites, to mimicking God Himself.[2]

To many people, perhaps the greatest miracle of the Bible is the Bible itself — the miraculous manner in which it has withstood countless rigorous tests of time. It has done so in an unparalleled descriptive artistic style.

Miracles have manifested in several ways throughout history. Some are more convincing than others. It has been reported that icons weep, Indian elephant icons drink milk, and that relics of saints or martyrs have miraculous power. The best documented, however, are the stigmata phenomena and people or places with supernatural powers of healing. The latter are often interfused with "apparitions" of angels or the blessed Virgin Mary.

Medjugoria, Batania, and Fatima are well-known places of miracles, but Bernadette's spring in Lourdes, France is the most frequently visited and best documented in the world. The waters of Bernadette's spring attract up to five million visitors every year. They wait in long lines sometimes for hours hoping to dip into the healing waters. Some arrive for spiritual cleansing, while others come to be cured of physical affliction. The spring's history began with the vision of a humble miller's daughter named Bernadette Soubirous. One hundred forty years ago, Lourdes was a quaint French village at the base of the Pyrenees Mountain range near the Spanish border. On February 11, 1858 in a grotto near town, an apparition of a woman in a blue and white gown appeared before Bernadette and beckoned her to dig in a specific place. As she dug, water began oozing from the ground.[3] The Roman Catholic Church authenticated Bernadette's vision in 1862.

So coveted is Bernadette's spring, as it is sometimes known, that a basilica was built over it, and in 1933 Bernadette Soubirous was proclaimed a saint by the Vatican. It is believed that Bernadette's apparition was the blessed Virgin Mary guiding this humble peasant girl to unearth waters of divine healing.[4]

Also credited with supernatural powers of healing are some stigmatics such as Padre Pio. Stigmatics are people who spontaneously display the wounds of Christ. St. Francis of Assisi was the first recorded stigmatic, displaying his wounds in 1224. In 1375, rays of light from a crucifix burned into the hands, feet, and chest of St. Katherine of Sienna, Italy. Anne Katherine Emerig of Germany endured annual Easter stigmata for thirteen years until her death in 1824. From 1899 to 1903, an Italian woman named Gemma Gullgani experienced stigmata only on Thursdays and Fridays, and another woman from Germany, Theresa Noyman, bled from her face, feet, and chest every weekend from the 1920s to the 1950s. All of these events are well documented. Some are on film.[5]

Extraordinary traumatic events such as the near-death experience (NDE) or even an alien abduction have also been known to trigger miraculous healing powers in people. Grace DiBicarri's NDE case in this chapter and the alien abduction experience of Elizabeth Robinson are examples (*see the timeline, 1997, in the chapter on Extraterrestrial Life*). Still many others, such as Joan Wester Anderson, have experienced miracles for no apparent rhyme or reason.

There are three basic theories regarding miracles:

1. Miracles are genuine and can be attributed to divine or other supernatural intervention. Some mechanisms that may trigger miracles are prayer, the near-death experience, stigmata, divine apparitions, or the alleged alien abduction experience.

2. Miracles are strictly physiologically based and the human organism possesses the ability to heal itself.

3. Some combination of numbers 1 and 2.

Angels are currently impossible to study with known human science, though more and more hospital personnel are coming forward with their eyewitness accounts of angels appearing around the dying. The medieval perception of the angel of death was that of the familiar drawn, faceless, skeletal figure cloaked in a dark robe and brandishing a scythe. The real angel is apparently no such creature. Angel encounters, as they are now called, occur more frequently than most people think. In fact they occur more often than not. According to researcher Leanord Day some angels may even appear as a cloud or mist, or in human or even animal form.[6]

Documented Cases
The Medical Miracle of Robert Gutherman

What began as a simple earache when he was fifteen, nearly evolved into a fatal illness. Robert was first diagnosed with an acute mastoid infection where part of the bone connecting the ear to the brain had been destroyed. This exposed the brain cover called the "dura mater." Had the infection progressed further, Robert would have acquired meningitis or possibly a brain abscess, either of which would have resulted in death. Robert was to undergo a procedure called a mastoidectomy, which would save his life, but which would result in permanent loss of hearing in one ear.

Robert's mother, a devout Roman Catholic, prayed for his recovery.

On the evening before Robert's operation, something remarkable occurred. Robert insisted that he could hear someone calling his name from the hall. The next morning Mrs. Gutherman, convinced Robert could now hear, talked the doctor into another ear exam rather than the intrusive surgery. Results indicated the infection had simply vanished and normal hearing had been restored. Robert's ear surgeon, Dr. Miles Turtz, was dumbfounded and could not explain this outcome. He had done nothing to achieve this result.

So remarkable was Robert Gutherman's recovery that the archdiocese of Philadelphia established several tribunal hearings to examine the case in detail. Acting on established Vatican procedure for investigating miracle claims, the tribunal interviewed key witnesses. Dr. Turtz outlined the medical details. He explained how the ossicals, the middle ear bones, were completely eradicated from so much infection. Upon further observation the next morning however, the ossicals had fused together to repair the hole in the eardrum. The doctor asked Mrs. Gutherman what she and her son were doing that his other patients were not. Mrs. Gutherman replied: "We pray."

Having dismissed medical reasons for Robert's recovery, the tribunal sought evidence that prayer had been instrumental in the cure. Mrs. Gutherman revealed her encounters with a sister of the Sacrament Order where Robert had once been an alter boy. She had gone to see the nuns to ask the Lord to help her bear Robert's pain. Then, according to Sister Ruth Catherine, she asked the Lord to heal her son. Mother Catherine Drexel, founder of the nun's order, died in 1955 but had remained the focus of the order's prayers. She was an heiress who had been very generous with the poor. The sisters placed great faith in Mother Catherine's healing abilities.

Later, the tribunal requested another examination of Robert's inner ear to prove that healing was attained by non-medical means. This exam was conducted with the latest technology thirteen years after Robert's original infection by Dr. Louis Lowry, a leading American ear specialist. Against all anticipated findings, there was no evidence of earlier damage. The eardrum and ossicals were normal. Professor Lowry had no medical or clinical explanation for the fact that there were no ossicals in 1974, but normal ossicals in 1987.

Robert Gutherman's miracle case was passed on from the archdiocese of Philadelphia to the Vatican and to the Pope himself. The case was scrutinized by the Vatican's medical and theological experts. Robert's case was next heard by the Cardinal's Congregation for the Causes of Saints in the Vatican's Apostolic Palace. Many cases fail at this rigorous final stage, but this committee passed Robert's case unanimously in 1987. Robert's cure was finally declared a miracle by the Pope. Mother Catherine Drexel was beatified as a saint in a Vatican ceremony in 1988. The Gutherman family was in attendance.[7]

Grace DiBicarri, otherwise known as "Amazing Grace"

People with incurable diseases flock to Danbury, Connecticut to seek the miraculous healing power of an evangelical faith healer appropriately named "Amazing Grace." Many believe Grace stimulates the innate self-healing capacity of individuals, which cures the medically incurable. Grace believes she has been blessed to be a healing conduit to God.

Grace had a near-death experience during which she "floated up into the heavens and saw a bright light." She wanted desperately to enter the light as it overwhelmed her with warmth and love, but she told herself, "No, I'm not ready, I'm not ready." Her spirit returned to her body and she awoke. She asked God thankfully what she could do. God told her simply to sing and leave the rest to him.

In a typical service, Grace claims that God guides her down the aisle and tells her to go left, right, or straight. She stops at the person she believes God has chosen. Grace feels that God directs her to certain people, many of whom are afflicted with incurable maladies. Grace's healing record is well documented by the medical profession in the Danbury, Connecticut area. Following are four of countless remarkable cases:

Harriett Grimaldi was diagnosed in 1987 with an incurable disease called scleroderma. Her physician, Ronald Chodosh of the Albert Einstein School of Medicine, claimed she was barely conscious and suffering with blood pressure problems, seizures, kidney failure, severe anemia, and fluid around her heart and lungs. Her prognosis was certain — death was imminent. She remained in the Phelpps Memorial Hospital intensive care unit for five months. After hearing of Grace DiBicarri, she persuaded the hospital to allow her to attend one of Grace's healing sessions. Her first attendance resulted in no measurable improvement. With each successive visit however, Grace prayed over her and she began to feel improved mobility. First, she could move her shoulders, and eventually, her hands. Over time, Harriett made a complete recovery and is now a volunteer gardener at Phelpps Hospital where she was once a terminal patient. Dr. Chodosh has no medical explanation for her survival, turnaround, improvement, or healing.

Carol Guilfoil had six physicians tell her that all she had to look forward to was a slow, perhaps agonizing life of dealing with multiple sclerosis. Carol attended one of Grace's gatherings, this time in a gymnasium. Grace approached her and asked what illness afflicted her. After Carol replied, Grace touched her forehead and Carol immediately fell backwards. Carol claims she was instantly and completely healed. Grace asked for Carol's cane and told her to walk from one end of the gymnasium to the other. Carol did so with complete astonishment. Normally an endeavor such as this would have resulted in certain injury from a fall. Neither Carol nor her husband had an explanation other than that a miracle had occurred.

A friend of chiropractor Dr. John Pagano had been clinically deaf in the right ear for over twenty years. Grace pointed to him during one meeting and told him he would be healed that night. As Dr. Pagano explained it, his friend's right ear suddenly popped. The pop was quite audible, and Grace asked the audience if they heard it. People around him did. From that moment on, he has had perfect hearing in his right ear.

Dr. Pagano revealed another case that involved a man suffering from a chronic herniated disk. Foey Datino had absolutely no faith in Grace whatsoever. He reluctantly attended one of Grace's healing sessions. His wife drove him, but he would not go in. Foey kept ducking from Grace hoping to remain unnoticed. Grace picked him out and told him to come forward. As Grace touched him, he fell backward as others had. While laying on the floor, he felt heat surge through his legs and into his thighs. He squirmed a bit and then straightened out. As the ushers began to help him up, Grace stopped them and said he would get up on his own. With no assistance, he stood straight up for the first time in years. He began crying in front of the people he had been embarrassed to be seen with.

Dr. Pagano believes that Grace in some way stimulates the healing forces within people, and further that the faith these people have in Grace or in God or in hope itself, is perhaps responsible for a self-induced healing. Grace on the other hand sees it differently: "It doesn't matter what religion you are. God loves all people of all faiths, all religions."

Grace DiBicarri accepts no money for her healing and suggests faith healing is not a substitute for conventional medicine.[8]

The Stigmata of Padre Pio

So well known was the stigmatic Padre Pio that the entire town of San Giovanni Rotando in Italy grew up around the simple friary where he lived and preached. His stigmata first appeared in 1918 and bled consistently for fifty years until his death in 1968. Worshipers came by the hundreds of thousands hoping to get close enough to him during mass to get a glimpse of the wounds of Christ he bore on his hands.

According to Friar Joseph Pius, Padre Pio received his stigmata on September 20, 1918. Father Pio was giving thanks in front of the crucifix in the friary chapel. Wounds on the resurrected body of Christ emitted rays of light energy that penetrated matching areas on Padre Pio's body. These rays of light opened wounds that had already secretly existed on the priest's body for eight years. From that day forward Padre Pio concealed his hands from public view except when he displayed them bleeding during mass. Monsignor Michael Buckley was privileged to have served mass with Padre Pio and witnessed that candlelight from the altar shined through the wounds.

Miracles of healing and the gift of prophecy were attributed to Padre Pio. Physicians who examined the priest throughout his life had no medical explanation for the stigmata. Photographs taken after his death in 1968 revealed only tiny scars on his hands and side. So inspirational were his stigmata during his life that over 100,000 people attended his funeral.[9]

Jack Almon and the Angel of Death

Skeptical by profession as a disciplined police officer, Jack Almon became a believer in the reality of angels on the evening of January 7, 1984. Eleven to twelve angels descended into his mother's hospital room during her final hours of life. The transparent beings appeared in human form around Jack and his mother and emanated a warm glow. Jack's mother died four hours after the angels ascended and to this day Jack remains convinced they came to usher his mother's spirit into heaven.[10]

Beyond the Facts

For the first time in our journey through the magic of our universe we enter the ethereal space of the supernatural. We find the phenomenon of miracles supported by two opposing theories: one based in science — of self-induced physiological activity, the other based in faith — of divine intervention or a connection with a more powerful universal force. Also interrelationships crop up between miracles, healing, the near-death experience, and prophecy in both the historical case of Padre Pio and the more contemporary case of Amazing Grace (*see the chapters on Extrasensory Perception and Life After Death*).

The phenomenon of miracles is genuine. Through clinical documentation, the cases presented herein suggest the existence of powers beyond normal human capacity. For some in the scientific community, these powers may be generated by human physiology and are indicative of our own untapped power (*see the chapter on Extrasensory Perception*). For spiritual and religious believers, these miraculous supernatural powers of healing are unquestionably signs of the power of God and our spiritual Universe.

Can science discover the supernatural or has human science defined itself to narrowly? If science is the most accurate template of knowledge of our physical world but the supernatural realm does exist, then why are the "truths" seemingly in conflict? What is the scientific method? Isn't it a process, not a result. Should mainstream science be limited by hypothesis? Where do hypothesis come from? Is the scientific method capable of dealing with supernatural phenomena?

Light once again plays a significant role in a universal anomaly. Rays of light energy emanate from a crucifix to open the stigmata of Padre Pio in 1918 as they did for Saint Katherine of Sienna in 1375. Light of unusual supernatural intensity seems to envelope angels as in the case of Jack Almon and the angels of death. With extraterrestrials, light energy was used in ways that defy the laws of known human science: Humans are transported through light beams into craft as with the Weiner twins, and light shafts are used to analyze water as in the Gosford incident (*see the Extraterrestrial timeline*). Many forms of light energy seem to be interwoven into our Universe in ways beyond current human understanding.

Finally, in all of its complex, brilliant diversity, in all of its color, in all of its overwhelming grandeur: the trees, our furry little pets, the oceans and mountains, ourselves; everything known to us — is not life itself the most astounding and enchanting miracle of them all?

Resources for Further Investigation
Leading Research Scientists and Investigators

Joan Wester Anderson
Joan Anderson has documented numerous cases of miracles and angels in her popular books.

Arthur C. Clarke
Well-known author, inventor, and documentary host, A. C. Clarke suggests stigmata may be caused by a dormant power of the mind that becomes energized under physical, spiritual, or emotional stress.

Dr. Peter Haas
A Professor of Religious Studies at Vanderbilt University, Dr. Haas is an authority on scientific research into miracles. He believes miracles are genuine and that the phenomenon deserves serious research.

Melvin Morse, M.D.
Dr. Morse is a leading authority on cases of miracles and life after death involving children.

Bernie S. Siegal, M.D.
Though at first a naturally skeptical physician, Dr. Siegal believes miracles are real. He has documented fascinating cases involving his own patients.

Paul Robert Walker
Author and researcher Paul Walker has retrieved numerous cases of miracles and other supernatural phenomena from the Internet. He has found that humans have a renewed interest in miracles, angels, and life beyond death for two reasons: People are looking beyond material wealth for happiness, and they believe the new millennium will bring a new unifying level of awareness for the human race. Walker also suggests the

non-physical Universe may be responsive to our prayers and expectations — a theory evidenced by recent discoveries in particle physics.[11]

Recommended Television Programs and Networks

Please consult the Directory of Television Networks in the back of the book for scheduling information and availability of home videos:

Angel, *Unsolved Mysteries*, 8 minutes
on Lifetime
air dates: 05/28/98

Angel Stories, 1995, 60 minutes
on The Learning Channel
air dates: 12/25/97, 12/25/98

"Angels," *Strange but True?* 1997, 15 minutes
on The Discovery Channel
air dates: 02/12/98, 05/17/98, 10/08/98

Entertaining Angels Unawares, 1995, 60 minutes
on The Learning Channel
air dates: 12/25/97, 12/25/98

"*Jesus*: Holy Child," *Mysteries of the Bible*, 1994, 60 minutes
on The Arts & Entertainment Network
air dates: 06/07/98

Lourdes, France, *Unsolved Mysteries*, 1994, 25 minutes
on Lifetime
air dates: 07/10/98, 02/24/98

"Magic and Miracles in the Old Testament," *Mysteries of the Bible*,
 1994, 60 minutes
on Arts & Entertainment Network
air dates: 06/18/98

Medjugorie, *Unsolved Mysteries*, 15 minutes
on Lifetime
air dates: 06/25/98

Mexico City, Our Lady of Guadeloupe, *Unsolved Mysteries*,
12 minutes
on Lifetime
air dates: 07/22/98

Miracles, *Unsolved Mysteries*, 9 minutes
on Lifetime
air dates: 05/29/98

"Miracles and Sainthood," *Strange But True?*, 1997, 15 minues
on The Discovery Channel
air dates: 03/12/98

Miracle of Fatima, *Unsolved Mysteries*, 15 minutes
on Lifetime
air dates: 07/29/98

Miracles of Prayer, *Unsolved Mysteries*, 10 minutes
on Lifetime
air dates: 09/07/98

Miracles of the Milk-Drinking Statues, *Extremely Weird*, 1995,
2 minutes
on The Learning Channel
air dates: 01/03/98, 01/31/98

Modern Miracle, *Unsolved Mysteries*, 7 minutes
on Lifetime
air dates: 03/19/98

"Mysteries from Heaven," *Arthur C. Clarke's Mysterious Universe*, 1994,
30 minutes
on The Discovery Channel
air dates: 10/17/98, 08/30/98

"Mysteries of India," *Arthur C. Clarke's Mysterious Universe*, 30 minutes
on The Discovery Channel
air dates: 03/07/98

Padre Pio, *Unsolved Mysteries*, 20 minutes
on Lifetime
air dates: 08/19/98

"Power of Prayer," *The Unexplained*, 1997, 60 minutes
on The Arts & Entertainment Network
air dates: 10/18/98

Rita Klaus, *Unsolved Mysteries*, 8 minutes
on Lifetime
air dates: 06/11/98, 06/29/98

Saving Angels, *Unsolved Mysteries*, 10 minutes
on Lifetime
air dates: 06/16/98

"Secrets of Survival," *The Unexplained*, 1998, 60 minutes
on The Arts & Entertainment Network
air dates: 02/26/98

Sightings, Series First Aired 1991, Went Into Syndication 1994
on The Sci-Fi Channel
air dates: 1991 through 1998

"STIGMATA The Wounds of Christ?" *Arthur C. Clarke's World of Strange Powers*, 1994, 30 minutes
on The Discovery Channel
air dates: 03/15/98

Stories of Miracles, Part I and Part II, 1996, 120 minutes
on The Learning Channel
air dates: 12/25/97, 12/25/98

Strictly Supernatural, 60 minutes
on The Discovery Channel
air dates: 10/20/97 through 10/22/97

The Shroud of Turin, *Unsolved Mysteries*, 1991, 12 minutes
on Lifetime
air dates: 08/03/98

Touched by an Angel (For my Mother, Jean Davis Moberg)
on CBS
airdates: Sunday evenings

Recommended Books
An Angel to Watch Over Me
by Joan Wester Anderson

Angels A to Z
by James R. Lewis and Evelyn Dorothy Oliver

Angels: The Mysterious Messengers
by Joan Wester Anderson

Celebration of Miracles
by Jodie Berndt

Every Day's A Miracle
by Paul Robert Walker

Know Your Angels
by John Ronner

Love, Medicine & Miracles
by Bernie S. Siegal, M.D.

Where Angels Walk
by Joan Wester Anderson

Where Miracles Happen
by Joan Wester Anderson

Recommended Internet Sites
Angel Art
http://www.lakeyart.com

Camelot Productions
The site of *The Magic of Our Universe*
http://www.camelotpublishing.com

Paranormal Phenomena Archive
http://www.in-search-of.com

The Arts and Entertainment Network
http://www.AandE.com

The Discovery Channel
http://www.discovery.com

The History Channel
http://www.HistoryChannel.com

The Learning Channel
http://www.tlc.com

The Ufomind Paranormal Index and Bookstore
http://www.ufomind.com

Unsolved Mysteries
http://www.unsolved.com

Your Public Broadcasting Station
http://www.pbs.org

Endnotes

[1] "Magic and Miracles in the Old Testament," *Mysteries of the Bible*, narr. Richard Kiley and Jean Simmons, writ. Tracey Benger and Susan Lutz, prod. Bram Roos, The Arts & Entertainment Network, 7 June 1998.

[2] "Magic and Miracles in the Old Testament," *Mysteries of the Bible*, 7 June 1998.

[3] Luck, Steve, ed. *Oxford Family Encyclopedia*, 1st edition, New York, New York: Oxford University Press, Inc. 1997 (408).

[4] *Unsolved Mysteries*, The Unexplained, narr. Robert Stack, writ. Raymond Bridgers, prod. Cosgrove Meurer Productions, Lifetime, 24 Feb. 1998.

[5] "STIGMATA The Wounds of Christ?," *Arthur C. Clarke's World of Strange Powers*, narr. Stanley Anderson, prod. Adam Hart-Davis, The Discovery Channel, 15 March 1998.

[6] "Angel of Death," *Sightings*, narr. Tim White, writ. Susan Michaels, prod. Kim Steer, Henry Winkler and Ann Daniel, The Sci-Fi Channel, 28 April 1998.

[7] "Miracles and Sainthood," *Strange But True?*, narr. Michael Aspel, prod. Ralph Jones and Simon Shaps, The Discovery Channel, 12 March 1998.

[8] "Amazing Grace," *Sightings*, narr. Tim White, writ. Susan Michaels, prod. Amber Benson, Lindsey Paddor, Henry Winkler and Ann Daniel, The Sci-Fi Channel, 23 Feb. 1998.

[9] "STIGMATA The Wounds of Christ," *Arthur C. Clarke's World of Strange Powers*, 15 March 1998.

[10] "Angel of Death," *Sightings*, 28 April 1998.

[11] Walker, Paul Robert, Interview, *Stories of Miracles*, narr. Devon O'Day, writ. Peter Shockey, prod. Peter Shockey, 25 Dec. 1998.

Life Beyond Death
and
Reincarnation

Life Beyond Death and Reincarnation

Definitions

Life Beyond Death. A proposed state of consciousness that occurs after physical death, which can be experienced during a near-death experience (NDE); the living spirit of humans; the next phase of existence after physical death in a series of existential phases.

Reincarnation. The process after physical death where the soul of a human, animal, or other form returns to Earth to live out another life in another physical form. The Eastern religion of Hinduism suggests that reincarnation occurs in either higher or lower forms depending on how the previous life was lived. The word *reincarnation* was formed in English around 1860 from the Latin prefix *re* meaning "again," combined with *incarnation,* derived from the Late Latin *incarnare* meaning "to make into flesh."

Statistics

• As of 1998, there were 410 books in print regarding life after death and reincarnation. One is in print from 1930, 1 in 1947, 6 in the 1960s, 21 in the 1970s, 74 in the 1980s, and a whopping 286 in the 1990s. One hundred twenty-eight of the 286 were published within the last four years. This astonishing recent output of books suggests a tremendous surge in both interest and activity in the afterlife (Numbers obtained from *R. R. Bowker's Books in Print,* the 1998 list).

• In 1997 there were approximately four hours of documentaries aired on life after death and reincarnation. In 1998 there were around twenty-eight hours of documentaries again suggesting a great increase in interest (Numbers derived from Gissen, Jay, ed., *The Cable Guide*, 1997, 1998).

• Noteable author P. M. H. Atwater claims that at least eight million Americans have died and lived to describe the details of their experience, and that ninety percent of these experiences are positive ("The Near Death Experience," *Life After Death*, 22 Dec. 1997).

• A consensus between a recent *Gallup* poll and near-death researchers puts the adult NDE figure closer to thirteen million Americans and suggests the worldwide numbers of all age groups is likely much larger (*Frequently Asked Questions about NDEs*, The International Association of Near Death Studies, <http://www.iands.org/faq.html> 31 Aug. 1998).

• Forty-two percent of all Americans report some contact with the dead (Greely, Reverend Andrew, Sociologist, "The Near Death Experience," *Life After Death*, 22 Dec. 1997).

• *Ascent of the Blessed*, painted by Hieronymous Bosch in the fifteenth century, depicts light beings or angels escorting the spirits of humans to the light at the end of the tunnel (Moody, Dr. Raymond A., *Life After Life*, video cassette, 1992).

• An Oxford University study revealed that sixty-six percent of nurses in England have reported mystical events triggered by near-death experiences of patients ("The Near Death Experience," *Life After Death*, 22 Dec. 1997).

• The overwhelming majority of Earth's inhabitants believe in life after death. A sizeable portion believe in reincarnation, and déjà vu may be an indication of the reality of this belief ("*Beyond the Grave:* The Afterlife," *In Search of History*, 10 Aug. 1998).

• Artist Gustove Dore depicted the tunnel of light in his nineteenth-century engraving (Moody, Dr. Raymond A., Life After Life, video cassette, 1992).

History

The greatest lifelong enigma of humanity is surely the contemplation of what happens to us when we die. What world, if any, awaits us on the other side of death's door?

Historically, evidence of mankind asking this question goes back to the Stone Age. Primitive humans once buried their dead in the fetal position suggesting the belief that they would be born again into a new human form. According to some researchers this ritual may be the earliest known example of belief in reincarnation.

Many millennia later, reincarnation took root in India and became the cornerstone of the oldest of today's major world religions — Hinduism. The goal of every Hindu is to break the wheel of *samsara* or the process of reincarnation. To accomplish this one must open their heart to the world, become compassionate, and satisfy all Earthly desires. Once the soul has matured in this fashion and there is no more karma to pay, then the soul rejoins its maker.

The revered priest called the Dalai Lama is believed by all Buddhists to be their reincarnated spiritual leader. In 1937 a two and-a-half-year old boy was confirmed as the reincarnated fourteenth Dalai Lama through his knowledge of objects owned by previous Dalai Lamas and by certain physical characteristics such as moles found in certain locations on the young boy's body.[1]

Other world cultures throughout history have been captivated by the notion of life after death or reincarnation. For centuries Native American tribes have based their lives around the spirit world. The Mayan symbol of death and rebirth is the skull (*see the chapter on Crystal Skulls*). Is it possible that these ancient civilizations developed a reverence for the afterlife through their positive near-death experiences?

Recorded evidence of near-death experiences or NDEs is found in the ancient Egyptian as well as the Tibetan *Books of the Dead*. In Egypt, small shafts projecting out from the center of the great pyramid of Giza are believed by some to be portals for the Pharaoh's soul to depart to the heavens, and in Greece, the philosophers Socrates, Plato, and Aristotle also wrote of reincarnation.

In the mid-nineteenth century, spiritualism ignited an American preoccupation with the afterlife, and in 1875 a Ukrainian immigrant named Madame Blavatsky kindled U.S. interest in reincarnation.[2] But serious scientific exploration of these phenomena has been ongoing only in recent decades. The true magic of what happens to humans when they die has only recently surfaced in the stories of those who have literally died and come back to tell us of their amazing journeys.

Perhaps the most significant aspect of the near-death experience is that it deeply and permanently affects the life of the experiencer. To these people this experience is absolutely real in every way. Also, patterns of NDEs are consistent worldwide throughout all cultures, all religions, and even among atheists. They occur in men, women, and children from all socioeconomic backgrounds.

Most of the ninety percent of positive near-death experiences[3] begin with a traumatic physical event such as an operation, an accident, or a heart attack. Although often declared clinically dead, a typical "NDE traveler," as I shall refer to him or her, begins the journey by first becoming aware of EMS or ER personnel talking amongst themselves or working on a patient in distress. Our traveler will then "pop out" of his body and begin to float over this scene as an observer.

In many cases it takes a while for the traveler to recognize that the body below is actually his own. At this point he begins to experience a level of peace and warmth, of love and joy, and of pure contentment beyond human explanation. They feel suddenly released from human pain and bondage, freed from the physical crisis of their ordeal. Then quite remarkably they realize they are able to telepathically understand the humans in the room below, or for that matter — humans in the hall or in the next room, or even outside. Some travelers describe complete euphoria, especially when they go outside. They feel completely free. They are no longer a wife, husband, daughter, or brother. They are simply themselves, and they are ecstatic to be where they are.[4]

Skeptics of course argue that this experience is simply the dying process of the physical human brain, that this is simply our own physiological "send-off" into the world of nothing.[5] Yet very specific details "learned" during their NDE, or during their resuscitation, and later recalled and confirmed seem to refute this contention — details either previously unknown to the patient, or available only to someone looking down on the operating table from above or "consciously listening" to frantic conversations among ER personnel.

Some people describe the ability to be anywhere geographically simply by thought. Apparently distance and time are not constraints in the world of human spirits. NDE travelers describe in detail their journey to see a loved one or friend. Upon their return to the land of breathing humans, they recall and describe in minute detail the clothes their loved ones were wearing, their conversations, or what they were doing at exactly that point in time. Their relatives or friends are overwhelmed when their once "dead" brother or sister recounts these events perfectly to the letter.

Some "consciospiritual" (*see the Glossary*) travelers even claim to have the ability to telepathically communicate with babies or small children, and still others travel into space to view the Earth from above. Renowned psychiatrist Carl Jung was one such space explorer during his near-death experience.

Eventually NDE travelers realize that other living humans are unable to see or hear them — a revelation that often seems to bring on the "tunnel-light" phase of their journey. They find themselves drawn toward a brilliant golden or white light often seen through a tunnel. At this point usually a spirit guide, either a deceased loved one or an angel will greet them and accompany them into the light. This light is like no other light they have ever seen. It is absolute pure love, pure warmth, and it surrounds them with complete understanding, empathy, and unconditional love.

From this all-consuming light of pure love often comes a powerful being of light. The traveler now finds himself in the presence of God. Some describe this being as the Creator, as the Virgin Mary, or simply as the all-powerful all-loving being. During their experience the traveler feels a oneness with the Universe. The light is so intense that it penetrates the traveler; it knows and understands everything about the traveler. Senses such as sight and smell become detailed and greatly enhanced. Some people experience vivid colorful gardens and waterfalls, beautiful music or chimes.

At this moment in the presence of the light being, the traveler will experience a panoply of his life's events occuring concurrently rather than in sequence. Every deed, every action, every thought from birth through his near-death experience is reviewed. During this replay the traveler sees not just his own life but how his life impacted those around him. The traveler is both viewing and participating in the events. Unanimously, the elements of life that surface as being the most important in these reviews are the small acts of love and kindness we perform for others. Financial wealth, achievement, or success are insignificant.

After spending time with this being of light, the traveler is usually asked to return to his body. This suggestion is always met with great resistance as they wish to stay in the presence of this understanding and loving being. They then recall being shoved back into a cold lifeless body. Pain returns. In some cases the traveler re-enters the body in the morgue or as in the case of Dr. George Rodonaia, during the beginning of an autopsy.[6]

NDEs tend to profoundly impact a person's life after the experience. Most significantly, people lose their fear of death forever

— as a result of learning that there is no death. They also become more appreciative of life and more compassionate and loving towards others. People's lives take on a greater importance, and they feel they have been returned to this world to fulfill a mission. They become not necessarily more religious, but more spiritual. Many write books or lecture about their experience, and some even quit their jobs to become ministers. They possess a much greater awareness of their spiritual existence and feel spiritually connected with the Universe. Death becomes the door to this connection. After the experience, some people demonstrate new supernatural ability such as telepathy, clairvoyance, or the power to heal[7] (*see the chapters on Extraterrestrial Life, Miracles and Angels, and Extrasensory Perception*).

Significantly, some people must realize that they cannot take their own life if they want to return to paradise, and those who have attempted suicide usually experience a negative NDE or are informed by the light being that they will have to relive those aspects of their life that led to their suicide. Overwhelmingly, the consistent message brought back with NDE travelers is the great importance of love and that life truly is eternal.[8]

Of the remaining ten percent of NDEs, most seem to be "hellish" experiences, while a few evoke feelings of nothingness. Some attempted-suicide victims also experience "hell." These people, like those with the positive experiences, can vividly smell, taste, hear, and see these events. A small group of people experience a state of nothingness, darkness, non-existence, or a feeling of emptiness. Some of these negative NDEs turn positive during the experience.

There are essentially two opposing schools of scientific thought regarding near-death experiences:

1. NDEs are purely physiological neurochemical reactions taking place in the brain, and the reason many experiences are similar is because our brains are similar.

2. There is a clear separation of the physical human body and the "consciospiritual" human being. The body dies and the consciousness and spirit enter a new phase of existence.

Most parapsychologists agree that notions of heaven and hell are cultural and religious in nature. They vary as the doctrines vary between Western religions such as Christianity and Eastern religions such as Buddhism, and traditional native beliefs.

Around the world, NDE experiments are being conducted to either prove or disprove the reality of the phenomenon. In cardiac units around southern England, objects are hidden, unknown to the patient and out of view, so that if the patient floats out of his body and he can later describe the object, an NDE would be confirmed.[9] Similar experiments are being conducted in the Netherlands[10] and in America with electronic message boards hidden from view.[11] Air force centrifuge experiments[12] and "Persinger's chamber" (*see Leading Research Scientists section*) have mimicked some NDE symptoms but do not produce the behavioral impact of real events. Test subjects don't write books or quit their jobs after the experience.

Documented Cases

Betty J. Eadie

Betty Eadie, perhaps one of people best known for her NDE, has written a best-selling book about her experience, *Embraced by the Light,* and she lectures around the world. During an operation when she was in her thirties, she claims that she literally died and went to heaven. As she entered her near-death experience, she was attracted to a point of light and was drawn toward it. The light grew in intensity and size and began to surround her with a very warm feeling of love. This light of pure love completely surrounded her and carried her to a well-maintained garden with a tremendous waterfall cascading down the side of a green, forested mountain into a beautiful sunlit gorge.

Everything in this place was very much alive and had spirit. The flowers were beyond any description. They moved and swayed in perfect harmony to a melody "very perfect for God." She moved closer to a pond in the gorge, leaned over and brushed the water, and gazed into it. There she witnessed for the first time the reflection of her own spirit. She was overwhelmed by its appearance shimmering in the water. She marveled at its harmony and magnificence and she knew this was heaven. Then Betty began traveling back through the tunnel and was told it was not yet her time. She was told she would share her experience with others.[13]

Pam Nesure

One of the most fascinating NDE cases occurred during Pam Nesure's multihour brain surgery. This case is significant because she was literally put to death and brought back to life while being monitored every minute with the most sophisticated medical instrumentation. After suffering from years of headaches, she was diagnosed in 1990 with an aneurysm deep in her brain. She entered the hospital for a radical new medical procedure called a hypothermic cardiac arrest operation. During surgery, she was first administered a general anesthetic, then put on a cardiopulmonary bypass machine. Her body was then cooled to $58°$F, at which time her heart went into ventricular fibrillation and came to a complete stop. Her cranium was opened for surgery. The blood from her head and complete circulatory system was drained into the bypass machine. At this point, her brain was without blood or any electrical activity. Her heart had stopped and she was not breathing. Her body temperature was 58ºF. Remarkably, she was in a state that met all the criteria for clinical physical death, and she remained there for some time.

During this procedure, Pam was lifted from her body and found herself hovering over the operating table. She realized it was her body, but didn't mind. She felt no pain and very much felt at peace. She then became aware of a light and a distant presence. She was pulled toward the light and realized the presence was her grandmother. Her grandmother was wearing light instead of clothes. Pam began to see more people, many of whom she knew. Many were relatives. They were all wearing light. Pam had never seen a light like this before anywhere. It was breathing, alive, warm, and comfortable. It was pure love. She was not at all afraid.[14] Significantly, Pam met two people she hadn't realized had passed away. There were many others she didn't know, yet they knew her. Somehow it was all connected.[15]

Eventually she knew it was time to return to her body. Her uncle brought her back. When she saw her body, she wished to stay in her new wonderful place, rather than enter her body. She then felt pushed back into it. She felt as if she had entered a pool of ice water. Her next conscious moment of physical life was opening her eyes and seeing her family around her.[16] Also of significance, upon her recovery Pam was able to describe in detail certain medical instruments used during her operation.[17]

George Rodonaia, Ph.D.

Dr. Rodonaia is a psychologist and Soviet dissident who in 1975 was invited to work in the U.S. On his way to the airport to come to America in 1976, Dr. Rodonaia was run down on a sidewalk by the K.G.B. After every resuscitative effort he was pronounced dead in a hospital emergency room.

At this time Dr. Rodonaia floated out of and above his body. He felt absolute freedom; he was fascinated with his telepathic ability to "see" the thoughts of the ER personnel below. His senses of smell and hearing were greatly enhanced. He looked upon his lifeless body with disdain and was ecstatic to be free from it. Remarkably, Dr. Rodonaia discovered he could be in other geographic locations simply by thinking about them. He could be in the hospital over his body, in Moscow, and in New York, all at the same time.

George also discovered he could telepathically and spiritually communicate with babies who were "just coming from that place where I was going." One little girl in the hospital had a broken hip and no one around her understood why she was crying. George consciospiritually told her to stop crying. She did so and smiled up at him.

On the sixth day after his return to his body, George told the baby's mother and physicians that she was crying because of her broken hip. Physicians later confirmed this diagnosis.

At some point George "realized" that he was actually dead. Yet he was not dead. As a psychologist and a scientist this contradiction scared George. Fear overcame him. George found himself in darkness; he found himself without answers. He was alone in the unknown. He realized he couldn't understand his circumstance, that his lack of knowledge had placed him in darkness. He was afraid of the darkness and he was afraid of being there without his body. George "remembered" the Hegelian dialectic where two equally yet opposing propositions are reconciled by a third proposition on a higher level of truth.

George began "reasoning" to himself. He thought "If I can think, then therefore I am. If I can think then why not think positively instead of negatively." He began to think about light — the opposite of darkness. A light appeared in the distance. His first thought was to go toward this light. George was greeted by his real biological parents. He "learned" from them that they were killed by the K.G.B. in Moscow. He had never known this before and had always thought they had abandoned him.

Then a complete holographic replay of George's entire life appeared around him. He found himself both the observer as well as the participant.

Love is what eventually brought George back to his body — love of the loved ones who wanted him to return to his earthly, physical existence. He did not at all wish to return, but he felt he must out of love.

George's body had been taken to the morgue, washed, and readied for an autopsy. They opened George's abdomen with a T- shaped incision. During this procedure George was pushed back down into his body. He immediately felt a tremendous headache and opened his eyes.

From his near-death experience George, a disciplined scientist, learned that we are alive because of love, that hell is being in darkness where he was at first, that hell is separation from light, separation from knowledge, from God, from love, and from infinity. George knows now why suicide is condemned by all religions. "If you commit suicide you will go into nowhere, into nothingness, you will go somewhere opposite of goodness."

George learned that love is everlasting: "This cannot be changed. Love is life. Love is what keeps this world alive. Love is an eternity. It is the basis of humankind. We are alive because of love. Life is an everlasting light of pure love. We cannot die. We are created to live forever. The dimension of the spirit is everlasting life. Death does not exist. Humans should not be afraid of death — it is only a railroad station where you change trains to go into another life."[18]

Vicki Umepeg

Another unique case is that of blind musician Vicki Umepeg. Vicki was in a bad car accident and was rushed to the hospital, where for the first time in her life, she could see. She floated out of her body and could clearly see the hall and hospital personnel before she went up through the ceiling. She was then sucked into a tunnel and ended up out on a lawn with magnificent flowers, birds, and angels. Upon her recovery, Vicki, a blind woman, was able to describe the hospital corridor, and the orderlies who had wheeled her in.[19]

Beth Young

Beth Young is among the ten percent who experience a negative NDE event. Beth was having marriage difficulties and wished to put herself in the hospital, perhaps for attention. She shot herself in the neck and was hospitalized in a coma for three days, sustained only by life support. Because she had lost so much blood, her prognosis was very grim. Her horrible vision began with very grotesque small creatures. They made holes in her everywhere, even in her eyes. She felt extremely ill from this experience but found she could not get sick, gag, or do anything about it. She could smell, but felt no pain. Just over her right shoulder she heard a heavy, raspy breathing getting closer. She could not turn to see what it was, nor did she wish to. She knew she was experiencing pure evil. The very moment before the entity was in view, she opened her eyes and was conscious again.[20]

The Reincarnation of Mary Sutton

Déjà Vu! Turn-of-the-century French meaning "already seen." A phrase that has lived with Jenny Cockell all her life — constantly toying with her sleeping mind through dreams: dreams of a church and of eight children, dreams of the name "Mary" and of a small cottage with only one arched door flanked by two arched windows, and dreams of maps — maps of a quaint seaside community.

The seaside village is Malahide, Ireland some three hundred miles from Jenny's home in England. Throughout her childhood, Jenny worked on the maps — getting the streets, the church, the jetty and cottage all just where they should be. She even detailed the buildings. All her life Jenny had been drawing maps of a town she had never seen in this life, but had lived in as a mother named Mary in a life before.

For years, Jenny considered other villages around Europe trying to find a match with her maps. She always returned to Malahide in her mind's eye.

One day she finally found the town of her dreams. There they were — the church on Church Street and the jetty — nearly identical to her childhood drawings. She came upon the ruins of her old cottage and

immediately felt a waft of déjà vu. Of what little structure remained of
the cottage, the arched window overgrown with vines and trees matched
her drawings with striking accuracy.

Jenny Cockell now knew with the deepest conviction that she was
the reincarnation of mother Mary, and that she once lived in this very
house. Through local newspaper ads and patience she further confirmed
her dreams. She located villagers who had known the family of that
cottage. Through them she found her marriage certificate dated 1917
and she also found her last name — Sutton. Her name had been Mary
Sutton. Then she tracked down birth certificates of six of the eight children — all of whom were still living aged in their sixties and seventies.

Few words could describe the feelings, the shock, the joy experienced in the strange but loving reunion of Mary Sutton and her children. They shared intimate stories, events, and details known only to
Mary and her children. The haunting dreams of Jenny Cockell's life all
came to life in Malahide, Ireland with Mary Sutton and her siblings.
Most remarkably, Jenny vividly recalled the moment of Mary's death in
childbirth and of her spirit leaving the body. This significant case of
reincarnation is well documented.[21]

Beyond the Facts

Although cases of reincarnation are important, the phenomenon of
life beyond death is more fascinating because of the medical monitoring and scientific documentation of the events.

In cases of miracles and angels, humans typically remain in the physical world and experience supernatural powers from a place beyond. Such
was the case with Robert Gutherman and Padre Pio. Grace DiBicarri, however, briefly visited this realm during her near-death experience and
returned to demonstrate miraculous powers of healing acquired during
her excursion. The NDEs in this chapter not only provide a much more
extensive view into the world beyond physical death, but also uncover
specific details that both support the reality of the phenomenon and

suggest the existence of an afterlife.

Betty Eadie's near-death experience illustrates both the typical pattern of a positive NDE and how each experience is tailored to the individual. She first experiences the warm loving light and then sees her own spirit reflected in a pond. Betty's NDE so greatly impacted her life that she wrote a book about it.

However with the cases of Pam Nesure and George Rodonaia, significant details surface that suggest some form of cognitive process transpired while the human cognitive device — the brain — was clinically dead and not functioning. (*Key case words and phrases illustrating this process have been underlined for easier reference*).

In Pam's case her vital signs were closely monitored so physicians knew she was clinically physically dead. Her brain was without blood or any electrical activity. Yet during this period she "learned" that two people had passed away, and she "saw" and later described a surgeon's drill used to open her cranium. She had no prior knowledge of this instrument or the death of her friends.

Even more remarkable is the case of psychologist Dr. Rodonaia where memory, telepathy, and reasoning were experienced along with learning during his episode of clinical physical death. After he "died," George immediately became aware of his new telepathic ability as he scoped the thoughts of the ER personnel and later as he consciospiritually communicated with the baby girl. Later on during his NDE, George's "reasoning" delivered him from darkness into light. Then his biological parents welcomed him into the light and he "learned" they were killed by the K.G.B., that they didn't abandon him as he had previously thought.

Considering the case of blind musician Vicki Umepeg, try to imagine being born blind and then experiencing clear "vision" of the world for the first time when you are unconscious and fighting for your physical life. Then after you awaken from the ordeal imagine being able to describe what you have seen.

Evidence of cognitive processes in these cases where the brain is clinically inactive seems to provide strong support for a form of human consciousness and intelligence that can exist without the human brain — a revelation that supports the existence of an afterlife.

Clearly something quite amazing is going on here, but the afterlife issue really gets interesting when considered in context with other universal anomalies such as extrasensory perception, hauntings, and extraterrestrial life.

Telepathy is a form of communication apparently common among some extraterrestrial civilizations as reported by alien abductees during their experiences (*see the Extraterrestrial timeline, 1993 and 1994*). Telepathy surfaces again in the phenomenon of life beyond death. Dr. George Rodonaia and others interviewed in Dr. Moody's documentary entitled *Life After Life* all claim to have communicated telepathically during their NDEs, but with a spiritual twist or "consciospiritually" as I call it. Medium James Van Praagh continues to demonstrate his successful telepathic ties with thousands of spirits as evidenced by his three-year waiting list for private client sessions, and psychic Peter James has proven his telepathic talents in countless hauntings investigations (*see the chapters on Hauntings and Extrasensory Perception*).

I find this telepathy revealed in many anomalies of great interest for two reasons: First, James Van Praagh's and Peter James's ability to link up with the spirit world lends further support to the existence of an afterlife; and second, extraterrestrial telepathy seems to suggest that telepathy may be a very common means of communication not only in the consciospiritual realm, but also throughout our physical Universe. Could telepathy be the language of the heavens?

Uncommon light energy predominates life beyond death. Throughout most stories of NDE travelers, the magnificent spiritual world of light is depicted consistently. Light becomes the path to heaven. It is the path to God. It is the path to the Universal Spirit. Light is the medium, perhaps, in which the Universal Spirit exists and communicates. The light of the near-death experience is warm and pervading. It is pure love and complete understanding. It is all that is good. It is both omniscient and omnipresent. Light is the opposite of darkness. Some NDEs that are negative at first often become positive when the traveler "contemplates" light or God. Negative NDEs such as Beth Young's tell us that life is good, that life and love of one's life are of ultimate significance. If we seek the light in times of trouble, when surrounded by darkness, when we find ourselves in "hell," and if we focus on that light, then we shall overcome darkness. This is the lesson to be learned from negative NDEs. Positive NDEs tell us that our Universe is a place of ultimate love. Together, all NDEs suggest that our Universe is filled with love and that we should love and respect life. The near-death experience is a conduit to our Spiritual Universe. It is a conduit to knowledge.

When we consider these revelations of a loving and peaceful Spiritual Universe together with the evidence that suggests extraterrestrial civilizations are peaceful, we are left with the encouraging possibility that life in at least two dimensions exists in peace.

No endeavor of near-death or afterlife research is complete without carefully considering cases of alien abductions, hauntings, miracles, angels, and extrasensory perception, specifically telepathy. What are the implications of near-death research and where might it take us? I will leave you at the end of this chapter with an amazing thought — one that I am sure both mainstream science and believers alike will love: Try to imagine human science someday confirming the very existence of God.

Resources for Further Investigation
Leading Research Scientists and Investigators

Atwater, P. M. H.
Researcher P. M. H. Atwater wrote the book *Coming Back to Life*, which explores the aftereffects of NDEs.

Susan Blackmore, Ph.D.

Once a parapsychologist herself, she is a professor of psychology at the University of Bristol in England and now debunks myths. Dr. Blackmore is a quintessential skeptic who is completely physiologically-oriented. She experienced her own NDE and believes NDEs are brain- and neurochemically-based. She has researched NDEs for twenty years, and suggests that every NDE event is simply a function of the brain.

Nancy Evans Bush

She is the founder of the International Association for Near Death Studies. She has been researching NDEs and negative NDEs, which she had herself where she experienced nothingness and non-existence.

Bruce Taub-Bynum, Ph.D.

He is the director of the Behavioral Medicine and Biofeedback Clinic at the University of Massachusetts. He has written *Transcending Psychoneurotic Disturbances, The Family Unconscious, Families and the Interpretation of Dreams* and has focused his research around preparation dreams and symbols of death and the cultural and religious aspects of NDEs.

Maggie Callahan

She is an RN, a hospice nurse, and is co-founder of an organization called Shades of the Rainbow, the goal of which is to restructure the human approach to dying. She wrote *Final Gifts* about understanding the special awareness, needs, and communications among those who are dying.

Mally Cox-Chapman

She interviewed fifty people about their NDEs, which resulted in *The Case for Heaven*, a book about near-death experiences as evidence of the afterlife.

Dr. Peter Fenwick

A neuropsychiatrist at The Institute of Psychiatry, England, he researches altered states of consciousness in the brain. He has researched four hundred NDEs and believes the experiences are real and are not brain-based.

Dr. Marie Louise Van Franz

A dream psychiatrist and dream analyst, she has analyzed over ten thousand dreams of the dying.

Tom Harpur

A theologian, Rhodes scholar, journalist, and author, he wrote *Life After Death*, which was made into a two-hour television documentary of the same name that aired on The Learning Channel. He studied NDEs for three years and is an exceptional source for information.

Dr. Raymond A. Moody, Jr.

Dr. Moody has documented and researched over two thousand cases of NDEs. Six of these were featured on his documentary entitled *Life After Life*. This video and his new video *Through the Tunnel and Beyond* are a must for anyone interested in the near-death experience.

Dr. Melvin Morse, M.D.

Based in Seattle at the University of Washington, Dr. Morse is an associate professor of pediatrics. He is a leading authority of NDEs in children and believes that through their NDE artwork we can preview the afterlife. He wrote *Parting Visions* about the uses and meanings of pre death, psychic, and spiritual experiences.

Dr. Michael Persinger

A professor of behavioral neurosciences at Laurention University, Dr. Persinger believes that NDEs are controlled by physiological brain chemistry. He developed Persinger's chamber — a research facility that can mimic some NDE symptoms in test subjects.

James Van Praagh

Mr. Van Praagh is a medium who telepathically receives messages from the domain of human spirits and relays them to humans in our physical world. Since 1984 he has passed on thousands of messages to relatives of the dead. He frequently appears on television and has a three-year waiting list for private readings.

Dr. Maurice S. Rawlings, MD

This cardiologist wrote *To Hell and Back* and is an authority on negative NDEs.

Dr. Kenneth Ring

A professor of psychology at the University of Connecticut, Dr. Ring is a strong believer in the NDE as a real experience. During his twenty years of research he has discovered a pronounced pattern in near-death experiences. He has found that the NDEs bring about a severe shock in the life of the experiencers. They acquire a sense of understanding everything; they feel an absolute unconditional acceptance of themselves as individuals; they are enraptured by this acceptance; they are returned from this experience with the memory of the NDE "burned" into them. There is something ultimate about their experience, as they refer to it as "the ultimate experience."

Dr. Michael Sabom

Dr. Sabom is a cardiologist who has researched over two hundred NDEs including that of Pam Nesure. He believes near-death experiences are an experience of dying rather than afterlife experience.

James A. Santucci

James A. Santucci is a professor of comparative religion at California State University at Fullerton. He is an authority on reincarnation as perceived by the world's religions.

Robert A. F. Thurman

Dr. Thurman draws our attention to a fascinating and logical relationship between natural continuity in the Universe and the continuation of the human soul after physical death. He is a professor of religion at Columbia University in New York.

Dr. Carey Williams

Dr. Williams believes reincarnation is a real phenomenon and that our innate characteristics such as how we dress, who we are attracted to, or the types of food we prefer are all hints to a previous existence. She believes our present life is a composite of previous lives.

Recommended Television Programs and Networks

Please consult the Directory of Television Networks in the back of the book for scheduling information and availability of home videos:

"After Life," *48 Hours*, 1998, 60 minutes
on CBS
air dates: 08/06/98

"*Beyond the Grave*, The Afterlife," *In Search of History*, 1998,
60 minutes
on The History Channel
air dates: 08/10/98

Bruce Kelly, Phobia, *Unsolved Mysteries*, 20 minutes
on Lifetime
air dates: 07/23/98

"*Coma*, The Silent Epidemic," 1997, 60 minutes
on The Discovery Channel
air dates: 03/22/98

Contact With Loved Ones, *Unsolved Mysteries*, 5 minutes
on Lifetime
air dates: 03/25/98

"Have We Lived Before?" *Arthur C. Clarke's World of Strange Powers*,
1985, 30 minutes
on The Discovery Channel
air dates: 03/22/98, 08/30/98

Heidi Wyrick, *Unsolved Mysteries*, 9 minutes
on Lifetime
air dates: 07/24/98, 02/27/98

"*Life After Death*, a Skeptical Inquiry," 1998, 60 minutes
on The Discovery Channel
air dates: 05/31/98

"Life After Death," *Strange but True?* 15 minutes
on The Discovery Channel
air dates: 02/18/98

"*Life After Death*, The Near Death Experience," 1996, 60 minutes
on The Learning Channel
air dates: 12/22/97

"Life After Death, Visions of Heaven," 1996, 60 minutes
on The Learning Channel
air dates: 12/22/97

Life After Death, Visitations, *Unsolved Mysteries,* 10 minutes
on Lifetime
air dates: 02/18/98, 06/26/98

Love and Devotion from Beyond the Grave, *Unsolved Mysteries,*
1994, 7 minutes
on Lifetime
air dates: 01/30/98, 09/12/98

Luiz Antonio Gasparetto, *Unsolved Mysteries,* 1995, 6 minutes
on Lifetime
air dates: 09/03/98

Matters of Life and Death, A Science Odyssey, 120 minutes
on Public Broadcasting System
air dates: 01/11/98

"Messages from the Dead?," *Arthur C. Clarke's World of Strange Powers,*
1985, 30 minutes
on The Discovery Channel
air dates: 07/26/98, 01/18/98

Mysteries of the AfterLife, *Unsolved Mysteries,* 30 minutes
on Lifetime
air dates: 09/17/98

NDE, *Unsolved Mysteries,* 1989, 20 minutes
on Lifetime
air dates: 07/16/98

"Near Death Experiences," *Arthur C. Clarke's Mysterious Universe,*
30 minutes
on The Discovery Channel
air dates: 05/03/98

Near Death Experience, *Unsolved Mysteries,* 9 minutes
on Lifetime
air dates: 07/24/98

Reincarnation, Georgia Rudolph, *Unsolved Mysteries,* 1991, 25 minutes
on Lifetime
air dates: 08/03/98

Reincarnation, Georgia Rudolph, *Unsolved Mysteries*, 1990,
7 minutes
on Lifetime
air dates: 06/04/98

Reincarnation, Pearl Harbor Victim, *Unsolved Mysteries*, 12 minutes
on Lifetime
air dates: 06/12/98

"Reincarnation," *The Unexplained*, 1998, 60 minutes
on The Arts & Entertainment Network
air dates: 10/15/98

Sacred Places & Mystic Spirits, Mysteries of the Unexplained, 1996,
60 minutes
on The Discovery Channel
air dates: 06/12/98

Sightings, Series First Aired 1991, Went Into Syndication 1994
on The Sci-Fi Channel
air dates: 1991 through 1998

Transcend the Grave, *Unsolved Mysteries*, 11 minutes
on Lifetime
air dates: 09/27/98

Recommended Books

Across Time and Death: A Mother's Search for Her Past Life Children
by Jenny Cockell

After the Light
by Kimberly Clark Sharp

Beyond the Light
by P. M. H. Atwater

Closer to the Light
by Melvin Morse, M. D.

Coming Back to Life
by P. M. H. Atwater

Dying to Live
by Susan Blackmore

Embraced by the Light
by Betty J. Eadie

Families and the Interpretations of Dreams
by Bruce Taub-Bynum, Ph.D.

Final Gifts
by Maggie Callahan

Life After Death
by Tom Harpur

Life After Life
by Dr. Raymond A. Moody, Jr.

Life at Death
by Kenneth Ring

Many Lives, Many Masters
by Brian L. Weiss

Mission to Millboro
by Marge Rieder

Parting Visions
by Dr. Melvin Morse, M. D.

Reincarnation: A New Horizon
by Dr. Carey Williams

Riding With the Lion
by Kyriacos Markides, Ph.D.

Saved by the Light
by Dannion Brinkley

Space, Time and Medicine
by Larry Dossey, M. D.

Talking to Heaven
by James Van Praagh

The Case for Heaven
by Mally Cox-Chapman

To Hell and Back
by Dr. Maurice S. Rawlings, M.D.

Recommended Videotapes, Audio Tapes, and CD-ROMS

Life After Life (video)
based on the book by Raymond A. Moody, Jr.
available from Della LLC: 800-841-3196

Through the Tunnel and Beyond (video)
based on the book by Raymond A. Moody, Jr.
available from Hinshaw Productions: 404-367-0013

Recommended Internet Sites

Camelot Productions
The site of *The Magic of Our Universe*
http://www.camelotpublishing.com

Dr. Raymond A. Moody, Jr.'s site on NDEs
http://www.lifeafterlife.com

Information on NDEs
http://www.ndeweb.com

Near Death Experiences
http://www.near-death.com

Paranormal Phenomena Archive
http://www.in-search-of.com

The Arts and Entertainment Network
http://www.AandE.com

The Discovery Channel
http://www.discovery.com

The History Channel
http://www.HistoryChannel.com

The International Association for Near Death Studies
Exceptional information on NDEs
http://www.iands.org

The Learning Channel
http://www.tlc.com

The Life Surrounding Death
http://www.Death-Dying.com

The Sci-Fi Channel
Sightings available through the Dominion site, which can further
access all major paranormal links
http://www.scifi.com/sightings

The Ufomind Paranormal Index and Bookstore
http://www.ufomind.com

Underground Paranormal Stories Exchange Network
http://www.paranormalnetwork.com

Unsolved Mysteries
http://www.unsolved.com

Your Public Broadcasting Station
http://www.pbs.org

Organizations
IANDS (International Association for Near-Death Studies)
A worldwide research organization founded in 1977.
P. O. Box 502
East Windsor Hill, CT   06028-0502
http://www.iands.org
860-644-5216
860-644-5759 (FAX)
office@iands.org

Endnotes

[1] *"Beyond the Grave:* The Afterlife," *In Search of History,* narr. David Ackroyd, ed. Diana Friedberg, A.C.E., prod. Lionel Friedberg, The Arts & Entertainment Network, 10 Aug. 1998.

[2] "Beyond the Grave: The Afterlife," *In Search of History,* 10 Aug. 1998.

[3] "The Near Death Experience," *Life After Death,* narr. Tom Harpur, writ. Tom Harpur, prod. Jim Hanley and David Brady, The Learning Channel, 22 Dec. 1997.

[4] *Life After Life,* video cassette, Della LLC, Nashville, Della LLC, 1992, color, 57 minutes.

[5] Blackmore, Susan, Ph.D., Interview, "The Near Death Experience," *Life After Death,* narr. Tom Harpur, writ. Tom Harpur, prod. Jim Hanley and David Brady, The Learning Channel, 22 Dec. 1997.

[6] *Life After Life,* video cassette, Della LLC, 1992.

[7] "Amazing Grace," *Sightings,* narr. Tim White, writ. Susan Michaels, prod. Amber Benson, Lindsey Paddor, Henry Winkler and Ann Daniel, The Sci-Fi Channel, 23 Feb. 1998.

[8] *Life After Life,* video cassette, Della LLC, 1992.

[9] *Strange But True?,* narr. Michael Aspel, ed. David Alpin, Jeremy Phillips, prod. Ralph Jones and Simon Shaps, The Discovery Channel, 18 Feb. 1998.

[10] "Near Death Experiences," *Arthur C. Clarke's Mysterious Universe,* narr. Stanley Anderson, prod. Adam Hart-David, The Discovery Channel, 3 May 1998.

[11] "Waiting Room of the Soul," *Sightings,* narr. Tim White, writ. Susan Michaels, prod. Henry Winkler and Ann Daniel, The Sci-Fi Channel, 10 Feb. 1998.

[12] "Near Death Experiences," *Arthur C. Clarke's Mysterious Universe,* 3 May 1998.

[13] Eadie, Betty J., Interview, "Visions of Heaven," *Life After Death,* narr. Tom Harpur, writ. Tom Harpur, prod. Jim Hanley and David Brady, The Learning Channel, 22 Dec. 1997.

[14] Nesure, Pam, Interview, "Visions of Heaven," *Life After Death,* narr. Tom Harpur, writ. Tom Harpur, prod. Jim Hanley and David Brady, The Learning Channel, 22 Dec. 1997.

[15] "Mary," Interview, *Sacred Places and Mystic Spirits,* Mysteries of the Unexplained, narr. James Coburn, writ. Robert Gardner, prod. Robert Gardner, The Discovery Channel, 12 June 1998.

[16] Nesure, Pam, Interview, "Visions of Heaven," *Life After Death,* 22 Dec. 1997.

[17] Nesure, Pam, Interview, *"After Life:* Heaven Can Wait," *48 Hours,* narr. Erin Moriarity, prod. CBS Worldwide, Inc., CBS, 6 Aug. 1998.

[18] Rodonaia, Dr. George, Interview, *Life After Life*, video cassette, Della LLC, 1992.

[19] Umepeg, Vicki, Interview, "Visions of Heaven," *Life After Death*, narr. Tom Harpur, writ. Tom Harpur, prod. Jim Hanley and David Brady, The Learning Channel, 22 Dec. 1997.

[20] Young, Beth, Interview, "Visions of Heaven," *Life After Death*, narr. Tom Harpur, writ. Tom Harpur, prod. Jim Hanley and David Brady, The Learning Channel, 22 Dec. 1997.

[21] "A Mother's Love," *Sightings*, narr. Tim White, writ. Susan Michaels, prod. Henry Winkler and Ann Daniel, The Sci-Fi Channel, 26 May 1998.

Hauntings

Hauntings

Definitions

Ghost. The soul or spirit of a deceased human being believed to inhabit or wander among the physical world of living humans. The word *ghost* originated in English before the year A.D. 900 and is derived from the Middle English word *gost* or *goost,* which in turn is derived from the Old English word *gast* which is similar to the German word *geist,* which means "spirit."

Poltergeist. An unsettled soul or spirit of a deceased human being that usually demonstrates its mischievous nature in the physical world of living humans through knockings, rappings, rattles, or other anomalous environmental activity. A poltergeist may manifest its existence through a series of progressive levels from mild to very violent activity. The word *poltergeist* originated around 1848 from the German words *polter* or *poltern,* "to knock" or "make noise" and *geist,* which means "spirit."

Statistics

• As of 1998, there were 221 books in print on the subject of hauntings including poltergeists and ghosts. One book in print dates back to 1971 and there are numbers of books in print for each year throughout the seventies and eighties. Book output increased steadily through the early 1990s with numbers doubling between 1994 and 1995 from 15 to 31, with 28 in 1996 and 20 in 1997. This increased output from 1992 forward suggests an increase both in interest and activity (Numbers obtained from *R. R. Bowker's Books in Print,* 1998 list).

• 1997 produced twenty-five hours and thirty minutes of documentary air time regarding hauntings, which included poltergeists and ghosts. In 1998 there were thirty-six hours of documentaries aired on the subject of hauntings (Numbers derived from Gissen, Jay. ed. *The Cable Guide*, 1997, 1998).

• Twenty-five percent of all Americans believe in ghosts (recent *Gallup Poll*).

• "Ghosts! Many parapsychologists believe that there are collections of electrical energy, and conventional scientists agree electromagnetism is all around us, but paranormal researchers take it one extraordinary step further. They believe electromagnetism has a personality, that it can be the outward manifestation of a tortured soul in limbo" (White, Tim, narrator, "Hauntings," *Sightings*, 4 June 1998).

• The differences between poltergeist activity and a haunting can be hard to distinguish. In the early stages of a poltergeist manifestation, it may be impossible. Haunts and poltergeists do share some basic aspects such as apparitions, strange noises, odors, moving or disappearing objects, and so on, but there are also some features that make them very different:

1. Hauntings are spirits of deceased human beings that frequently appear in specific places. Poltergeists may not be spirits at all. One theory is that poltergeists are mass forms of energy that a living person is unknowingly controlling. In some cases extreme poltergeist activity has been linked to demons.

2. Hauntings are usually related to a specific place or tragic way of death. Poltergeists, however, are usually linked directly to a specific person or object.

3. Hauntings are appearances of a ghost or ghosts in areas known to the deceased before their deaths. Poltergeists can be triggered by a living person's trauma in any area, at any time.

4. Haunting activities are continuous over time, concentrated in the same area. Poltergeists build up over time to a climax, then start over. They can travel anywhere.

5. Hauntings are not violent. Most poltergeists nearing the climax of their energy can become dangerous to the living, inflicting both mental and physical terror in extreme cases (Ghosts and Poltergeists, <http://www.zerotime.com/ghosts/polter.htm>, 31 August 1998).

- There are five levels of poltergeist events:

1. An attack on human senses that is characterized by cold spots, strange noises, odd odors, footstep sounds, disturbed pets, and the feeling of being watched.

2. Evidence of communication that is characterized by whispers, laughs or giggles, moans, moving shadows, breezes, visible clouds, strong static electricity, and marks on walls or floors.

3. Evidence of electrical control that is characterized by electric lights and appliances turning on and off, unseen hands grabbing or touching people, writing on walls or pattern markings, doors opening and closing or locking and unlocking, hearing words or voices clearly, full apparitions or dark figures, and levels of communication with humans such as strange telephone calls.

4. Evidence of trickery that is characterized by flying or moving or disappearing objects that reappear elsewhere, shaking furniture, fire starting, frightening entities, humans being pushed or shaken, illusions or visions, speaking in ordering tones, victims feeling dizzy or nauseous, windows, mirrors or other objects breaking for no reason, and levitation.

5. Evidence of dangerous activity that is characterized by biting, slapping, punching, rape, animated objects, victims becoming "possessed," the use of household electrical systems to cause harm, fires, and burning,

flying knives or sharp objects, blood on walls, floors, and ceilings, heavy objects falling, threatening writings or visual signs (Ghosts and Poltergeists, <http://www. zerotime.com/ghosts/polter.htm>, 31 August 1998).

• America's only legally haunted house exists in Nyack, New York. A previous owner neglected to tell Jeff and Patrice Stambovsky, who purchased the house, that it was haunted. Two weeks after the sale, the Stambovskys sued for their purchase price and won, thus proving in a court of law that ghosts exist ("Encounters, Hauntings, Investigations," *Sightings*, 14 Sept. 1998).

• More than a thousand people per year see or feel evil spirits at Sterling Castle in Scotland, and since its construction in the fifteenth century, countless other residents and visitors have experienced haunting phenomena from mere apparitions to downright demons. Over one hundred of these haunts are believed to be permanent residents ("Encounters, Hauntings, Investigations," *Sightings*, 14 Sept. 1998).

• Over fifty percent of the citizens living in Great Britain believe in ghosts, and one in seven claims to have seen one ("Ghosts," *Strange But True?*, 28 June 1998).

• "Place memory" is the term for present hauntings originating from retained past energy at locations of great anguish and torment (*Sightings*, 20 Aug. 1998).

• A "classic haunt" is characterized by the unique history of an establishment, usually a school or a hotel or a restaurant, along with a variety of multiple witnesses who continue to experience haunting phenomena (Chacon, Christopher, Scientific Paranormal Investigator and Founder of O.S.I.R., Interview, "Haunted High," *Sightings*, 6 Jan. 1998).

• "Of the eight hundred investigations, haunts, and poltergeist phenomena that I've been on, seventy percent of them appeared to have rational explanations or definitive answers. However, there is another thirty percent which apparently we cannot find a rational explanation for, they defy the known laws of nature and physics, at least as we know them today" (Chacon, Christopher, Director, O.S.I.R., Interview, "Haunted High," *Sightings*, 6 Jan. 1998).

• The Ouija Board was originally designed as a game and was first marketed in 1899. The word "Ouija" comes from the French word *Oui* and the German word *ja* both meaning "yes" ("Ghostly Voices," *Unnatural History*, 26 May 1998).

• Humans have been reporting haunting phenomena for over two thousand years (*Haunted Places*, Thrills, Chills and Spills, 31 May 1998).

• "This phenomenon is part of our experienced reality. It's been reported since the beginning of time. It has come up in all cultures" (Gaynor, Kerry, Parapsychologist, Interview, "*The Living Dead*, Speaking From the Grave," *Sightings*, 25 Oct. 1998).

• "I think the interest in paranormal phenomena is certainly increasing, in fact the establishment of paranormal events is increasing" (Hauck, Dennis William, Paranormal Researcher and Author, Interview, "Restless Spirits," *Sightings*, 6 Sept. 1998).

Some of the most haunted places in the world:
- The *Queen Mary* Hotel and Convention Center, San Diego, California, dubbed by Peter James as the most haunted place in America with 600 residual haunts in residence.
- Sterling Castle in Scotland, home of the Green Lady and one hundred other spirits.
- Berry Pomeroy Castle in southern England, home of the Blue Lady and the White Lady and uninhabited since 1688 because of hauntings.
- The Treasurer's House, York, England, home to a regiment of Roman soldiers.

- Alcatraz Island, San Francisco, California.
- Dover Castle, White Cliffs, Dover, England.
- The Ten Bells Pub, London, England.
- Chillingham Castle, northern England.
- The aircraft carrier *U.S.S. Cabot.*
- The Drum Barracks, Wilmington, California.
- Brookdale Lodge, near San Francisco, California.
- Valley Forge, Pennsylvania Civil War battlefield.
- Fredericksburg, Pennsylvania Civil War battlefield.
- Moss Beach Distillery, San Francisco, California.
- Bobby Mackey's Music World.
- The Excalibur nightclub, Chicago.
- The Black Swann Inn, San Antonio, Texas.
- The Stewart Indian School, Stewart, Nevada.
- Resurrection Cemetery, home of Resurrection Mary in Chicago.
- The Whaley House in California.
- St. Petersburg High School, St. Petersburg, Florida.
- The Winchester House, San Jose, California.
- The Joshua Ward House, Salem, Massachusetts.
- La Posadas Hotel, Santa Fe, New Mexico.
- Manressa Castle, Port Townsend, Washington.
- The White House, Washington, DC.
- The Benton Homestead, circa 1720, Tollant, Massachusetts.
- House of the Seven Gables, Salem, Massachusetts, former home of Nathaniel Hawthorne, now home to the ghost of Suzanne Ingersoll.
- John Stones Inn in Ashland, Massachusetts.
- The Myrtles Plantation in New Orleans, Louisiana, home of Chloe, a former slave girl.
- Cemetery #1 in New Orleans, home of the spirit of former voodoo priestess Marie Leveaux.
- The LaLaRi Mansion in New Orleans, home to numerous black slave spirits.

- The *Delta Queen* riverboat on the Mississippi River in New Orleans, home to the ghost of Mary Green, the former owner and captain.
- The Le Petit Theatre in New Orleans.
- The Dock Street Theatre in Charleston, South Carolina.
- The Thomas Rose House in Charleston, South Carolina.
- The Old Exchange Building in Charleston, South Carolina.
- The Battery Carriage House Inn in Charleston, South Carolina, home of the Gentleman Ghost.
- The 1837 bed-and-breakfast in Charleston, South Carolina, home of the slave child George.
- Maxwell's Jazz Club, New Orleans.
- The Southern Nights bed-and-breakfast, New Orleans.
- The Bourbon Orleans Hotel, New Orleans.
- The Octagon House, Washington, DC.
- The Comedy Store, Hollywood, California.

History

The roots of hauntings plunge some three thousand years back into the Celtic origins of Sowen rituals, known today as All Hallows' Eve or Halloween. One very particular night between the bountiful harvest and the bitter cold winter, between the long warm days and the short cold days, transpired the most important night of Gaelic prayers. Their priests called Druids, would pray in thanks for the harvest and in fear of the cold approaching winter. On that transitional night called Sowen, the Celts believed the boundary between light and dark, between life and death, was so thin that the spirits of the dead could pass through back and forth at will.[1] On that night was born an eternal awareness of spirits reentering the world of the living.

Atrocities of the Middle Ages that occurred to the west of Ireland released spirits into such bastions as Scotland's Sterling Castle, home today of the Green Lady and ninety-nine other haunts, and Chillingham Castle, a bit further south in England, home of Lady Gray and of the Radiant Boy.

Ironically, it was a Puritan disdain for Halloween that may have released some of the first human spirits into the New World in 1692 to haunt people forever. The witch trials of Salem resulted in nineteen innocent hangings and one man put to death under the weight of enormous rocks. One of those responsible for the torture and killing of witches was George Corwin, the sheriff of Salem in 1692. Corwin's house once stood where the Joshua Ward House stands today, which is one of the most haunted sites in all of New England.[2]

As the colonists settled along America's east coast, so their dead began to fill up the cemeteries. Ample eyewitness testimony today suggests that the colonial spirit world also began to fill up during the eighteenth century in places like New England, Charleston, and New Orleans (*see Some of the World's Most Haunted Places section above*).

The nineteenth-century preoccupation with life beyond death began in the spring of 1848 in the New York village of Hydesville. Two sisters, Margaret and Catherine Fox, decided after great frustration, to attempt to relate to the nagging spirit that was rapping and knocking loudly throughout their quaint farmhouse. Catherine would snap her fingers twice and the spirit would knock twice back. This deliberate attempt to communicate with the spirit world became known as "spiritualism." It is the science, philosophy, and religion of continuing life. Margaret and Catherine had become the country's first "mediums."[3]

Spiritualism spread rapidly across America. By 1853 there were as many as twenty-five-thousand mediums[4] attempting to communicate with the spiritual members of the next phase of human existence. The goal of the movement was to scientifically prove that human spirits did exist and that it was possible to establish communication with them. Spiritualists do not believe in death, only different phases of life connected through mediumship.

Fakery ran rampant during this time and eventually even the now-famous Fox sisters drew criticism. But one man named Daniel Douglas Holmes made believers out of nearly all who witnessed his uncanny talent. At one seance he convinced poet Elizabeth Barrett Browning by having spirit hands place a garland on her head. Holmes' trademark was his ability to levitate and materialize objects including himself, and while many other frauds were exposed, he remained untouched. Today, the world center for spiritualists is the Lily Dale Assembly on Cassadaga Lake in western New York State.[5]

As America grew throughout the nineteenth century, so did reports of ghostly phenomena. Wherever violent quick deaths occurred, restless spirits were born. From the early days of the Puritan settlements and witch trials in New England, through the American Revolution and the slavery issue of Charleston in the late 1700s, to the San Francisco gold rush robbery killings of 1849, then back to the Civil War of the mid-nineteenth century, young America was a violent place to be. Many died and became haunting legends.

Many such landmarks where America's future course was set are now the focus of a new breed of spiritualist. Today, they are called paranormal investigators. These ghost hunters use a vast complete array of detective tools, everything from the proven extrasensory skills of psychic investigators to an arsenal of sophisticated instrumentation used to monitor haunting environments. Though still struggling to become a mainstream scientific endeavor, ghost hunting has entered the information age of technology.

Some instruments used in investigations are the hydrothermograph for detecting temperature changes, the thermovision camera for detecting thermal image deviations, special radioactivity monitors as well as electromagnetic and geomagnetic field monitors, several different types of surveillance systems, video cameras, closed circuit television, and Polaroid film. Every environmental characteristic is examined, including the visual, physical, audible, chemical, electrical, magnetic, geophysical, thermal and residual. Deviations between a normal environment and a suspected anomalous environment usually indicate the presence of a spirit. Because this science is still young, humans have yet to develop a device that will irrefutably point to a ghost.

Prevailing theories regarding hauntings are:[6]

1. Spirits of the dead that return to complete a task or to pursue revenge, justice, or to interact in some way with living humans.

2. Spirits are emotional tracers that linger after physical death, acting like a shadow pressed into the space-time plane.

3. Spirits are memories somehow sustained in some type of psychic ether.

4. Spirits are residual images that get replayed over and over again.

5. Spirits are caused by the human imagination.

Theory #1 is substantiated by the most evidence.

Documented Cases
The Heartland Ghost

In a quaint little house on a quiet street in our American heartland, lived a young family of three who experienced the haunting of hauntings. The television documentary, *Sightings*, a leader in scientific ghost investigations worldwide, became involved with Tony, Deborah, and Taylor Pickman in what was to become a landmark case packed with high-tech evidence and multiple videotaped eyewitnesses.

Early in 1993, shortly after they moved into their home, the Pickmans' freshly snapped baby pictures came back from the developers with distorted blobs of light and color covering the image of baby Taylor. The photographic anomalies continued through countless rolls of film and two different cameras. The concerned young family turned to psychic Barbara Conner who determined the entity causing the photographic anomalies was a restless little girl named Sallie. The photos were authenticated as a genuine anomaly, and not a double exposure or a hoax, by visual effects specialist Edson Williams. Soon after these episodes, the most bizarre behavior began to occur, it would continue throughout the incident and would become the signature of the six-year Heartland investigation. Significantly, this entire case was video-taped by *Sightings* from beginning to end.

Out of thin air, Tony's arms, back, and chest became the target of scratches, not tiny ones mind you, but long, deep, welted scratches that would form and begin to bleed right in front of everyone's eyes, even on camera. Environmental and medical causes were officially ruled out. Also, the air immediately around Tony turned very cold during these events. Paranormal investigator Howard Heim entered the picture and measured the temperate and electromagnetic fluctuations. Then, a lonely rose resting in a vase on the kitchen windowsill was found to be burned on the inside of some of its petals, and the scratches on Tony continued to appear.

Sightings, now entrenched in this case, invited internationally esteemed psychic Peter James to join them in pursuit of the answers to the cause of Sallie's frustration. With no previous case knowledge, Peter psychically identified Sallie, along with many other case details, in the presence of many witnesses. Courthouse and cemetery records confirmed Peter's suggestions that Sallie Isabel Hall died in this house from pneumonia in 1905 and was buried in the town cemetery.

Tony's scratches continued to appear with no apparent rhyme or reason, but it was not a hoax, not self-inflicted wounds, and not an allergy or any medical condition. Then *Sightings* got down to business. They brought in parapsychologist Kerry Gaynor along with every instrument known to exist for paranormal research. Closed-circuit cameras were set up in every room, and the kitchen was transformed into the base of operations with oscilloscopes, frequency counters, audio monitors, and a handheld thermal energy system that detected cold spots.

Throughout their vigil, the team monitored anomalies with all their instruments as the scratches continued to form on Tony. The Pickmans finally left their house after three years of Sallie's bizarre mayhem. Wondering whether Sallie moved with them or stayed behind, *Sightings* called in Peter James once again to psychically survey the house. Confirmation of Sallie's presence came in the form of burns to Peter's face.

Two years later, after several other tenants had come and gone, Sallie still remained on that quaint, quiet, heartland street, according to Peter James, who once again came to survey the home. Sallie never again displayed as many transgressions against other occupants as she had inflicted upon Tony. Peter believes Sallie will remain in that house for a long time, until she finally realizes her physical form no longer exists.[7]

Hard Evidence

The landmark Heartland Ghost case provides the best physical evidence to date of the existence of the human spirit. The actual scratches forming on Tony's skin along with other anomalous activity were all monitored, recorded, filmed, and witnessed by highly credible multiple eyewitnesses. The sprit Sallie was verified by two reputable psychics, and her life and background were confirmed by courthouse and cemetery records.

Beyond the Facts

Hauntings are similar to miracles and angels in that members of the spirit world interact with our physical world. In cases of life beyond death, humans "traveled" in spirit form to the spirit realm, then returned to the physical world of Earth.

In some cases, ghosts may be restless human spirits going through what we now know to be a negative near-death experience. According to

Kerry Gaynor, quick violent deaths are the most common cause of hauntings.[8] Suicide is surely one of the most negative violent acts known. Sometimes near-death experiences or NDEs are negative at first but become positive after the spirit discovers the light. Could hauntings be frustrated human spirits who either don't know to look for the light or who may have been a suicide victim? According to most NDE "travelers" both positive and negative, suicide, the destruction of one's own physical life does not occur without spiritual consequences. Suicide is shunned by all religions. Is it possible that these spirits are forced to roam among the physical world of humans until they have learned the true meaning and gift of their own life?

Considering the Heartland Ghost case, the Pickmans experienced firsthand the phenomenon of a lingering, unsettled human spirit, and the reality of our unseen Universe became starkly apparent, regardless of what die-hard skeptics they may have previously been. This event is quite undeniable, having been witnessed by so many credible people, having been recorded both on video and audio tape from beginning to end, and having been monitored with every available high-tech environmental instrument. This is a very significant case because it was scientifically monitored. Furthermore, mainstream science has recently found hard evidence for the human extrasensory system — thus lending further credibility to genuine psychics such as Peter James. (See the chapter Extrasensory Perception). One fascinating observation to me is that Sallie died in 1905 yet some ninety years later her spirit was confirmed by psychic Peter James as that of a little girl. Do human spirits age in the spirit realm?

Although not apparent in the Heartland case, the element of unusual light energy surfaces from time to time among cases of reputable psychics and investigators. They will tell a restless haunt to "Go into the light; it's okay; move into the light." My theory is that the light they refer to is the same light described in positive NDEs and is likely the same light that opened the stigmata of Padre Pio in 1918 and Saint Katherine of Sienna in 1375 (*see the chapters on Miracles and Angels, and Life beyond Death and Reincarnation*).

When we consider all the evidence of miracles and angels, life beyond death and reincarnation, and hauntings; when we consider all of the known haunted places in our world, there remains little doubt that humans are both physical and spiritual beings.

Resources for Further Investigation
Leading Research Scientists and Investigators

Loyd Auerbach
Parapsychologist Loyd Auerbach works mostly with a magnetometer and with genuine psychics in his pursuit of evidence. He believes the human consciousness or spirit survives physical death and impacts the environment. He has found that a magnetometer can pick up traces of the impact because geomagnetic and electromagnetic fields are affected by the spirit. Psychics are able to read electromagnetic fields around people.

Richard S. Broughton
Mr. Broughton is the director of the Institute of Parapsychology in Durham, North Carolina. He believes there is good evidence that people can detect environmental anomalies or spirits through ESP.

Steven Lee Carson
A historian and a lecturer on hauntings, Steve Carson is an authority on ghosts in the White House, United States Capitol, and other Washington landmarks.

Christopher Chacon
Christopher Chacon is a paranormal investigator and the founder and director of O.S.I.R. Chacon and his organization employ perhaps the most extensive array of sophisticated equipment in the business to monitor the environment, to differentiate a normal environment from one with anomalies or spirits. Chacon and O.S.I.R. are used extensively in television documentary investigations.

Tony Cornell

Tony Cornell is a paranormal investigator from Cambridge, England. He is specifically well versed on the haunted history of British Isles castles. After over eight hundred investigations, he believes ghosts and poltergeists are real phenomena. Tony first gathers historical information on the site, and employs psychics to identify hot spots. He then uses environmental monitoring equipment to confirm the presence of an entity by detecting changes relating to sound, sight, heat, geomagnetic, and electromagnetic fields. Cornell is an authority on Pomeroy and Chillingham Castles, and is often interviewed for television documentaries.

Kerry Gaynor

Parapsychologist and paranormal investigator Kerry Gaynor is very well known for his work on the Entity and the Poltergeist cases. Gaynor has investigated over 850 cases over the last twenty years. He has worked closely with the *Sightings* investigations, including the Heartland haunting.

William Guggenheim

He is an after death communications researcher.

Dennis William Hauck

Hauck is a paranormal researcher, author, and editor from Sacramento, California. Dennis Hauck has investigated hauntings and other paranormal hot spots for over ten years. He has compiled *The National Directory of Haunted Places,* which began as a case reference manual for fellow researchers, but has become a travel guide to over two thousand paranormal sites throughout all fifty states. The guide is updated every two years to remove sites no longer under investigation and to add new sites harboring unexplained phenomena.

Peter James

Peter James is perhaps one of the most talented psychic mediums in the world, with the ability to, in most cases, instantaneously determine the number, names, and backgrounds of haunts in any given environment. His findings are confirmed with courthouse records and other historical documentation. He believes the *Queen Mary* is the most haunted place in America.

Randy Liebeck

Mr. Liebeck is a paranormal investigator.

Dr. Michaeleen Maher

Dr. Maher is a psychic investigator specializing in statistical research.

Annette Martin

She is a professional psychic.

Joe Nickell

Mr. Nickell believes that ghosts are all within the imaginative minds of people who believe in ghosts.

Patrick Polk

Polk is a folklorist knowledgeable on hauntings. His studies are based at the University of California in Los Angeles.

Dr. William Roll

One of America's best-known parapsychologists, Dr. Roll has investigated many leading cases.

Paul Scarzo

Paul Scarzo has been successful at photographing spirits by using a stereographic 3-D camera with four lenses. He takes a picture, actually four pictures at once, every time an electrostatic voltmeter or some other instrument picks up an anomalous reading. Occasionally an entity will show up in one of four shots.

Richard Senate

Mr. Senate is a paranormal investigator, historian, parapsychologist, and psychic investigator. He is very knowledgeable about history in addition to being a phenomenal psychic. He is often interviewed for television documentaries.

Deryck Seymour

He is a paranormal author, historian, and the leading authority on Pomeroy Castle having investigated it for over sixty-five years.

Recommended Television Programs and Networks

Please consult the Directory of Television Networks in the back of the book for scheduling information and availability of home videos:

Allan Mann, *Unsolved Mysteries*, 1994, 20 minutes
on Lifetime
air dates: 02/27/98, 04/24/98

Archaeology/Anthropology, *A&E Classroom*, 1997, 60 minutes
on The Arts & Entertainment Network
air dates: 04/10/98

Bus Crash, San Antonio, *Beyond Bizarre*, 1998, 12 minutes
on The Discovery Channel
air dates: 06/02/98

Civil War Ghosts, *Unsolved Mysteries*, 1994, 1992, 12 minutes
on Lifetime
air dates: 01/30/98, 07/16/98, 03/06/98, 09/21/98

Comedy Store Haunting, *Unsolved Mysteries*, 9 minutes
on Lifetime
air dates: 05/18/98

"Fairies, Phantoms and Fantastic Photographs," *Arthur C. Clarke's World of Strange Powers*, 1985, 60 minutes
on The Discovery Channel
air dates: 01/10/98

"Ghosts, Apparitions, and Haunted Houses," *Arthur C. Clarke's World of Strange Powers*, 1994, 60 minutes
on The Discovery Channel
air dates: 09/20/98, 02/15/98

"Ghosts," *Strange but True?*, 1997, 15 minutes
on The Discovery Channel
air dates: 02/05/98

"Haunted Castle," *Strange but True?* 1997, 15 minutes
on The Discovery Channel
air dates: 05/10/98

"*Haunted History*, Charleston," 1998, 60 minutes
on The History Channel
air dates: 10/29/98

Haunted History of Halloween, 1997, 60 minutes
on The History Channel
air dates: 10/23/98

"Haunted History, New England," 1998, 60 minutes
on The History Channel
air dates: 10/27/98

"Haunted History, New Orleans," 1998, 60 minutes
on The History Channel
air dates: 10/27/98

"Haunted History, San Francisco," 1998, 60 minutes
on The History Channel
air dates: 10/29/98

Haunted Places, Thrills Chills and Spills, 1997, 60 minutes
on The Discovery Channel
air dates: 05/31/98

Haunted Ranch House, *Unsolved Mysteries*, 1996, 9 minutes
on Lifetime
air dates: 05/26/98

"Hellfire Corner," *Strange but True?*, 1997, 30 minutes
on The Discovery Channel
air dates: 02/05/98, 06/20/98

In The Grip of Evil, 1997, 60 minutes
on The Discovery Channel
air dates: 11/28/97, 05/31/98

La Placada Hotel, *Unsolved Mysteries*, 1994, 13 minutes
on Lifetime
air dates: 02/27/98, 08/12/98

Moss Beach Distillery, *Unsolved Mysteries*, 1994, 12 minutes
on Lifetime
air dates: 01/30/98, 07/16/98, 03/06/98, 09/21/98

Poltergeist or Psychokinetic, *Unsolved Mysteries*, 1993, 25 minutes
on Lifetime
air dates: 07/06/98

"Poltergeists," *Strange but True?*, 1997, 30 minutes
on The Discovery Channel
air dates: 01/25/98

"Poltergeist," *The Unexplained*, 1997, 60 minutes
on The Arts & Entertainment Network
air dates: 05/17/98

Resurrection Mary, *Unsolved Mysteries*, 1994, 10 minutes
on Lifetime
air dates: 01/30/98, 03/06/98, 09/21/98

Sightings, Series First Aired 1991, Went Into Syndication 1994
on The Sci-Fi Channel
air dates: 1991 through 1998

"Spirits of Place - Hauntings and Ghosts," *Arthur C. Clarke's Mysterious Universe*, 1995, 30 minutes
on The Discovery Channel
air dates: 06/08/98

"The Curse of James Dean's Car" *Extremely Weird*, 1995, 2 minutes
on The Learning Channel
air dates: 01/03/98, 01/31/98

"The Curse of the Nimrud Treasure," *Extremely Weird*, 1995,
2 minutes
on The Learning Channel
air dates: 01/03/98, 01/31/98

"The Curse of Tut's Tomb" *Extremely Weird*, 1995, 2 minutes
on The Learning Channel
air dates: 01/03/98, 01/31/98

"Things That Go Bump in the Night," *Arthur C. Clarke's World of Strange Powers*, 1985, 30 minutes
on The Discovery Channel
air dates: 08/23/98, 02/08/98

Would You Believe It? 60 minutes
on The Discovery Channel
air dates: 11/28/97

Recommended Books
Hell's Gate: Terror at Bobby Mackey's Music World
by Doug Hensley

Hollywood Haunted
by Laurie Jacobson

Reincarnation
by Julian T. Buxton, III and Carey Williams

Sightings
by Susan Michaels

Spirits of San Antonio
by Docia Schultz Williams

The National Directory of Haunted Places
by Dennis William Hauck

Recommended Videotapes, Audio Tapes, and CD-ROMS
The Ghost Report (video)
from *Sightings*

Recommended Internet Sites
Apparitions and Hauntings
http://www.infidels.org

Camelot Productions
The site of *The Magic of Our Universe*
http://www.camelotpublishing.com

Paranormal Phenomena Archive
http://www.in-search-of.com

ParaStore Books: 500 British Ghosts and Hauntings
http://www.parascope.com

The Arts and Entertainment Network
http://www.AandE.com

The Discovery Channel
http://www.discovery.com

The Spirit Website
Exceptional information source regarding hauntings
http://www.ghosthunter.org

The Ufomind Paranormal Index and Bookstore
http://www.ufomind.com

Unsolved Mysteries
http://www.unsolved.com

Organizations
The Center for Inquiry
1310 Sweet Home Road
P. O. Box 664
Amherst, NY 14226-0664
716-636-7571
716-636-1733 (FAX)
CFIFLYNN@aol.com
The debunking center of paranormal phenomena.

CSICOP (The Committee for the Scientific Investigation of the Paranormal)
Box 703
Amherst, NY 14226
716-636-1425
INFO@CSICOP.org
www.csicop.org
Paul Kurtz, Chairman
Their goal is to bring together scientists, skeptics, and academics to look into the many paranormal claims across the board — afterlife, poltergeists, ghostly hauntings, UFOs and to try to find objective explanations. *The Skeptical Inquirer* is their journal reporting on their investigations.

GRS (Ghost Research Society)
P. O. Box 205
Oak Lawn, IL 60454
dkaczmarck@ghostresearch.log
www.ghostresearch.org
Dale D. Kaczmarck, President

HH (Haunt Hunters)
2188 Sycamore Hill Court
Chesterfield, MO 63017
Instrumental Transcommunication
Mark Macy
This organization claims to have successfully communicated with spirits through television, telephone, fax machines and e-mail.

ISPR (International Society for Paranormal Research)
P. O. Box 291159
Los Angeles, CA   90027
323-644-8866
ghost@hauntings.com
www.hauntings.com
Larry Montz, Parapsychologist
They conduct scientific investigations of phenomena using scientific methodology.

OPI (Office of Paranormal Investigation)
P. O. Box 875
Orinda, CA   94563-0875
415-781-1707
415-553-2588
Loyd Auerbach, Director
www.mindreader.com

OSIR (The Office of Scientific Investigation and Research)
Christopher Chacon, Founder and Director
Peter Akroyd, John Berry

Poltergeist Research Institute
Dr. Barrie Colvin, Founder
A group of hand-picked international scientists investigating poltergeist activity worldwide.

The Center for Paranormal Studies
Silver Springs, Florida
James Bosworth, Research Scientist, Founder
Russell W. McCarty, Paranormal Researcher, Founder
Andrew Nichols, Parapsychologist

The Rhine Research Center
Institute for Parapsychology
402 N. Buchanan Blvd.
Durham, North Carolina   27701-1728
919-688-8241
919-683-4338 (FAX)
www.rhine.org
info@rhine.org

The Society of Psychical Research
University of Nottingham, England

Endnotes

[1] *Haunted History of Halloween*, narr. Harry Smith, writ. Jeff Swimmer, prod. Jeff Swimmer, The History Channel, 23 Oct. 1998.

[2] "*Haunted History*, New England," narr. Michael Dorn, ed. Bradley Holmes, prod. Craig Haffner and Donna Lusitana, The History Channel, 26 Oct. 1998.

[3] *Ghostly Voices*, Unnatural History, narr. Mark Hamill, writ. Michael Tetrick, prod. Michael Tetrick, The Learning Channel, 26 April 1998.

[4] *Ghostly Voices*, Unnatural History, 26 April 1998.

[5] *Ghostly Voices*, Unnatural History, 26 April 1998.

[6] "Encounters, Hauntings Investigations," *Sightings*, narr. Tim White, writ. Susan Michaels, prod. Paul Hall and Mark Cowen, The Sci-Fi Channel, 14 Sept. 1998.

[7] "*The Living Dead*, Speaking From the Grave," *Sightings*, narr. Tim White, writ. Susan Michaels, prod. Henry Winkler and Ann Daniel, The Sci-Fi Channel, 25 Oct. 1998.

[8] Gaynor, Kerry, Interview, "Encounters, Hauntings Investigations," *Sightings*, narr. Tim White, writ. Susan Michaels, prod. Henry Winkler and Ann Daniel, The Sci-Fi Channel, 14 Sept. 1998.

Extrasensory Perception

The Known Elements of Psi

Telepathy
Identical Twins

Clairvoyance
Mediums
Remote Viewing
Psychic Detectives
Animal Clairvoyance
Dowsing

Precognition
Prophecy
Nostradamus
Jules Verne
Gordon-Michael Scallion
Edgar Cayce

Psychokinesis and Telekinesis
Psychic Healers

The Force comes from all living things.
It surrounds us, it penetrates us,
it bonds the galaxy together....

— **Obi-Wan Kenobi,** *Star Wars*

Extrasensory Perception

Definitions

Extrasensory Perception (ESP). Information or knowledge perceived or communicated outside of the known human sensory system. Current ESP research, known in science as "psi," encompasses the phenomena of telepathy, clairvoyance, precognition, and the related phenomena of psychokinesis and telekinesis. The term *extrasensory perception* first appeared in written English around 1935. Around 1942, the term "*psi*" was derived from the word *psychic*.

Telepathy. The extrasensory transfer of information between the minds of beings. The word was created around 1883 from the Greek *têle*, which means "far," and the Greek *patheia*, which means "feeling."

Clairvoyance. The extrasensory perception of people, objects, or events that are isolated from the viewer by either space or time. The word first appeared in English around 1845 and is derived from the French *clairvoyant*, which means "clear seeing."

Precognition. Extrasensory knowledge of a circumstance or event that has not yet occurred. The word originated around 1425 from the late Middle English *cognicioun*, which was derived from the Latin *cognoscene*, "to know," and the Latin *prea*, which means "beforehand."

Psychokinesis. Moving or deforming solid objects through focused mental application. The word was first documented in English around 1914 and is derived from *psycho*, from the Greek *psyche*, which means "mind, spirit, or soul," and the Greek *kinesis*, "to move."

Telekinesis. The movement of information from a distance through focused mental application. The word was first used in English around 1890, the combination of the Greek prefix *têle*, meaning "far," and the Greek *kinesis*, which means "to move."

Statistics

- As of 1998, there were 399 books in print on the subject of extrasensory perception including all the categories on the title page of this section. The number of books in print remained steady through 1992, then doubled in 1993 from 16 to 32. Publications doubled again from 33 in 1995 to 61 in 1997. This activity suggests increased awareness of the phenomenon (Numbers obtained from *R. R. Bowker's Books in Print*, 1998 list).

- Nearly forty-six hours of documentaries related to ESP or psi were aired in 1997, and an astounding 275 hours aired in 1998. Without a doubt, this six hundred percent increase indicates an amazing jump in human interest in psi-related phenomena (Numbers derived from Gissen, Jay, ed., *The Cable Guide*, 1997, 1998).

- Over four thousand sets of twins attend the annual Twin's Days Festival in Twinsburg, Ohio ("Identical Twins," *Strange But True?*, 19 March 1998).

- Sixty percent of Americans claim to have experienced some form of extrasensory perception (Miller, Kenneth, "Psychics: Science or Seance? A Reporter Visits the Twilight Zone," *Life*, June 1998: 88–103).

- Fifty percent of Americans believe in extrasensory perception (1991 *Gallup Poll*).

- "Our normal idea of where information comes from has to be expanded. In other words, there are ways of getting information not only through normal means but through some other means" (Radin, Dean, Ph.D., Interview, *Invisible Forces*, Science of the Impossible, 19 July 1998).

• Evidence suggests an additional sensory system exists, through which humans and possibly other animals can gather information (May, Ed, Senior Research Physicist, Stanford Research Institute, Interview, *Invisible Forces*, Science of the Impossible, 19 July 1998).

• The Biblical prophet is defined as "one whose eye has opened," meaning one who has a different range of experience than most people (Huffman, Herbert B., Prof. of Old Testament, Drew University, Interview, "*Prophets*: Soul Catchers," *Mysteries of the Bible*, 28 Nov. 1998).

• Animal behavior specialist, author, and researcher Rupert Sheldrake theorizes that psychic abilities are very common in animals. Animals connect and bond with other animals and with humans through what is called a morphic field (Sheldrake, Rupert, Interview, *Sightings*, In the News, 23 July 1998).

• In 1943, while dowsing with a pendulum, wildcatter Ace Gutowski discovered Oklahoma's largest oil field — directly underneath the state capitol building, of all places ("An Element of the Divine," *Arthur C. Clarke's World of Strange Powers*, 12 July 1998).

• Under clinically controlled conditions, healer Dean Kraft has destroyed cancerous hela cells in a test tube, has effectively lowered the blood pressure of lab rats, and a Howard University study showed a forty percent improvement rate in patients treated by Kraft ("Healers," *Sightings*, 17 Feb. 1998).

• The historical and cross-cultural persistence of psi experiences such as telepathy, clairvoyance, remote viewing, precognition, and psychokinesis suggests that human understanding of consciousness, space, and time may be incomplete, possibly in fundamental ways (Radin, Dean, Ph.D., *Consciousness Research Laboratory*, <http://www.psiresearch.org>, 26 Jan. 1999).

- The first U.S. patent for a psi-based effect was granted to Princeton University researchers on November 3, 1998 (Radin, Dean, Ph.D., *Consciousness Research Laboratory*, <http://www.psiresearch.org>, 26 Jan. 1999).

- "Until recently, many mainstream scientists have assumed (without scientific examination) that psi-like events could be explained entirely as a combination of delusions, misunderstandings about coincidences, wishful thinking, and perceptual and cognitive distortions" (Radin, Dean, Ph.D., *Consciousness Research Laboratory*, <http://www.psiresearch.org>, 26 Jan. 1999).

History

The best-documented facet of extrasensory perception, which transcends human history, is that of precognition — the ability to foretell the future. Claims of prophecy far outweigh any other form of psi, although some ancient "precognitive" events remain fodder for debate.

Five thousand years ago, Babylonian astrologers assisted their kings with important decisions regarding kingdom rule. Throughout the centuries, shaman prophecies have been reverently heeded in many parts of the world.[1] In the Bible, prophecy appeared with Samuel, who was divinely chosen around 1050 B.C. to reverse waning faith and growing paganism. Other popular Old Testament prophets were Elijah in 886 B.C., Amos in 792 B.C., Isaiah in 742 B.C., Jeremiah in 626 B.C., and Ezekiel in 593 B.C.[2] Hebrew scripture documents these prophets however, as evidence that the covenant of righteousness and compassion was upheld, more than for their precognitive predictions.[3]

One of the oldest and most fascinating Biblical accounts of prophecy occurred in ancient Egypt about four thousand years ago. Genesis 41:28 tells of a young dream interpreter named Joseph who correctly deciphered the reigning Pharaoh's dream and saved a nation.

As the dream played out, seven scrawny cows consumed seven fat cows; then seven barren ears of corn devoured seven full ears. Joseph's interpretation predicted seven bountiful years of harvest followed by seven lean years. Joseph suggested the Pharaoh store grain during the first seven years for sustenance during the following period of drought. Joseph's prediction held true and thousands of Egyptians were spared starvation and certain death. Because of his accuracy Joseph was appointed counselor to the Pharaoh.[4]

Around A.D. 95 St. John the Divine[5] wrote the final book of the New Testament, the prophecy of the Apocalypse. Ironically, he penned the book of Revelation while basking on the quiet, beautiful Greek island of Patmos.[6] Perhaps a little more time must pass before his prediction comes true. Eight hundred years later[7] the Maya of northern Central America and southern Mexico accurately predicted their own demise by the Spanish conquest of 1518.[8]

Fifteen years earlier in the sixteenth century, notable prophet Michel de Nostredame was born in the southeastern region of France known as Provence.[9] Early on he practiced astrology and medicine. He became an admired physician who implemented medical procedures contrary to those of other practitioners, which were successful in healing plague-ravaged Europeans. Beginning in 1547 Nostradamus began predicting the future — some claim with immaculate precision. In a room solely devoted to his predictions he used a black mirror he called his "doorway to the future" and a book entitled *The Mysteries of Egyptology* for inspiration. He completed his collection of prophecies, *Centuries,* in the year 1555.[10] The book contained over nine hundred predictions in rhyming verse called quatrains that were arranged in hundred-verse segments — hence the title.[11]

Nostradamus evaded the prying eyes of the Inquisition by jumbling the chronological order of his verses[12] and by writing the quatrains in code: a blend of different languages, anagrams, and symbolism.[13] Some scholars credit him with predicting the rise and fall of Napoleon and Hitler, the atomic annihilation of Hiroshima and Nagasaki, and the assassination of JFK, among many others.[14] Nostradamus and the twelfth-century Irish prophet St. Malachi independently predicted that the name of the last of 112 popes would be "Peter the Roman."[15] Malachi lived three hundred years before Nostradamus.

Another Frenchman, novelist Jules Verne, was the Gene Roddenberry of the nineteenth century. More a futurist than a prophet, he spawned epics such as *Twenty Thousand Leagues Under the Sea* in 1869, which depicted the nuclear submarine one hundred years before its time. He also wrote *From the Earth to the Moon*, which contains a nearly perfect nineteenth-century version of the Apollo mission right down to the launching pad in Florida and the splashdown in the Pacific. His English counterpart H. G. Wells followed suit with the futuristic classics *The Time Machine* and *The War of the Worlds*.[16]

The Victorian era in England also ushered in the formal scientific study of extrasensory perception with the funding of the London-based Society for Psychical Research in 1882.[17] Early research included field-work and debunking some spirit mediums as frauds. Across the Atlantic and five years before the SPR opened its doors, perhaps the best-documented genuine prophet of our time was born in rural Kentucky. His name was Edgar Cayce[18] (*see the case study on Edgar Cayce*).

Further inroads into the scientific study of psi transpired just north of Cayce's birthplace some fifty years later. Two botanists, Joseph Banks Rhine and his wife, Louise, were attending a lecture on spiritualism given by celebrated novelist Sir Arthur Conan Doyle. The Rhines were so captivated by Doyle's Chicago speech that they changed careers and established the science of parapsychology in the U.S. in 1927.[19]

Adjacent to Duke University in Durham, N.C., the nonprofit Rhine Research Center houses four staff parapsychologists who "explore the unusual types of experiences that suggest capabilities as yet unrecognized in the domain of human personality, and who investigate those capabilities thoroughly by exact scientific methods." Rhine parapsychologists now coordinate their work with other research facilities worldwide, including the Consciousness Research Lab in California, The University of Edinburgh in Scotland, The Princeton Engineering Anomalies Research Lab, The University of Amsterdam, Franklin Pierce College in New Hampshire, and the Cognitive Sciences Lab in California, to mention a few. The Rhine Center's open-minded and encouraging objectives are to coordinate its psi research with other relevant disciplines and to establish a more cohesive learning relationship between the academic community, independent researchers, and the general public.[20]

In addition to Richard S. Broughton of the Rhine Center, another scientist who speaks good layman's English is the esteemed author and director of the Consciousness Research Laboratory, Dean Radin. His web site offers outstandingly detailed, yet readable information regarding worldwide psi research. Over the past few decades, Radin and his colleagues have amassed convincing evidence from continuously repeated controlled experiments suggesting the reality of psi phenomena in humans (see Recommended Internet Sites and Organizations).

Currently some highly significant and fascinating research is exploring the strong psi bond between animals, as well as between animals and humans. Researcher Rupert Sheldrake explains these common links in terms of morphic fields (see the Glossary). A morphic field is the observable force that bonds flocks of birds or schools of fish. Veterinarian Michael Fox, a Washington, D.C. animal surgeon, suggests that wandering lost animals hundreds of miles from home find their way back by tuning into an empathetic emotional realm he calls the empathosphere.[21] Dogs are now being used for early detection of everything from melanoma[22] to epileptic seizures[23] to earthquakes.[24]

All around the world, people with all kinds of psi continue to demonstrate remarkable innate abilities. The annual Twins Day Festival in Twinsburg, Ohio, of all places, is literally a telepathic field day.[25] Psychic detectives such as Dorothy Allison, Noreen Renier, and Carol Pate consistently amaze law enforcement officers by helping them solve unsolvable cases. Well-known clairvoyants Peter James and James Van Praagh are booked far in advance for documentary interviews, talk shows, and performances, and psychic hot lines have ballooned into a billion-dollar business in a little more than a decade.[26] Contemporary prophets such as Gordon-Michael Scallion continue to hit their mark more often than not, while healers Dean Kraft, Jack Gray,[27] and Grace DiBicarri continually defy medical science with their miracles.

The weight of the evidence strongly suggests that an innate extrasensory system exists virtually untapped in humans and other animals. Moreover, some humans such as Edgar Cayce have accessed this system at will and have subconsciously traveled through the space–time continuum. This other-dimensional realm in the space around us has been referred to as hyperspace by New York University physicist Micho Kaku,[28] as the ether by other scholars,[29] and as the empathosphere by veterinarian Michael Fox.[30] I call it the consciospiritual dimension.

Documented Cases

The Remarkable Story of Jim and Jim

There is little question that identical twins provide psi research with the most fascinating case studies and data regarding telepathy. One story of twins separated at birth illustrates just how strong the invisible bond can be. In the case of Jim Lewis and Jim Springer, their bond transcends time and space.

Born nameless on August 19, 1939 in Bradford, Ohio, identical twin boys were placed for adoption by their mother because of hard times.

Earnest and Sarah Springer claimed one of the boys, and Jess and Lucille Lewis adopted his brother two weeks later. The twins were separated from each other for the next forty years. In February of 1979, after thirty-three years of searching, Jim Lewis finally found his brother living only fourteen miles away. Jim Springer lived thirty-nine years of his life thinking his twin had died at birth. The stories they shared about their time apart were astonishing. For starters they both preferred the same brand of beer — Miller Lite. In school, they both hated spelling but liked math; both named their dogs "Toy"; later in life they both became police officers; both men first married women named Linda, got divorced, then married women named Betty; both sets of Jim and Betty had sons they named James Allen; both men smoked the same brand of cigarettes; both built identical white benches around trees in their gardens and built workshops in their basements; they even vacationed for years at the same place in Florida, not knowing they were both on the same stretch of beach.

Eventually Jim Lewis and Jim Springer were invited to the Minnesota Center for Twins Research to participate in a series of tests. The two men answered the questions identically and were consequently asked by researchers to retake the exams.[31]

The Amazing Clairvoyance of Peter James

As a child of five, Peter James discovered that he had playmates on the playground who were not known to the other children, but it wasn't until three years later that he knew for sure that he was playing with children of the spirit world.[32] Peter James is quite simply one of the most gifted clairvoyant mediums on the planet.

Not only can Peter communicate with residents of the spirit realm, but he also claims to see spirits as well. He finds a similarity between his ability to see human spirits and the ability of other humans to see human beings. Peter tells us that spirits have personality: Some are quiet and shy, while others are friendly, and still others are not so friendly. Peter knows from experience that humans and spirits coexist in parallel worlds.

The minute Peter James sets foot in a haunted dwelling, he immediately begins to perceive elements key to the spirit's identity. Clues surface in his mind and names appear. At first they are disjointed words and images, but soon they take on meaning and specific relevance to the history of the people and places involved. These names can later be confirmed with the owners of the premises or with official records. Such was the case in the moving Heartland investigation (*see the Hauntings chapter*) where Peter identified the spirit Sallie, who was later confirmed in both cemetery and courthouse documents.[33, 34]

Peter has investigated hundreds of cases, many with the *Sightings* group, including the case of the *Queen Mary*, which he claims is the most haunted place in America, and that of the Black Swan Inn in San Antonio, Texas.[35] In every case Peter immediately psychically retrieved details previously known only by the *Sightings* team, in courthouse records, or by the owner of the property.

Clairvoyant Remote Viewer Joe McMoneagle

Joe McMoneagle's clairvoyance began with a near-death experience. McMoneagle was serving as a U.S. Army intelligence officer in July of 1970 when an episode of near-fatal illness triggered an NDE. After his recovery, Joe McMoneagle realized he had acquired psychic ability.

From 1978 through 1984 Joe worked as a military remote viewer with the U.S. Army Intelligence and Security Command (INSCOM), located in Arlington, Virginia.[36] During his military career, he targeted remote sites in the Soviet Union, Libya, Iran, and Iraq.[37] He worked on over 350 cases, including the Iranian hostage crisis, and he was able to describe eighty percent of the target items of interest to military intelligence. Joe completed his military career as a Special Projects Intelligence Officer.

Later, McMoneagle worked with director Ed May at the Stanford Research Institute in the CIA's remote viewing project called STARGATE.[38] He currently works with Dean Radin at the Cognitive Sciences Laboratory on a project for remote viewing of future technologies.[39] His success rate in controlled experiments is around fifty percent — remarkable considering that guessing would result in about a twenty percent success rate. Typically, Joe will select the correct target from a group of five that have been randomly generated by a computer. His civilian clientele pay him $1,500 per day to travel clairvoyantly to their assignments.[40]

Clairvoyant Detective Dorothy Allison

Dorothy Allison is an unimposing woman, small in stature, with curly brown hair and glasses. But she has the face of a woman who knows another realm of existence. Her career spans twenty-five years, and she has worked on over four thousand law enforcement cases worldwide, locating over one hundred missing persons and solving seemingly unsolvable murders. She has helped with cases such as the Son of Sam, Atlanta serial killer Wayne Williams, and John Wayne Gayce. Dorothy was asked by Detective Joe Kozenczack to help locate the last of the thirty-four bodies in the Gayce case in Chicago. She informed Joe the body would turn up on April 9 along a river near a bridge. On April 9 Joe received a phone call from a county sheriff with news of a body found along a river by a bridge. It was number thirty-four.

Like many psychic investigators Dorothy uses psychometry (*see the Glossary*) to gain an extrasensory empathetic image of the crime scene, the victim, or the criminal. As soon as Dorothy touches an item belonging to the victim, images flash in her mind — abstract at first, such as numbers and names or words. As law enforcement officers drive around with Dorothy, these symbols become addresses, street names, or significant locations. These clues often produce new leads and Dorothy can often visualize the killer. Dorothy only becomes involved in cases through a written invitation from a law enforcement office. She does not volunteer her services.[41]

A Cancer Sniffer Named Boo

London oncologist Dr. Hywell Williams conducted research on patients with melanoma skin cancer at Kings College. While reviewing his journal entries one day, he came upon a peculiar comment in the log: "Dog sniffed at mole!!" An assistant had entered it regarding Bonita Whitfield of London. Dr. Williams remembered removing the mole but was unaware of the dog connection. Intrigued by the note, he called Mrs. Whitfield to discuss the matter. Bonita claimed that on many occasions while standing at the sink in her kitchen, she would feel her dog Boo come up from behind and start sniffing her leg. Boo would always sniff in the same area, and Bonita would shoo her away. For several months Boo continued this erratic behavior until one day Bonita felt a lump on the back of her leg. She soon discovered the lump was a mole —one that had never been there before.

One summer day Boo actually tried to bite off the mole. She kept nipping at it — behavior very uncharacteristic of Boo. Finally Bonita told her friend, a nurse, about the mole. Her friend immediately suggested that a doctor should look at it. The mole was removed, biopsied, and found to be melanoma. One more year and the lethal cancer would have spread throughout Bonita's entire body. Boo had saved her master's life.[42]

Ted Kauffman, Dowser Extraordinaire

A smaller, thin version of Burl Ives, Ted Kauffman has enjoyed twenty-one years of dowsing success. Two of his triumphs near Lake George in upstate New York astonished respected officials of the U.S. Forest service, the local sheriff's department, and the Gore Mountain Ski Center, and provide exceptional examples of dowsing methods.

Primarily, Ted combs the Earth for water using a divining rod. For a desperate client in the Adirondack Mountains, he competed with state engineers to see who could locate the best drilling spot. Gore Mountain Ski Center nearly had to close its slopes after a nest of beavers rendered their water supply unfit to drink. With their high-tech drilling equipment, the state geological engineers found a source of blackish-yellow water not much better than the beaver's hole. Ted on the other hand located eighty-two gallons a minute of crystal clear water using only a Y-shaped stick.

Over the years Ted had also helped forest ranger Vic Sasse locate lost adventurers. Ted's expertise was called upon for a serious task in the winter of 1981. Two men were missing in the Lake George area and local authorities had exhausted all the search possibilities. Ted came armed not with a stick, but with a pendulum and a survey map. In the presence of another forest ranger, Ted held his pendulum over the map and concentrated his cleared mind on its point. He began asking questions referring to the lost men: "Are they alive?" The pendulum slowly swung counterclockwise, which means no. "Are they in the U.S.?" This time it swung clockwise for yes. "Are they in the Lake George Area?" The pendulum swung yes again.

Then, Ted swept the pendulum over the survey map to further home in on the lost men. He first located the vertical line, then the horizontal. Sheriff Ed Litwa drew intersecting lines on the map to show where Ted claimed the men were located — right in the middle of Lake George. Naturally, Sheriff Litwa thought Ted had completely lost his mind. How could the men be lost in the middle of a frozen lake?

Ted's day in court came on April 2, 1981 when the body of Jack Montgomery, one of the men, surfaced not a mile from Ted's map location. In June of that year Sheriff Litwa took Ted out on the lake to help him find the missing truck. Again Ted brought his pendulum. Ted directed them to a specific spot on the lake and instructed them to drop anchor. Divers went down for a look around, then resurfaced. On a lake twenty-three miles long, two miles wide in places, and forty-eight feet deep, the anchor had landed right in the bed of a blue Ford pickup — Jack Montgomery's truck.[43]

The Amazing Sleeping Prophet, Edgar Cayce

Born in the Kentucky countryside in 1877, Edgar Cayce would communicate with his dead grandfather even as a young boy. But he had little idea that he would become one of the most celebrated and best-documented visionaries in human history. During his life of sixty-eight years Cayce would produce fourteen thousand psychic readings, of which over nine thousand would be medical readings or diagnoses. He would also help cure thousands of medically incurable afflictions, and he would interpret over one thousand dreams.[44]

It began with an apparition of a beautiful woman he saw while playing in the woods as a boy. The apparition asked him what he wanted to do with his life, to which he replied: "I want to help people." The voice of the woman helped Edgar, then age thirteen, launch his altruistic career when he was having difficulty spelling words. She told him to lay his head down and sleep on his spelling book. When he awoke, not only could he spell words, but he also knew which words were on which pages, the page numbers, and all the other information on every page in the book.[45]

Cayce's strange ability surfaced again in the year 1900 after he had turned twenty-three and had married and settled down. Mysteriously, he lost his voice for a year and a half. Physicians tried everything, but to no avail. His parents finally suggested hypnosis. Cayce was placed in deep hypnotic sleep, and the session was monitored and documented by his personal physician. Family and friends witnessed in complete amazement as Cayce began to talk. He began describing parts of his own throat in perfect anatomical detail, along with the precise problem such as constriction of blood flow in the throat. When he awoke from the session, he coughed up a little blood, then resumed normal speech. This event was Edgar Cayce's first medical reading.[46] Later in life, Cayce would use his power to save his wife from tuberculosis and to restore his son's eyesight.[47]

A typical reading would be conducted in Cayce's study with his wife Gertrude reading the case objective and his secretary Gladys Davis writing everything down. Edgar would enter a self-induced, sleep-like trance and then would apparently enter the space–time continuum. He would then travel through a patient's body and determine the exact diagnosis and appropriate cure. Upon his return to consciousness he would remember no part of the reading.[48]

Occasionally during his readings he would blurt out an unrelated nonmedical prophecy. For instance, he predicted the stock market crash of 1929, the exact dates of World War II — both beginning and end, the discovery of laser light and the Dead Sea Scrolls, and the demise of Russian Communist rule. Cayce predicted major Earth changes such as complete reversal of the Earth's poles and magnetic fields, and great disruptions in land mass.[49]

Not surprisingly, Edgar Cayce was extremely psychic in the conscious world as well. He could easily read minds or read hands in a card game, and he could see the aura or life-force surrounding people. Cayce claimed that under normal circumstances these auras were a particular pattern of color. Mood swings would change the color. For example, when a person was mad, his aura would be red.[50]

In 1914 Edgar and Gertrude Cayce had two sons, Edgar Evans and Hugh Lenn. In 1925 Cayce moved to Virginia Beach, Virginia, and by 1931 he had established The Association for Research and Enlightenment to house his readings. Edgar Cayce departed our physical world on January 3, 1945, leaving to its people over 120,000 pages of readings, tremendous inspiration for self-discovery, and priceless insight into the universal mind.[51] Physicians and scholars from around the world continue to consult his readings.

Psychic Healer Dean Kraft

When medical science has exhausted all possibilities, Dean Kraft takes over. While being clinically observed by the medical profession, he has caused paralyzed patients to walk and cancer patients to go into remission.[52] He has even destroyed cancer cells in a test tube.

At age 21, Dean Kraft was headed for the stage as a musician; then one day, just for fun, he placed his hands over his brother-in-law's headache and it vanished. He quickly realized he possessed a unique ability. He was gifted with some form of telekinetic energy that could be disbursed at will to heal the sick. Dean's laying on of hands is intuitive, not planned. He follows his hands as they move over a patient's afflicted area; then he visualizes the affliction being reduced by the energy flowing through his hands. Dean's hands vibrate and emit heat as they pass over the patient.

Forty-three-year-old Nelda Buss was a terminal patient dying of Lou Gehrig's disease. When she finally became a quadriplegic, she was given six months to live and consequently gave away all of her clothing except for her death dress. Fortunately, Nelda had heard of Dean Kraft, a connection that dramatically saved her life. After Dean's laying on of hands, Nelda could at first move only her toes, then her fingers, then her back muscles, then her hands, arms, and legs. A woman hopelessly preparing for death was brought back from the brink by an energy unseen and unknown, from the hands of a total stranger — a kind, gifted man named Dean Kraft.[53]

Hard Evidence

The primary source of hard evidence in psi research is controlled laboratory experiments, although scholarly, analytical, and theoretical research and case studies do contribute to the field. Exacting worldwide scientific research over the past sixty years has produced increasingly persuasive data for psi phenomena such as psychokinesis, telepathy, and remote viewing.

Major psi experiments include psychokinesis on random number generators, psychokinesis on living systems, ESP in the *ganzfeld,* which means "whole field," and remote viewing. Positive results have been obtained through strictly controlled repetition of experiments by many researchers worldwide — for the purpose of reproducing results, adding experimental controls, or extending the scope of the experimentation (Radin, Dean, Ph.D., *Consciousness Research Laboratory,* <http://www.psiresearch.org>, 26 Jan. 1999). (*For further technical details inquire at Dr. Radin's site and also refer to Resources for Further Investigation.*)

Beyond the Facts

Our journey through the magic of our universe culminates in the ethereal realm of space and time and with its integral relationship to ourselves. We are amazed to discover mainstream science heavily entrenched in research of an invisible energy force — the extrasensory or psi system of humans. Even more astonishing is their hard evidence suggesting that humans and other animals possess an additional sensory system that can perceive information. Moreover, this consistent, scientifically documented evidence suggests that our understanding of space, time, and consciousness may be fundamentally incomplete.

These revelations are astonishing for several reasons. For one, they imply that mainstream science is giving credence to the existence of psi-related phenomena such as the case studies considered in this chapter. When evidence for an ethereal realm is elicited by the hard, cold, black-and-white, proof-positive methods of mainstream science, we have a major accomplishment on our hands. I shall bravely extrapolate this evidence to include other phenomena.

Since phenomena such as certain miracles, the near-death experience, and hauntings may be related to psi experiences through the concept of hyperspace or what I call the consciospiritual realm, then theoretically, by association, recent discoveries in psi research may also suggest the scientific existence of these phenomena. We shall see how well this theory weathers the storm of time. One important fact to remember is that until very recently, mainstream science, by their own admission, explained away psi experiences as delusions and ridiculed scientists involved in psi research (*see Statistics*) — not unlike the historical chiding of Galileo when he faithfully supported the Copernican view of the Earth orbiting the Sun. Perhaps recent scientific accomplishments in psi research are the first step toward serious research of what animal researcher Michael Fox calls the empathosphere, or what Michio Kaku calls hyperspace, or what I call the consciospiritual realm. The empathosphere, an emotional or empathetic realm, and hyperspace, a cognitive dimension, are similar in theory with the consciospiritual realm, with the exception that the consciospiritual realm is empathic, emotional, cognitive, *and* spiritual.

When we openly consider *all* the related case evidence — such as the cognitive near-death experience of George Rodonaia, the medically documented miracles of Grace DiBicarri, and the precognitive and diagnostic readings of Edgar Cayce, we begin to suspect a grand connection. All these people experienced the consciospiritual realm in some fashion. George "traveled" there, communicated with others in that realm, returned to this dimension, then was so moved by his experience that he quit his job and became a minister. Grace also experienced a powerful being from this other realm, then returned with profound, acquired, medically proven powers of healing. Edgar Cayce first experienced this realm through his boyhood vision of a "beautiful lady" in the woods, then began a career of no less than twenty-one thousand trips through the consciospiritual realm. Even Tom McMoneagle first had an NDE from which he acquired remote viewing — an ability clinically proven to be beyond chance by thirty percent. These facts make it imperative for scientists to periodically pull their heads out of their technical journals and articles, step back from their micro-data world of research, and consider how investigating certain relationships may help develop the universal picture.

Consider telepathy for example, a psi phenomenon evidenced in the alien abduction cases researched by Harvard scientist John E. Mack. Telepathy or consciospiritual communication is also commonly evidenced in the near-death experiences researched by Dr. Raymond Moody. One of science's virtues is also its problem — as science necessarily becomes immersed in detailed analysis, scientists grow blinders to other potential evidence. Related evidence, perhaps anecdotal at first, may lead to further scientific scrutiny, which may in turn significantly contribute to ongoing research — all of which may eventually lead to proof — perhaps to the ultimate proof.

Only within the past few years have documentary producers begun to group similar anomalies together, not necessarily in any order, for miniseries. "*Strange Beings and UFOs*," Mysteries of the Unexplained, a one-hour segment of an exceptional three-hour series, documents research of extraterrestrial implants in humans, whereas "*Aliens. Where Are They?*," Science of the Impossible, one hour in a series of five one-hour shows, apparently prefers to ignore the mountains of evidence suggesting alien visitation. In stark contrast however, *Invisible Forces*, Science of the Impossible provides a complete and riveting exposé on psi research. Watching these miniseries and others such as related episodes of *The Understanding Festival* are highly recommended for anyone interested in universal anomalies.

All psi research, all the discoveries about animal behavior, such as dogs sniffing cancerous moles and the morphic fields bonding animals and humans together, and the telekinetic healing power of Dean Kraft —all of these and more have been studied only during the most recent inkling of human history. The very first psi research patent was awarded as recently as November 3, 1998. Are we living in a very special age of human enlightenment? What do you think?

The most amazing fact facing us at this evolutionary moment is that our science, the human measurement of knowledge, is for the first time, by its own strict standards, proving the reality of that which it once thought was illusion. For the very first time in our existence we are truly beginning to understand the interconnectedness of our universal living space. I suggest there simply is no discovery more powerful or more significant to human beings than understanding how all life everywhere, even extraterrestrial life, may be connected by invisible forces and unbounded by the historical parameters of time and space.

Resources for Further Investigation
Leading Research Scientists and Investigators

Of the many scientists involved in psi research, the following researchers are the most frequently interviewed liaisons between the technical scientific arena and the general public. Others such as Ingo Swann and John Hogue are provided to thoroughly represent the entire field of psi research.

Loyd Auerbach

A popular parapsychologist, Loyd Auerbach is perhaps best known for his research of a psychic's ability to detect the electromagnetic field of human spirits.

Dr. Susan Blackmore

As a psychologist rather than a parapsychologist, Dr. Blackmore contributes to psi research from the University of Bristol in England. As with near-death research, Susan believes psi phenomena are brain-based rather than supernatural.

Richard Broughton

He is the acting director of the Rhine Research Center's Institute for Parapsychology in Durham, N.C. Their basic objective is to understand human potential and to bridge the gap between the academic community, independent researchers, scientists, and the general public.

Arthur C. Clarke

Well-known author and host of his own documentary series, Arthur Clarke often features case studies about all types of psi. His viewpoint is conservative but open-minded.

Ed Dames

Now president of his own remote viewing intelligence gathering company called PsiTech, Ed was involved with the CIA in developing remote viewing as an intelligence tool.

Dr. Michael Fox

Dr. Michael Fox is a veterinarian practicing in Washington, D.C. His theory of animal bonding focuses on an emotional realm called the empathosphere, through which animals empathatically sense the location of their siblings or their owners.

Robert Grant

He is the coordinator of the Association of Research and Enlightenment — the archive of Edgar Cayce's 14,000 prophetic and diagnostic readings located in Virginia Beach, Virginia.

Dr. Douglas B. Henderson

Dr. Henderson is a psychology professor at the University of Wisconsin. He has been interviewed for *Unsolved Mysteries*.

John Hogue

Among the most, if not *the* most, knowledgeable scholar of the sixteenth-century prophet Michel de Nostradame, Hogue has written several books that propose to decipher Nostradamus' prophecies.

Peter James

He is one of the most reputable psychic investigators in the country if not the world (*see case study on Peter James*).

Dr. Ed May

Ed May is perhaps best known for his involvement in remote viewing at the Stanaford Research Institute. Dr. May directed the U.S. government-funded program for several years and his base of operations is the Cognitive Sciences Laboratory in Palo Alto, California.

Joe McMoneagle

Also involved with remote viewing at the Stanford Institute, Joe McMoneagle now operates from his home in Virginia for private clients (*see case study on Mr. McMoneagle*).

Robert Monroe

Robert Monroe is founder of the Monroe Institute. His wife, Laurie, is acting president. Their research focuses on out-of-body experiences.

Joe Nickell

Mr. Nickell works with the Centre of Inquiry International in an ongoing effort to debunk paranormal activity. He is often interviewed for television documentaries to provide the skeptical viewpoint.

Dr. Dean Radin

Dean Radin, Ph.D., is among those few mainstream scientists providing great exposure of psi research to the general public. He has compiled a very popular web site (http://www.psiresearch.org) and has written a popular book *The Conscious Universe*, both of which delve into all aspects of psi research in plain English. His Consciousness Research Lab is located in Palo Alto, California.

Dr. Nancy Segal

She is a researcher specializing in the bond between identical twins.

Rupert Sheldrake

A leading researcher in psychic bonds between animals, Rupert Sheldrake believes animals and animals, or animals and humans, are psychically connected through morphic fields. His book *Seven Experiments That Could Change the World* explores this and other theories. He researched animal behavior for fourteen years at Cambridge University in England. Sheldrake conducts his research from Santa Cruz, California and is optimistic that dogs can be used as an early warning system for earthquakes.

Lynn Sparrow

Lynn Sparrow is an Edgar Cayce historian.

Ingo Swann

Mr. Swann is a remote viewer who has worked at the Stanford Research Institute. Major Ed Dames learned remote viewing from Ingo Swann.

Dr. Richard Wiseman

A parapsychologist and paranormal investigator, Dr. Wiseman works from his base at England's University of Hertfordshire.

Recommended Television Programs and Networks

Please consult the Directory of Television Networks in the back of the book for scheduling information and availability of home videos:

"An Element of the Divine," *Arthur C. Clarke's World of Strange Powers,*1985, 30 minutes
on the Discovery Channel
air dates: 07/12/98

Ancient Prophecies, The series, 60 minutes
on The Learning Channel
air dates: 01/09/98

"Animal Faith Healers," *Strange but True?,* 1997, 15 minutes
on The Discovery Channel
air dates: 05/10/98

"Dowsers," *Strange but True?,* 1997, 15 minutes
on The Discovery Channel
air dates: 02/12/98, 05/17/98, 10/08/98

"Faith Healers," *Strange but True?,* 1997, 15 minutes
on The Discovery Channel
air dates: 02/05/98

"From Mind to Mind," *Arthur C. Clarke's World of Strange Powers, 1985,* 30 minutes
on The Discovery Channel
air dates: 09/06/98

"Identical Twin," *Strange but True?,* 1997, 30 minutes
on The Discovery Channel
air dates: 03/19/98, 06/28/98

"Into Thin Air," *Arthur C. Clarke's Mysterious Universe*, 1995,
30 minutes
on The Discovery Channel
air dates: 09/06/98, 01/24/98

Invisible Forces, Science of the Impossible, 60 minutes
on The Discovery Channel
air dates: 0715/98, 07/19/98

"Metal Bending, Magic and Mind Over Matter," *Arthur C. Clarke's*
World of Strange Powers, 1985, 30 minutes
on The Discovery Channel
air dates: 01/25/98

"Morphic Fields," *Strange but True?*, 1997, 15 minutes
on The Discovery Channel
air dates: 05/24/98

"Prophecies," *In Search of History*, 1997, 60 minutes
on The History Channel
air dates: 03/13/98, 07/28/98

"*Prophets*: Soul Catchers," *Mysteries of the Bible*, 60 minutes
on The Arts & Entertainment Network
air dates: 11/28/98

"Psychic Animals," *Animal X*, 1998, 30 minutes
on The Discovery Channel
air dates: 05/21/98

"Psychic Detectives," *Arthur C. Clarke's Mysterious Universe*, 1994,
30 minutes
on The Discovery Channel
air dates: 10/24/98

"Psychic Spies," *The Unexplained*, 60 minutes
on The Arts & Entertainment Network
air dates: 02/12/98

"Psychics," *Strange but True?*, 1997, 30 minutes
on The Discovery Channel
air dates: 02/01/98

Secrets of the Super Psychics, 1997, 60 minutes
on The Learning Channel
air dates: 02/01/98, 05/28/98

Sightings, Series First Aired 1991, Went Into Syndication 1994
on The Sci-Fi Channel
air dates: 1991 through 1998

"Strange Powers of Animals," *Arthur C. Clarke's Mysterious Universe,*
1995, 30 minutes
on The Discovery Channel
air dates: 02/14/98, 08/23/98

"Strange Powers the Verdict," *Arthur C. Clarke's World of Strange
Powers,* 1985, 30 minutes
on The Discovery Channel
air dates: 08/02/98, 03/08/98

"*Supertwins:* Triplets, Quads and More", 1995, 120 minutes
on The Learning Channel
air dates: 05/10/98

The Mystery of Twins, 1996, 60 minutes
on The Learning Channel
air dates: 05/10/98

The Science of Twins, 1996, 60 minutes
on The Discovery Channel
air dates: 04/24/98

"The Twin Connection," *The Unexplained,* 60 minutes
on The Arts & Entertainment Network
air dates: 01/15/98, 08/16/98

"Twins," *Extremely Weird,* 1995, 7 minutes
on The Learning Channel
air dates: 01/03/98, 01/31/98

"Warnings From the Future," *Arthur C. Clarke's World of Strange
Powers,* 1985, 30 minutes
on The Discovery Channel
air dates: 02/01/98

Recommended Books
Journeys Out of the Body
by Robert Monroe

Living Without Your Twin
by Betty Jean Case

Mind Trek
by Joe McMoneagle

Nostradamus and the Millennium
by John Hogue

Nostradamus: The Complete Prophecies
by John Hogue

Parapsychology and the Unconscious
by Jule Eisenbud, Psychiatrist

Phoenix Rising
by Mary Summer Rain

Prophecies of the Psalms
by J. R. Church

Psychic Dreaming
by Loyd Auerbach

Seven Experiments That Could Change the World
by Rupert Sheldrake

Sightings
by Susan Michaels

Talking to Heaven
by James Van Praagh

The Conscious Universe
by Dean Radin, Ph.D.

The Healing Journey
by Dr. Carl Simonton

The Millennium Book of Prophecy
by John Hogue

Recommended Videotapes, Audio Tapes, and CD-ROMS

The Psi Explorer (CD-ROM)
Contact the Conscious Research Lab for availability
http://www.psiresearch.org

The Psychic Experience (video)
from *Sightings*

Recommended Internet Sites

Camelot Productions
The site of *The Magic of Our Universe*
http://www.camelotpublications.com

Consciousness Research Laboratory
Excellent general information and frequently asked questions about parapsychology.
http://www.psiresearch.org

Dowsers
http://tqd.advanced.org/3205/Dows.html

Gordon-Michael Scallion Earth Changes Report
Web site of prophet Gordon-Michael Scallion
http://www.ecrnews.com

Nostradamus history and analysis
http://www.activemind.com

Paranormal Phenomena Archive
http://www.in-search-of.com

The Arts and Entertainment Network
http://www.AandE.com

The Discovery Channel
http://www.discovery.com

The History Channel
http://www.HistoryChannel.com

The Learning Channel
http://www.tlc.com

The Sci-Fi Channel
Sightings available through the Dominion site, which can further access all major paranormal links
http://www.scifi.com/sightings

The Ufomind Paranormal Index and Bookstore
http://www.ufomind.com

Unsolved Mysteries
http://www.unsolved.com

Organizations

AAAS (American Association for the Advancement of Science)
1200 New York Avenue, N.W.
Washington, DC 20005
202-326-6400
http://www.aaas.org

ARE (Association of Research and Enlightenment Library)
215 67th Street
Virginia Beach, VA 23451
757-428-3588
800-333-4499 (U.S. and Canada only)
http://www.are-cayce.com
ARE houses the psychic readings of Edgar Cayce.

Cognitive Science Laboratory
c/o Laboratories for Fundamental Research
Palo Alto, CA
http://www.lfr.org/csl/index.html

Consciousness Research Laboratory
http://www.psiresearch.org
e-mail: info@PsiResearch.org
Dean Radin, Ph.D., director

IANDS (International Association for Near Death Studies)
A worldwide research organization founded in 1977.
P. O. Box 502
East Windsor Hill, CT   06028-0502
860-644-5216
860-644-5759 (FAX)
http://www.iands.org

Koestler Parapsychology Unit
Department of Psychology
University of Edinburgh
7, George Square, Edinburgh   EH8 9JZ
United Kingdom
+44(0)1316503348
http://moebius.psy.ed.ac.uk/text/t_index.html

Monroe Institute
62 Robert Mountain Road
Faber, VA 22938-2317
804-361-1252
804-361-1237 (FAX)
http://www.monroeinstitute.org
e-mail: monroeinst@aol.com
Robert A. Monroe, founder
Laurie A. Monroe, president

PEAR (Princeton Engineering Anomalies Research)
C-131, Engineering Quadrangle
Princeton University
Princeton, NJ 08544
609-258-5950
609-258-1993 (FAX)
http://www.Princeton.edu/?pear
pearlab@princeton.edu (e-mail)

Rhine Research Center
Institute for Parapsychology
402 N. Buchanan Blvd.
Durham, NC 27701-1728
919-688-8241
919 683-4338 (FAX)
http://www.rhine.org

Twinless Twins Support Group International
11220 Saint Joe Road
Fort Wayne, IN 46835
219-627-5414
941-924-2900
http://www.fwi.com/twinless
e-mail: twinless@iserv.net
Dr. Raymond Brandt, founder
Twinless Twins is a support group for twins who have lost a twin.

Endnotes

[1] "Prophecies," *In Search of History*, narr. David Ackroyd, ed. Shelley Stocking, prod. Bram Roos, David M. Frank and Frank Kosa, The History Channel, 13 March 1998.

[2] *"Prophets*: Soul Catchers," *Mysteries of the Bible*, narr. Richard Kiley and Jean Simmons, ed. Duane Tudahl, prod. Bram Roos, David M. Frank and Gayle Kirschenbaum, The Arts & Entertainment Network, 28 Nov. 1998.

[3] "Prophecies," *In Search of History*, 13 March 1998.

[4] "Prophecies," *In Search of History*, 13 March 1998.

[5] Luck, Steve, ed. *Oxford Family Encyclopedia*, 1st edition, New York, New York: Oxford University Press, Inc. 1997 (567).

[6] "Prophecies," *In Search of History*, 13 March 1998.

[7] "Prophecies," *In Search of History*, 13 March 1998.

[8] Luck, Steve, ed. *Oxford Family Encyclopedia*, 1997 (178, 183, 435).

[9] *Ancient Prophecies*, narr. David McCallum, ed. Michael Andrews, prod. Graeme Whifler and Paul Klein, The Learning Channel, 9 Jan. 1998.

[10] *Ancient Prophecies*, 9 Jan. 1998.

[11] "Prophecies," *Unnatural History*, narr. Mark Hammill, prod. Andrea Matzke, The Learning Channel, 26 May 1998.

[12] Luck, Steve, ed. *Oxford Family Encyclopedia*, 1997 (488).

[13] Cannon, Delores, Interview, *Ancient Prophecies*, narr. David McCallum, ed. Michael Andrews, prod. Graeme Whifler and Paul Klein, The Learning Channel, 9 Jan. 1998.

[14] *Ancient Prophecies*, 9 Jan. 1998.

[15] *Ancient Prophecies*, 9 Jan. 1998

[16] "Prophecies," *Unnatural History*, 26 May 1998.

[17] Luck, Steve, ed. *Oxford Family Encyclopedia*, 1997 (246).

[18] *Ancient Prophecies*, 9 Jan. 1998.

[19] Miller, Kenneth, "Psychics: Science or seance? A reporter visits the twilight zone," *Life*, New York, June 1998: 88-103.

[20] *Rhine Research Center* (Inst. for Parapsychology), <http://www.rhine.org/>, 9 Sept. 1998.

[21] Fox, Dr. Michael, Interview, "Strange Powers of Animals," *Arthur C. Clarke's Mysterious Universe*, narr. Ed Green, writ. Cathryn Garland, prod. Simon Westcott, The Discovery Channel, 23 Aug. 1998.

[22] "Strange Powers of Animals," *Arthur C. Clarke's Mysterious Universe*, narr. Ed Green, writ. Cathryn Garland, prod. Simon Westcott, The Discovery Channel, 23 Aug. 1998.

[23] "Seizure Alert Dogs," *Sightings*, narr. Tim White, writ. Susan Michaels, prod. Henry Winkler and Ann Daniel, The Sci-Fi Channel, 2 Sept. 1998.

[24] "Animal Telepathy," *Strange But True?*, narr. Michael Aspel, prod. Bob Reid, The Discovery Channel, 24 May 1998.

[25] "Identical Twins," *Strange But True?*, narr. Michael Aspel, prod. Bob Reid, The Discovery Channel, 19 Mar. 1998.

[26] *Life*, June 1998: 88-103.

[27] "Healers," *Sightings*, narr. Tim White, writ. Susan Michaels, prod. Joanne L. Fish, Henry Winkler and Ann Daniel, The Sci-Fi Channel, 17 Feb. 1998.

[28] Kaku, Michio, Physicist, City Univ., NY, Interview, *Invisible Forces*, Science of the Impossible, narr. Michael Goldfarb, ed. Jason Farrow, prod. Chris Lent, John Blake and George Caney, The Discovery Channel, 19 July, 1998.

[29] "Fire In The Brain," *Sightings*, narr. Tim White, writ. Susan Michaels, prod. Henry Winkler and Ann Daniel, The Sci-Fi Channel, 23 Dec. 1998.

[30] Fox, Dr. Michael, Interview, "Strange Powers of Animals," *Arthur C. Clarke's Mysterious Universe*, 23 Aug. 1998

[31] "Identical Twins," *Strange But True?*, 19 Mar. 1998.

[32] "Profilers," *Sightings*, narr. Tim White, writ. Susan Michaels, prod. Ruth Rafidi, Michael Kriz, Henry Winkler and Ann Daniel, The Sci-Fi Channel, 4 May 1998.

[33] "*The Living Dead*, Speaking from the Grave," *Sightings*, narr. Tim White, writ. Susan Michaels, prod. Henry Winkler and Ann Daniel, The Sci-Fi Channel, 25 Oct. 1998.

[34] "Profilers," *Sightings*, 4 May 1998.

[35] "Black Swan Haunting," *Sightings*, narr. Tim White, prod. Michael Burns, Henry Winkler and Ann Daniel, The Sci-Fi Channel, 5 May 1998.

[36] "Joseph McMoneagle," *Doc Hambone*, <http://www.io.com/?hambone/web/mcmoneagle.html>, 27 Jan. 1999.

[37] McMoneagle, Joe, Interview, *Invisible Forces*, Science of the Impossible, narr. Michael Goldfarb, ed. Jason Farrow, prod. Chris Lent, John Blake and George Caney, The Discovery Channel, 19 July 1998.

[38] May, Ed, Interview, *Invisible Forces*, Science of the Impossible, narr. Michael Goldfarb, ed. Jason Farrow, prod. Chris Lent, John Blake and George Caney, The Discovery Channel, 19 July 1998.

[39] "Joseph McMoneagle," *Doc Hambone*, 27 Jan. 1999.

[40] *Life*, June 1998: 88-103.

[41] "Psychic Detective," *Sightings*, narr. Tim White, writ. Susan Michaels, prod. Henry Winkler and Ann Daniel, The Sci-Fi Channel, 7 Sept. 1998.

[42] "Strange Powers of Animals," *Arthur C. Clarke's Mysterious Universe*, narr. Ed Green, writ. Cathryn Garland, prod. Simon Westcott, The Discovery Channel, 23 Aug. 1998.

[43] "Dowsers," *Strange But True?*, narr. Michael Aspel, ed. David Alpin, Jeremy Phillips, prod. Ralph Jones and Simon Shaps, The Discovery Channel, 12 Feb. 1998.

[44] Grant, Robert, Interview, *Ancient Prophecies*, narr. David McCallum, ed. Michael Andrews, prod. Graeme Whifler and Paul Klein, The Learning Channel, 9 Jan. 1998.

[45] Sparrow, Lynn, Interview, *Ancient Prophecies*, narr. David McCallum, ed. Michael Andrews, prod. Graeme Whifler and Paul Klein, The Learning Channel, 9 Jan. 1998.

[46] *Unsolved Mysteries*, The Unexplained, narr. Robert Stack, writ. Raymond Bridgers, prod. Cosgrove Muerer Productions, Lifetime, 27 July 1998.

[47] *Ancient Prophecies*, 9 Jan. 1998.

[48] *Ancient Prophecies*, 9 Jan. 1998.

[49] *Ancient Prophecies*, 9 Jan. 1998.

[50] *Ancient Prophecies*, 9 Jan. 1998.

[51] *Unsolved Mysteries*, The Unexplained, 27 July 1998.

[52] Goldstein, Marcy, M.D., Interview, "Healers," *Sightings*, narr. Tim White, writ. Susan Michaels, prod. Joanne L. Fish, The Sci-Fi Channel, 17 Feb. 1998.

[53] "Healers," *Sightings*, 17 Feb. 1998.

Conclusion

Conclusion

So just what is the Magic of Our Universe?

The magic of our universe begins as a seed within our own imaginations. It may be the sighting of a UFO, some unfamiliar creature in a lake, a human spirit, or a near brush with death. At the outset, this seed may appear to be an illusion because it exists beyond the boundaries of the Universe as it is currently understood by humans. Courage is the essential fertilizer — courage to pursue and comprehend with unbiased minds the hidden mysteries of our universal living space. Without courage, and belief in our theories, the seed shall wither and die. With courage the seed will sprout, and with an open-minded perspective of a limitless Universe, it will grow rapidly. For those wearing blinders the seed shall again only wither and die.

Our seedling grows and branches out in a thousand directions. As we follow one branch fueled by courage, the illusion starts to become transformed. We begin to collect evidence. Being open-minded and intelligent, we consider all evidence. We consider all possibilities regardless of how improbable they may seem, or how greatly they challenge our human zone of comfort. As evidence piles upon evidence, the trunk and branch of our tree grows thicker and stronger. Anecdotal evidence turns to hard evidence and hard evidence ultimately leads us to proof. The seed that once appeared to be an illusion has now become reality. This reality is incorporated back into the ever-growing human condition. We would not have made it to proof without courage, and proof will yield yet a thousand more seeds.

In every universal anomaly encountered during our exploration, we found the age-old human conflict between skepticism and belief, between mainstream science and those scientists who believe that the evidence points to the reality of the unexplained, between those who consider the Universe in current human terms and those who explore it in universal terms. With few exceptions, every documentary regarding parapsychology, the supernatural, and the unexplained incorporates the controversy of skepticism versus belief. But, the issue is not about skepticism or belief. The real issue is about conducting thorough scientific research. It is about those scientists with blinders who ignore significant verifiable evidence. It is about those investigators who wrongly isolate and criticize one event removed from its overall historical context. The profusion of documentary bantering between skeptics and believers provides an accurate perspective of the current human mindset toward the unexplained. Television truly is the best poll, the best barometer of human thinking. It is also among the finest libraries available to mankind. When we combine and scrutinize many documentaries regarding one subject such as life beyond death, we are overwhelmed with facts, details, and cases that complete the picture, that help define our real Universe.

To me, the true magic of our Universe is found in the evidence that suggests unexplained phenomena such as extraterrestrial life are real. The magic is the transformation of illusion into reality.

When considering extraterrestrial life, the overwhelming mountain of evidence on UFOs does not intrigue me nearly as much as evidence such as the acquired advanced artistic styles of alien abductee twins, Jim and Jack Weiner, or the newly acquired healing powers of Australian abductee Elizabeth Robinson. Of gripping fascination to me are details suggesting that highly creative changes in the human condition have occurred from interaction with extraterrestrials. I believe this is yet another hint, another signal from one highly advanced civilization to the humans of Earth, which reveals the reality of what some people still perceive as illusion. Could these supernatural gifts bestowed upon us be a discreet display of peaceful creative alien communication? These astonishing details are to me the true great "magic" of our Universe. They are the "beanstalk" seeds of science that will grow to limitless heights for those with open minds.

With respect to hauntings, the magic is revealed in the scratches the spirit Sallie causes to appear on the skin of Tony Pickman. With crystal skulls, the magic shows up first in their mysterious origins, and second when psychics channel through them to the origins and depths of the Universe. With Bigfoot, it is the strong possibility that *Homo sapiens* may not be the only hominid walking planet Earth. With respect to both "Nessie" and Bigfoot, it is the possibility that other supposedly extinct species are alive and well and living in remote wilderness areas of our world.

With respect to less contemporary anomalies such as vampires, it is the significance of good science that becomes apparent. The physiological characteristics of dying from the Black Death are revealed as the likely source of "vampires," rather than some nocturnal man-eating, womanizing bat.

Life beyond death, reincarnation, miracles and angels, hauntings, the Philadelphia Experiment, and extrasensory perception, which includes prophecy, I believe, are all anomalies interconnected through the universal mind and universal spirit, or what I call the "consciospiritual" Universe. Miraculous supernatural powers of healing were acquired by Grace DiBiccari during her near-death experience. Pam Nesure also tapped into the consciospiritual Universe during her clinically confirmed brush with death. Edgar Cayce, psychic detective Dorothy Allison, medium James Van Praagh, psychic Peter James, and healer Dean Kraft have all demonstrated some form of interactivity amazingly at will with the consciospiritual dimension.

These anomalies, along with the superior technology of advanced extraterrestrial civilizations, all share an interactivity of elements of our hidden Universe such as the electromagnetic field, the geomagnetic field, the gravitational field, morphic fields with animals and the nonlinear space-time continuum. Indeed, it would not surprise me to someday see Einstein's unified field theory proven through open-minded research of "field-related" paranormal phenomena.

Extraterrestrials, in my opinion, have mastered the electromagnetic spectrum and likely possess a working knowledge of the unified field theory for transportation, teleportation and other purposes. For those readers unfamiliar with Einstein's unified field theory, also known as the grand unified theory, it is the holy grail of physics (*see the Glossary*). To prove it would be equivalent to learning how to make gold from toothpaste.

The concept of light or luminous energy is of course part of the electromagnetic spectrum. During our exploration of universal anomalies, we discovered light being used in ways far beyond those of current human understanding. Extraterrestrials in particular have displayed fascinating aptitude in the use of light energy. At the Height 611 incident in Delnivorsk, Siberia, a UFO was sighted searching for a crashed probe. The beam of the search-light was invisible and the search-light illuminated only the ground surface it touched. Light energy seems to be used also for teleportation of both humans and aliens into and from extraterrestrial craft. Notable descriptions of this activity were given by the Weiner twins in the Allagash abduction case and more recently by Kelly Cahill in Australia.

Advanced use of light energy is prevalent among other phenomena as well, such as the near-death experience (NDE), hauntings, some accounts of miracles and angels, and the Philadelphia Experiment. Of these, NDE descriptions are most remarkable in that human spirits seem to exist as light energy. Could extraterrestrials be aware of this? Do they experience NDEs? I believe we have only tapped the surface of the interconnected function of light throughout our mysterious hidden Universe. The Mayan word for crystal is "limbal" meaning light knowledge, and even today the authors of the Dead Sea Scrolls are still known as the Sons of Light. The Dead Sea Scrolls document the epoch of Christ and contain the oldest version of the Hebrew Old Testament by one thousand years.[1]

Unquestionably, the most exciting aspect of our journey is that we have traveled to the absolute cutting edge of human science, a place of monumental discoveries, the kind that alter our perspective of the Universe, discoveries that could catapult humanity millennia forward in technological advancement. Our journey is not unlike the trip back through time and space through the Hubble Space Telescope to the place where stars are born — the Eagle Nebulae. A place so magnificent and so beautiful and so unreal to humans that it seems sometimes to be the very home of God (*look it up on the Internet: http://antwrp.gsfc.nasa.gov/apod*). Yet, very significant details of near-death cases may truly lead us to the realm of God — to the realm of Light.

Prior to his near-death experience, George Rodonaia was an agnostic psychologist. He is now an ordained minister. Other previously atheist NDE travelers have quit their jobs to become ministers. Betty Eadie and many others have written books about their NDEs (*see the list of videos and books in the reference section of Life Beyond Death and Reincarnation*). From all NDE lab experiments, such as the air force centrifuge or Persinger's Chamber, mainstream science has yet to produce one person so moved by the experience that they quit their job or wrote a book about it.

Not unlike the alien abduction experience, the NDE is a powerful element hidden in our Universe that dramatically alters human behavior — more so perhaps than any earthly experience. Monumental experiences that affect the human condition, journeys to the consciospiritual realm — these illusions that become vivid and permanent pages of real human history — are to me the true great "magic" of our Universe.

Can humans benefit from an open-minded exploration of the unexplained? The possibilities are as limitless as the sea of space itself. As Einstein so eloquently put it: "The most beautiful thing we can experience is the mysterious. It is the source of all science." A much more timely and relevant question, however, might be: Will we require help as a planetary society facing global climatic changes in the coming decades?

The answer to that question has very recently been announced to us quite loudly from our own Mother Earth. Within the past five years, far ahead of all predictions, two tremendous segments of the Larson ice shelf in Antarctica have broken off. One chunk, the size of Connecticut, roughly 4,800 square miles, separated as recently as March of 1998.[2] El Niños and their residual effects are also occurring more frequently due to global warming, and two prophets have independently created nearly identical future maps showing the United States land mass reduced by twenty percent. The World Wildlife Fund has discovered a thirty percent decrease in the living plant index since 1970, which represents a one-third reduction in our planet's plant life within only the past thirty years of all of human history.[3]

All is not lost however and there is time for us to fix global climatic problems. But humanity must awaken to the environmental cries of Mother Earth. President Clinton's personal sex life received twenty-eight hours of CNN Headline news coverage per week on the average, while the catastrophic effects of global warming filled only ten total minutes of weekly air time. As Americans grew weary of hearing about Monica Lewinsky and Paula Jones, California and Manhattan slowly become underwater reefs. Does humanity require global assistance from peaceful, highly intelligent, highly advanced extraterrestrial civilizations? As outlandish as it may sound to some of us, this possibility cannot be ignored considering the current lack of human awareness.

The humans of Earth have reached a crossroad. We can follow the dinosaurs down the path to extinction, or we can wake up, grow up and with open minds consider all possibilities and leave no stone unturned in our pursuit of solutions. We may find the most appropriate answers hiding in the most unlikely places.

I leave you now to contemplate a most powerful true story of great hope. It is a human story of inspiration, of cooperation, and of great courage. It is a story of peace:

Snow! Lots of snow covered the frozen ground and fir trees of the Ardenne Forest along southern Belgium in the winter of 1944. Soldiers, both American and German, with their cold steel rifles blazing at one another in a rain of bullets, would ensure that the Battle of the Bulge would become the costliest of any United States wartime battle in terms of lost human life.

The night was Christmas Eve. Separated from their troop, four young soldiers from the American side wandered lost, hungry, and tired through the Ardenne Forest. One was lame with a bullet lodged in his thigh. Through the woods they spotted a log cabin with smoke streaming from the stone chimney and candlelight flickering in the windows. To these cold men, no sight could look more promising.

After several knocks on the door, a young German boy and his mother came out to greet them. The four asked if they could come inside to warm up and give their friend a chance to rest. Speaking no English but understanding their cold faces and shaking hands, the mother, named Elizabeth, invited them in. She knew very well that harboring the enemy would be paid for with her own life. But the woman and the boy were most hospitable. Elizabeth tended the wounded leg of the one soldier and made them all feel as comfortable as her meager existence would allow. She instructed her son, Fritz, to put more potatoes in the pot so that the men could join them for Christmas Eve dinner.

As the men settled around the barnwood plank table, another knock rang at the door. This time Fritz answered and was shocked to find four German soldiers standing in the snow where only moments before, the Americans had stood. They too had lost their unit and sought refuge from the cold. When a trembling Elizabeth explained that there were four Americans inside, the Germans lifted their weapons in readiness. Motherhood and the Christmas spirit instilled strength in Elizabeth's voice as she insisted that nothing was going to interfere with her peaceful dinner on Christmas Eve. She instructed the men to store their weapons in the woodshed and then join them inside by the fire. The Germans obeyed with some reluctance, and as they entered the cabin, four startled Americans then grabbed their guns. Elizabeth again quickly intervened and instructed Fritz to take all weapons to the woodshed. Minding the rules of this brave woman's house, the Americans slowly obliged.

A tense chill at first permeated the air. Then, the aroma of chicken and potatoes along with the warmth of the fire began to put senseless wartime grievances in a more appropriate place of insignificance. The men offered each other cigarettes and began to talk. One German spoke limited English and asked if the wounded man was feeling pain. He squatted down beside him, inspected his leg, removed a first aid kit from his backpack, and began dressing the American's wounded leg.

Before long, all sat down at the table with four Americans on one side, the four Germans facing them from the other, and Fritz and Elizabeth at the ends. Everyone's face was washed in candlelight. It was as if they were one big happy family. Elizabeth began to say grace. She thanked the Lord for everyone being together and at peace during such a horrible war. She was thankful for their meager dinner on that Christmas Eve and for the little possessions they had. As she continued with her prayer, the room fell completely silent and still except for the flicker of candlelight and the flames crackling in the fireplace: "Let's all promise to be friendly to each other forever if possible. Let's also pray for an end to the terrible war so that everyone can go home." As those words came out of Elizabeth's mouth, tears began to drip down the faces of all eight soldiers sitting at the table.

There they sat, eight soldiers stripped of their weapons, of their aggression, of their hatred — humbled and warmed by the kind words of a brave matriarch, charmed by the hospitality of a young boy. Whereas only the day before they would have gunned one another down in cold blood, there they sat, face to face, brother to brother, human to human. All of their differences and the cold harsh trappings of war had gone up the chimney with the smoke from the fire and had dissipated into the thin winter air.

The memories of that Christmas Eve in 1944, of that warm cabin, that island of light and hope surrounded by the cold dark winter of war, those memories burned deeply into the minds and hearts of Fritz and

Elizabeth. They remained forever embedded in the souls of eight men who had come to realize that regardless of what color their uniforms were, regardless of what language they spoke, regardless of their differences, that they were all ultimately human beings walking on the same ground sharing the same Earth.[4]

It is in the humbled human spirit of those eight soldiers on that Christmas Eve, that we must all place ourselves as we together face the future of the human race. Through cooperation we must set aside our differences and with open minds look for solutions to our global problems together. It is time for all humans, for all scientists, for both skeptics and believers to seek common ground, to consider all evidence regarding the fascinating phenomena hiding in our Universe, for therein we may find the answers to life's greatest challenges. It is time for our military to sit down with the people it protects, to share with us even some of its vast secrets of extraterrestrial life, so that through this knowledge we may build confidence to accept the reality that we are only one of countless universal communities.

Our established measurement of knowledge, our human science, is only now just beginning to confirm that humans are so much more than merely flesh and bones — that we possess unrealized sensory capacities — and that our universe is interconnected through a previously unknown realm where time and space exist in some non linear form. It is time for us to consider our Universe in the fascinating reality of universal possibilities rather than within the historical confinement of human understanding. For it is only then through open minds that the true great Magic of Our Universe shall be revealed to us in all of its magnificent splendor.

CONCLUSION

Endnotes

[1] "*Dead Sea Scrolls*: Unraveling the Mystery," writ. Bo Landin and Jane Wilson, and Sterling Van Wagenen, prod. Sterling Van Wagenen and Bo Landin, The Discovery Channel, 9 Nov. 1998.

[2] "*Climatic Catastrophe*, narr. Joe Frank, ed. Eric Wise, Ken Lubbert, prod. Eric Nelson, The Learning Channel, 1 Nov. 1998.

[3] *CNN Headline News*, 14 October 1998.

[4] "Battle of the Bulge. Christmas Eve, *Unsolved Mysteries*, narr. Robert Stack, writ. Raymond Bridgers, Terry Dunn Meurer, prod. Terry Dunn Meurer, John Cosgrove, Lifetime, 3 Sept. 1998.

Reference Section

A Statistical Synopsis of Our Universe

A Directory of Television Networks

Glossary

List of Works Used

Reference Section

A Statistical Synopsis of Our Universe

The Origin of the Universe

Current theory suggests that around tweleve[1] to fifteen billion years ago, a dimensionless point of infinite mass and density exploded in what is referred to as the "Big Bang." Around six billion years later the first stars appeared through nuclear fusion. Our own Sun formed around four billion years after that, and the humans of Earth evolved yet another five billion years later. Today the Universe continues to expand.[2]

Galaxies

By current scientific calculations there are hundreds of billions of galaxies in the known Universe. They range in size from 2,000 light-years in diameter to large masses of star systems at least eighty times larger. Our galaxy is 100,000 light-years across its disk. Its central bulge is 30,000 light-years in diameter, and its spherical halo is 300,000 light-years in diameter. Currently, the farthest observable galaxy is roughly twelve billion light-years from Earth.

Most galaxies have no definable shape. Those that do, range in shape from "spirals' like our own, to spirals with bars across the center called "barred spirals," to "elliptical discs" and "elliptical spheres."[3]

Star Systems

Current science estimates there are at least 100 billion stars similar to our own within our home galaxy. Our solar system is around 28,000 light-years from the center or about two-thirds the distance from the central bulge to the outer edge of the disk. Our Sun and nine planets orbit the center once every 200 million years.[4] Four or five billion years from now, our Sun will burn out. The largest stars that die become black holes.[5]

The Hubble Space Telescope

In April of 1990, the Hubble Space Telescope was launched into space. No other scientific achievement since the dawn of civilization has expanded and enriched human knowledge of the Universe as dramatically as this device. For a projected fifteen years it will orbit 330 miles above the Earth at five miles per second. It is forty-five feet long and weighs twenty-five thousand pounds. It produces pictures of the Universe ten times clearer than any telescope on Earth because it has no atmosphere to cloud its vision. Its development and construction employed some ten thousand scientists and engineers for twenty years.

The Hubble Telescope is really a time machine. It can provide an image of our distant Universe as it would have appeared five billion years ago. It also provides an endless stream of detailed information and photographs that enable astronomers to further define galaxies, nebulae, star systems, various types and ages of stars, planets, and moons. The most exciting current research underway is the "Origins Program," which locates star systems similar to ours, images planets within those systems, then searches for traces of life on those planets.[6]

Resources for Further Investigation

Recommended Television Programs and Networks

Please consult the Directory of Television Networks further back in this section for scheduling information and availability of home videos:

> *"Black Holes,* The Ultimate Abyss," 1996, 60 minutes
> on The Discovery Channel
> air dates: 10/5/97, 3/29/98, 7/25/98

"Cosmic Storms, " *Ultrascience*, 1998, 30 minutes
on The Discovery Channel
air dates: 2/25/98

"*Hubble*, Secrets From Space," 1997, 60 minutes
on The Discovery Channel
air dates: 3/7/98

Solar Empire Series, 1997, four 60-minute programs
on The Learning Channel
air dates: 8/3/97, 12/12/97, 5/24/98

Steven Hawking's Universe, 1996, three 60-minute programs
on PBS
air dates: 11/3/97, 11/10/97, 11/17/97

The Universe, Understanding Festival, 1996, 60 minutes
on The Learning Channel
air dates: 8/29/98, 11/21/98

Recommended Books

A Journey Through Time
by Jay Barbree and Martin Caidin

Oxford Atlas of the World, 5th Edition
by Oxford University Press

Endnotes

[1] "The Universe," *Understanding Festival*, narr. Candice Bergen, writ. Dale Minor and Jonathan Ward, ed. Art Binkowski and Walter Cronkite, prod. Ron Bowman, Dan Everett and Jonathan Ward, The Learning Channel, 21 Nov. 1998.

[2] *Oxford Atlas of the World*, 5th edition, New York, New York: Oxford University Press, Inc., 1997. (2)

[3] *Oxford Atlas of the World*, 1997.(2)

[4] *Oxford Atlas of the World*, 1997.(2)

[5] "Hubble: Secrets From Space," *Sci-Trek*, narr. Martin Sheen, writ. Mark Brice, ed. Bill Moore, prod. Mark Brice, The Discovery Channel, 2 May 1998.

[6] "Hubble: Secrets From Space," *Sci-Trek*, 2 May 1998.

A Directory of Television Networks

The following list of television networks is provided for readers and viewers interested in program scheduling, home video availability, or general information. A scheduling tip: To avoid missing programs, you may wish to order the monthly cable guide from your cable carrier, then circle your selections at the beginning of each month to plan your viewing in advance.

A & E and The History Channel
The Arts and Entertainment Network
Viewer Relations (please specify A&E or The History Channel)
235 East 45th Street
New York, NY 10017
212-210-1340 viewer relations 10:00 A.M. to 5:00 P.M. E.T.
888-708-1776 toll free for videotape orders
http://www.AandE.com or http://www.HistoryChannel.com

CNN, TNT, and TBS
Turner Cable Networks
One CNN Center
Box 105366
Atlanta, GA 30348
404-827-1500 viewer relations
http://www.cnn.com

Discovery Channel and The Learning Channel
Discovery Communications
Viewer Relations
P. O. Box 665
Florence, KY 41022
888-404-5969 viewer relations 8:00 A.M. to 6:00 P.M. E.T.
http://www.discovery.com or http://www.tlc.com

Lifetime Network
Viewer Relations
309 West 49th Street
New York, NY 10019
212-424-7000 viewer relations 9:00 A.M. to 5:00 P.M. E.T.
http://www.unsolved.com

The Sci-Fi Channel
Viewer Relations
1230 Avenue of the Americas
New York, NY 10020
212-413-5679 viewer comment line
212-408-9100 viewer relations
http://www.scifi.com

PBS
National Offices
1320 Braddock Place
Alexandria, VA 22314-1698
800-PLAY PBS
http://www.pbs.org

PBS
UNC-TV (serves Southeastern States)
Viewer Services
P. O. Box 14900
Research Triangle Park, NC 27709
919-549-7000
http://www.pbs.org

Glossary

anomaly, n., pl. -lies. A deviation from that which is normal, standard or common. The word *anomaly* originated around 1570 and is derived from the Greek word *anomalia.*

channeling, n. The extrasensory conveyance of information from the spirit realm to the physical world usually while in a self-induced trance-like state. The word first appeared in England around 1575.

clairvoyance, n. The extrasensory perception of people, objects, or events isolated in space and/or time from the viewer. The word first appeared in English around 1845 and is derived from the French *clairvoyant* meaning "clear seeing."

consciospiritual, adj. Of or refering to a state of existence where both the human consciousness and sprit survive physical death and exist in the consciospiritual dimenison, the realm of knowledge, the realm of light, the realm of God. The word *consciospiritual* was first documented in English in the 1999 publication "The Magic of Our Universe: Beyond the Facts," and is derived from *conscio* from the 1630 English word *conscious* meaning "self-awareness," combined with the Middle English *spiritual,* derived from the Latin *spirito* meaning "spirit."

consciospiritualism, n. The doctrine that both the human consciousness and spirit, or human essence, survives physical death, exists in the consciospiritual realm and communicates with living humans either through an extrasensory medium or a human having experienced a near-death experience. The word *consciospiritualism* was first documented in English in the 1999 publication "The Magic of Our Universe: Beyond the Facts," and is derived from *conscio* from the 1630 English word *conscious* meaning "self-awareness," combined with the Middle English *spiritual,* derived from the Latin *spirito* meaning "spirit," combined with the suffix *ism* from the Greek *ismos* meaning "practice" or "doctrine."

cryptozoology, n. The investigation and research of unknown, unverified, or unclassified animals with the objective of proving their existence. The word *cryptozoology* was formed around 1970 from the words *crypto* and *zoology.*

empathy, n. The state in which a person identifies with, is sensitive to, understands, and vicariously experiences the feelings, thoughts, or situation of another person. The word *empathy* originated around

1903 from the Greek word *empatheia,* which literally means "passion" or affection. *empatheia* is further derived from *em* and *pathos,* which means "feelings."

empirical, adj. Based upon or derived from experiment, experience, or observation alone without consideration of theoretical or systematic methodology. The word *empirical* was formed around 1565 from *empiric* and *al.*

extrasensory perception (ESP), n.   Information or knowledge perceived or communicated outside of the known human sensory system. Current research of ESP, preferably known to science as "psi" encompasses the phenomena of telepathy, clairvoyance, precognition, and the related phenomena of psychokinesis and telekinesis. The term *extrasensory perception* first appeared in written English around 1935. *Psi* was derived around 1942 from the word *psychic.*

hominid, n. Any one of an erect, bipedal primate of the Hominidae family comprising the genera Australopithecus, presumed extinct, and Home, the genus of the species *Homo sapiens sapiens* or modern man. The word *hominid* was formed around 1887 from the Neolatin word *Hominidae.*

hominoid, n. Any one of a primate mammal of the Hominoidea super family comprising all presumed extinct and modern great apes and humans. The word was formed around 1939 from the Neolatin *Hominoidae.*

humanoid, n. A being that resembles a human. **humanoid**, adj. bearing resemblance to a human. The word *humanoid* was formed around 1919 from *human* and *oid.*

hypnosis, n. A sleeplike trance either self-induced or induced by another person usually for the purpose of making suggestions or commands readily acceptable, or for the purpose of accessing the subconscious. The word *hypnosis* was formed around 1878 from *hypn* or *hypnotic* and *osis.*

ichthyosaur, n. Any one of a marine reptile presumed extinct from the order Ichthyosauria streamlined for aquatic life with an average length of 25 ft., an average round girth of 5 ft., a powerful tail and four flippers for swimming, a pointed snout with teeth, and an erect caudal fin. The word *ichthyosaur* was formed around 1830 from combining the Neolatin *ichthyo,* derived from the Greek *ichthys* meaning "fish," together with the Greek *sauros* meaning "lizard."

kelpie, n. A mythical horse-like water creature of Scottish legend believed to drown wayfarers or warn potential drowning victims. The word originated around 1747 from the Scotch Gaelic *cailpeach* meaning "heifer."

mosasaur, n. Any one of a marine reptile presumed extinct of the family Mosasauridae comprising large carnivorous aquatic lizards common during the Upper Cretaceous period, with paddle-like limbs for swimming. The word was formed around 1835 from the Neolatin genus name *Mosasaurus,* which is derived from combining the Latin *Mosa* the Meuse River in western Europe, the site of first discovery, together with the Greek *sauros* meaning lizard.

paranormal, adj. Referring to an event, person, place, or object not explainable through science. The word was formed around 1918 from the Greek prefix *para* meaning "beyond," combined with *normal.* **paranormal**, n.

piezoelectric effect. The property created when a nonconducting crystal is squeezed, resulting in a positive electric charge on one side and a negative electric charge on the other, in turn creating an electric field detectable as voltage. The word *piezoelectric* was formed around 1893 from combining the Greek word *piezein,* meaning "to press together" with *electric.*

Pleistocene, adj. Referring to the earlier era of the Quaternary period, or the corresponding geological and widespread ice formations, that began around two million years ago and ended ten thousand years ago. **Pleistocene**, n. The Pleistocene epoch. The word *Pleistocene* was derived around 1838 from the Greek *pleistos* meaning "most," combined with the suffix *cene,* a variation of *ceno* from the Greek *kainos* meaning "new" or "recent."

plesiosaur, n. Any one of an aquatic reptile presumed extinct of the genus Plesiousaurus common during the Jurassic and Cretaceous periods, having an elongated neck and small head, with an average length of 40 ft., rounded, slightly flattened torso 7 ft. in average diameter, and four modified limbs resembling paddles. The word *plesiosaur* was derived around 1830 from the Neolatin *Plesiosaurus,* a combination of the Greek *plesios* meaning "close," and the Greek *sauros* meaning "lizard".

precognition, n. Extrasensory knowledge of a circumstance or event that has not yet occurred. The word originated in the late Middle English language around 1425 from the late Middle English *cognicioun* further derived from the Latin *cognoscene* meaning "to know," combined with the Latin *prea* meaning "beforehand."

premonition, n.   The anxious anticipation, feeling, or impression of a future event. The word *premonition* was first documented in English around 1450 in the late Middle English language and is derived from Middle French, further from Late Latin *praemonition*, and further from Latin *praemonere* meaning "to warn in advance."

psychometry, n.   The ability to divine facts concerning an object or its proprietor through proximity to or contact with the object. The word originated in English form around 1848 by combining *psycho* from the Greek *psycho* meaning "mind, spirit, or soul," together with *metry* from the Greek *metria* meaning "to measure."

science, n.   Knowledge of the physical world acquired through systematic analysis and testing. The word *science* was first documented in the Middle English language around 1325 and is derived from Middle French and further from the Latin *scientia* meaning "having knowledge."

science, n.   (An interesting definition from the Internet) "Science is a set of laws by which we test reality (truth). It is a template used to organize the stream of consciousness we humans are immersed in daily. We use it to organize, count, catalog, and validate our experiences. We feel pretty good about our template (scientific beliefs) until some phenomenon comes along that doesn't fit the patterns of its structure.

At this point, we might consider the accuracy of our beliefs, whether they are perfect enough to cover ALL of human experience. Maybe they need to be modified or expanded: what if we don't know everything.

But rather than examine our tools we foolishly label the experience as false, a freak, or the experience/reporter as unreliable in some way. Even worse, we try to trim and shape the experience to force it into the structure of the template. Doing so, we can say we understand it, even though the experience has been violated and frauded." (Courtesy Leroy Kattein <http://www. ndeweb.com/FAQ09.htm> 2 September 1998).

scientific method, n.   A systematic procedure for acquiring knowledge where a problem is recognized, all pertinent data are collected and analyzed, from which a working hypothesis is established and tested. This phrase was first coined around 1853.

Sherpa, n.   Any one of, or a group of (pl.), a Tibetan people residing in southeastern Nepal in the high Himalayas south of Mt. Everest, who frequently provide support as packers and guides for mountain expeditions. The word was first known to the Western world around 1850.

skeptic, n.   An advocate of skepticism who doubts or questions the reality or validity of an alleged truth, fact, or religion. The word *skeptic* originated around 1580 and is derived from the Greek *skeptikos* meaning "to examine thoughtfully."

spiritualism, n.   The doctrine that the human spirit survives physical death exists in the spirit realm and communicates with living humans typically through an extrasensory medium. The word *spiritualism* was formed around 1800 from the Middle English *spiritual* derived from the Latin *spirito* meaning "spirit" combined with the suffix *ism* from the Greek *ismos* meaning "practice" or "doctrine."

supernatural, adj., n.   Of or referring to a state of existence above, beyond, or outside of the natural comprehensible universe; or or referring to God or an unnatural superhuman entity. The word *supernatural* was first written in English around 1525 and is derived from the Middle Latin *supernaturalis* further derived from the Latin prefix *super* meaning "above" or "beyond" combined with the Latin *natura* meaning "nature."

telepathy, n.   The extrasensory transfer of information between the minds of beings. The word was formed around 1883 from the Greek *tête* meaning "far" combined with the Greek *patheia* meaning "feeling."

ufology, n.   The study of UFOs. The word *ufology* was formed around 1956 from UFO meaning unidentified flying objects, combined with *logy* meaning "body of knowledge."

unified field theory, n.   A general theory proposing to unify the four basic forces of the known universe: gravity or gravitational fields, electromagnitism or electromagnetic fields, the strong nuclear force or the force binding subatomic particles known as quarks tightly together, and the weak nuclear force or the force binding atomic particles together. The phrase was formed around 1978. Also known as the Grand Unified Theory.

List of Works Used

"Abduction: Horror or Hype." *Sightings*. narr. Tim White. prod. Henry Winkler and Ann Daniel. writ. Susan Michaels. The Sci-Fi Channel. 1 Jan. 1998.

Alien Hunters. We Are Not Alone. narr. Colin Stinton. prod. Sara Woodford. The Learning Channel. 3 May 1998.

"*Alien Secrets*: Area 51." narr. Bruce Burgess. prod. Bruce Burgess. The Learning Channel. 8 Dec. 1997.

"*Aliens*: Where Are They?." Science of the Impossible. narr. Michael Goldfarb. ed. Hugh Williams and Peter Clark. prod. Chris Lent. John Blake and George Carey. The Discovery Channel. 13 July 1998.

"Allagash Abduction." *Sightings*. In The News. narr. Tim White. writ. Susan Michaels. prod. Henry Winkler and Ann Daniel. The Sci-Fi Channel. 4 Feb. 1998.

"Amazing Grace." *Sightings*. narr. Tim White. writ. Susan Michaels. prod. Amber Benson. Lindsey Paddor. Henry Winkler and Ann Daniel. The Sci-Fi Channel. 23 Feb. 1998.

"A Mother's Love." *Sightings*. narr. Tim White. writ. Susan Michaels. prod. Henry Winkler and Ann Daniel. The Sci-Fi Channel. 26 May 1998.

Ancient Prophecies. narr. David McCallum. ed. Michael Andrews. prod. Graeme Whifler and Paul Klein. The Learning Channel. 9 Jan. 1998.

"Ancient Wisdom." *Arthur C. Clark's Mysterious World*. narr. Stanley Anderson. prod. John Fairley. The Discovery Channel. 31 May 1998.

"An Element of the Divine." *Arthur C. Clarke's World of Strange Powers*. narr. Stanley Anderson. prod. Adam Hart-Davis. The Discovery Channel. 12 July 1998.

"Angel of Death." *Sightings*. narr. Tim White. writ. Susan Michaels. prod. Kim Steer. Henry Winkler and Ann Daniel. The Sci-Fi Channel. 28 April 1998.

"Animal Telepathy." *Strange But True?*. narr. Michael Aspel. prod. Bob Reid. The Discovery Channel. 24 May 1998.

AP Washington. *AP The Wire*. December 15, 1997. <http://www.nacomm.org/news/ 1997/ qtr4/etpoll.htm>. 26 August 1998.

"Area 51, Nevada." *Sightings*. In The News. narr. Tim White. writ. Susan Michaels. prod. Henry Winkler and Ann Daniel. The Sci-Fi Channel. 18 Feb. 1998.

Arnold, Larry. Interview. "Spontaneous Human Combustion." *The Unexplained*. narr. Norm Woodel. writ. Gaylon Emerzian. prod. Gaylon Emerzian. The Discovery Channel. 19 Feb. 1998

Atomic Archive. AJ Software & Multimedia. <http://www.atomicarchive.com/ Timeline/ Time1940.html>. 22 Nov. 1998

"Avebury Mystery Lights." *Sightings*. narr. Tim White. writ. Susan Michaels. prod. Henry Winkler and Ann Daniel. The Sci-Fi Channel. 20 Jan. 1998.

Battle of the Bulge. Christmas Eve. *Unsolved Mysteries*. narr. Robert Stack. writ. Raymond Bridgers and Terry Dunn Meurer. prod. Terry Dunn Meurer and John Cosgrove. Lifetime. 3 Sept. 1998.

"*Beyond the Grave*: The Afterlife." *In Search of History*. narr. David Ackroyd. ed. Diana Friedberg. A.C.E. prod. Lionel Friedberg. The Arts & Entertainment Network. 10 Aug. 1998.

Bielek, Al. Author. Interview. *New Visions of the Future*. Ancient Prophecies III. narr. David McCallum. prod. Paul Klein. The Learning Cnannel. 28 June 1998.

"Bigfoot." *Ancient Mysteries*. narr. Leonard Nemoy. writ. Rob Englehardt. prod. James P. Taylor, Sr. The Arts & Entertainment Network. 29 March 1998.

"Bigfoot, Skunk Ape, Sasquatch, Salawa." *Animal X.* narr. Betsy Aidem. writ. Wendy Wilson and Cathryn Garland. prod. Shauna Stafford. Julie Mapleston and Melenie Ambrose. The Discovery Channel. 17 May 1998.

Blackmore, Susan, Ph.D. Interview. "The Near Death Experience." *Life After Death.* narr. Tom Harpur. writ. Tom Harpur. prod. Jim Hanley and David Brady. The Learning Channel. 22 Dec. 1997.

"Black Swan Haunting." *Sightings.* narr. Tim White. prod. Michael Burns. Henry Winkler and Ann Daniel. The Sci-Fi Channel. 5 May 1998.

Byrne, Peter. Director. Bigfoot Research Project. "Bigfoot." *Ancient Mysteries.* narr. Leonard Nemoy. writ. Rob Englehardt. prod. James P. Taylor, Sr. The Arts and Entertainment Network. 29 March 1998.

Bullard, Dr. Thomas. Indiana University. Interview. "The Secrets of Alien Abduction." *Sightings.* In Depth and Beyond. narr. Tim White. writ. Susan Michaels. prod. Henry Winkler and Ann Daniel. The Sci-Fi Channel. 14 March 1998.

Cahill, Kelly. and Others. Interviews. "*Oz Encounters.* UFO's in Australia." narr. Martin Sacks. writ. Debbie Byme. prod. DebbieByme. The Discovery Channel. 27 Sept. 1998.

Cannon, Delores. Interview. *Ancient Prophecies.* narr. David McCallum. ed. Michael Andrews. prod. Graeme Whifler and Paul Klein. The Learning Channel. 9 Jan. 1998

"Case Closed." *Sightings.* narr. Tim White. writ. Susan Michael. prod. Joyce Goldstein. The Sci-Fi Channel. 28 April 1998.

Chacon, Christopher. Scientific Paranormal Investigator and Founder of O.S.I.R. Interview. "Haunted High." *Sightings.* narr. Tim White. writ. Susan Michaels. prod. Henry Winkler and Ann Daniel. The Sci-Fi Channel. 6 Jan. 1998.

"Clear Intent." *Sightings.* narr. Tim White. writ. Susan Michaels. prod. Phillip Davis. The Sci-Fi Channel. 5 Feb. 1998.

"*Climatic Catastrophe.* narr. Joe Frank. ed. Eric Wise and Ken Lubbert. prod. Eric Nelson. The Learning Channel. 1 Nov. 1998.

"Close Encounters of the Fourth Kind." *Sightings.* In the News. narr. Tim White. writ. Susan Michaels. prod. Rob Morhaim. The Sci-Fi Channel. 5 March 1998.

"Cluster UFO." *Sightings.* narr. Tim White. writ. Susan Michaels. prod. Philip Davis and Rob Sharkey. The Sci-Fi Channel. 17 March 1998.

CNN Headline News. 14 Oct. 1998.

CNN Headline News. 15 Dec. 1998.

CNN Interactive. *CNN/Time Poll.* June 10, 1997. <http://www.nacomm.org/news/1997/qtr2/ cnnpoll.htm>. 26 August 1998.

Coleman, Loren. Investigator and Author of *Tom Slick and the Search for the Yeti.* Interview. "The Abominable Snowman." *In Search of History.* narr. David Ackroyd. prod. Tim Evans. The History Channel. 30 April 1998.

"Colorado Cattle Mutations." *Sightings.* narr. Tim White. writ. Susan Michaels. prod. Kim Steer. The Sci-Fi Channel. 30 Dec. 1997.

"Contact Israel." *Sightings.* In The News. narr. Tim White. writ. Susan Michaels. prod. Henry Winkler and Ann Daniel. The Sci-Fi Channel. 11 March 1998.

"Contact at Socorro." *Sightings.* narr. Tim White. writ. Susan Michaels. prod. Rob Morhaim. The Sci-Fi Channel. 5 March 1998.

"Creatures of the Abyss." *Sci Trek.* narr. Will Lyman. ed. David Hope. prod. Nicolas Kent and Vanessa Phillips. The Discovery Channel. 8 August 1998.

"Crop Circles." *Sightings.* Update. narr. Tim White. writ. Susan Michaels. prod. Henry Winkler and Ann Daniel. The Sci-Fi Channel. 29 March 1998.

"*Dead Sea Scrolls*: Unraveling the Mystery." writ. Bo Landin, Jane Wilson and Sterling Van Wagenen. prod. Sterling Van Wagenen and Bo Landin. The Discovery Channel. 9 Nov. 1998.

"Deliberate Deception." *Sightings*. narr. Tim White. writ. Susan Michaels. prod. Philip Davis. The Sci-Fi Channel. 25 March 1998.

Dilletoso, Jim. Interview. "Cluster UFO." Sightings. narr. Tim White. writ. Susan Michaels. prod. Phillip Donis and Robert Sharkey. The Sci-Fi Channel. 17 March 1998.

Discovery News. ABC News. 3 July 1998.

"Dowsers." *Strange But True?*. narr. Michael Aspel. ed. David Alpin and Jeremy Phillips. prod. Ralph Jones and Simon Shaps. The Discovery Channel. 12 Feb. 1998.

Eadie, Betty J. Interview. "Visions of Heaven." *Life After Death*. narr. Tom Harpur. writ. Tom Harpur. prod. Jim Hanley and David Brady. The Learning Channel. 22 Dec. 1997.

Ellis, Richard. Interview. *Strange Beings and UFOs*. Mysteries of the Unexplained. narr. James Coburn. writ. Shamus Culhane. prod. Joel Westrook. The Discovery Channel. 5 April 1998.

"Encounters, Hauntings Investigations." *Sightings*. narr. Tim White. writ. Susan Michaels. prod. Paul Hall and Mark Cowen. The Sci-Fi Channel. 14 Sept. 1998.

"Extraterrestrial Life." *The Unexplained*. narr. Norm Woodel. writ. Jamie Ceaser. Rollie Hudson. prod. Jamie Ceaser. The Arts & Entertainment Network. 9 March 1998.

"Falling Phenomena." *Arthur C. Clarke's Mysterious Universe*. narr. Ed Green. writ. Cathryn Garland. prod. Simon Westcott. The Discovery Channel. 31 May 1998.

"Fire In The Brain." *Sightings*. narr. Tim White. writ. Susan Michaels. prod. Henry Winkler and Ann Daniel. The Sci-Fi Channel. 23 Dec. 1998.

Fowler, Raymond E. Interview. "UFO's: Japan." *Sightings*. narr. Tim White. writ. Susan Michaels. prod. Henry Winkler and Ann Daniel. The Sci-Fi Channel. 19 March 1998.

Fox, Dr. Michael. Interview. "Strange Powers of Animals." *Arthur C. Clarke's Mysterious Universe*. narr. Ed Green. writ. Cathryn Garland. prod. Simon Westcott. The Discovery Channel. 23 Aug. 1998.

Frequently Asked Questions about NDEs. The International Association of Near Death Studies. <http://www.iands.org/fag.html>. 31 Aug. 1998.

Friedman, Stanton. Interview with Larry King. *The UFO Cover-up?* Live from Area 51. A TNT Larry King Special. narr. Larry King. writ. Tom Farmer. prod. Carrie Stevenson. TNT. 13 Sept. 1998.

Gaynor, Kerry. Interview. "Encounters, Hauntings Investigations." *Sightings*. narr. Tim White. writ. Susan Michaels. prod. Henry Winkler and Ann Daniel. The Sci-Fi Channel. 14 Sept. 1998.

Gaynor, Kerry. Parapsychologist. Interview. "*The Living Dead*. Speaking from the Grave." narr. Tim White. writ. Susan Michaels. prod. Henry Winkler and Ann Daniel. The Sci-Fi Channel. 25 Oct. 1998.

Ghostly Voices. Unnatural History. narr. Mark Hamill. writ. Michael Tetrick. prod. Michael Tetrick. The Learning Channel. 26 May 1998.

Ghosts and Poltergeists. <http://www.zerotime.com/ghosts/poter.htm>. 31 August 1998.

"Ghosts." *Strange But True?*. narr. Michael Aspel. series eds. David Alpin and Jeremy Phillips. prod. Ralph Jones and Simon Shaps. The Discovery Channel. 28 June 1998.

Gill, G. W. President. The American Board of Anthropology. Interview. "Bigfoot," *Ancient Mysteries*. narr. Leonard Nemoy. writ. Rob Englehardt. prod. James P. Taylor, Sr. The Arts and Entertainment Network. 29 March 1998.

Gissen, Jay. ed. *The Cable Guide*. Horsham, Pennsylvania: TVSM, Inc., 1998.

Goldstein, Marcy. M.D. Interview. "Healers." *Sightings*. narr. Tim White. writ. Susan Michaels. prod. Joanne L. Fish. The Sci-Fi Channel. 17 Feb. 1998.

Good, Tim. Interview. "*UFO's*: The 100 Year Cover-up." *Sightings*. In Depth and Beyond. narr. Tim White. writ. Susan Michaels. prod. Henry Winkler and Ann Daniel. 1 Jan. 1998.

Goodall, James. 133 Airlift Wing. Interview. "*Alien Secrets*: Area 51." narr. Bruce Burgess. prod. Bruce Burgess. The Learning Channel. 8 Dec. 1997.

Gorham, Joan. ed. *Mass Media 95/96*. 2nd ed. Guilford, Connecticut: The Dushkin Publishing Group, Inc., 1995.

Grant, Robert. Interview. *Ancient Prophecies*. narr. David McCallum. ed. Michael Andrews. prod. Graeme Whifler and Paul Klein. The Learning Channel. 9 Jan. 1998.

Greenwell, Richard. Secretary. International Society of Cryptozoologists. Interview. "The Abominable Snowman." *In Search of History*. narr. David Ackroyd. prod. Tim Evans. The History Channel. 30 April 1998.

Greer, Dr. Steven. Director of CSETI. Interview with Larry King. *The UFO Cover-up?* Live from Area 51. A TNT Larry King Special. narr. Larry King. writ. Tom Farmer. prod. Carrie Stevenson. TNT. 13 Sept. 1998.

"Gulf Breeze Encounters." *Sightings*. narr. Tim White. writ. Susan Michaels. prod. Henry Winkler and Ann Daniel. The Sci-Fi Channel. 10 May 1998.

Haggerty, Chief Paul. Retired. Upper Darby Fire Dept. Interview. "Spontaneous Human Combustion." narr. Norm Woodel. writ. Gaylon Emerzian. prod. Gaylon Emerzian. The Discovery Channel. *The Unexplained*. 19 Feb. 1998.

Hauck, Dennis William. Paranormal Researcher and Author. Interview. "Restless Sprits." *Sightings*. narr. Tim White. writ. Susan Michaels. prod. Michael Burns. Henry Winkler and Ann Daniel. The Sci-Fi Channel. 6 Sept. 1998.

Haunted Places. Thrills, Chills and Spills. narr. Henry Strozier. writ. Bruce Cooke and Douglas Paynter. prod. Bruce Cooke and Douglas Paynter. The Discovery Channel. 31 May 1998.

Haunted History. "New England." narr. Michael Dorn. ed. Bradley Holmes. prod. Craig Haffner and Donna Lusitana. The History Channel. 26 Oct. 1998.

Haunted History of Halloween. narr. Harry Smith. writ. Jeff Swimmer. prod. Jeff Swimmer. The History Channel. 23 Oct. 1998.

"Hauntings" *Sightings*. narr. Tim White. writ. Susan Michaels. prod. Henry Winkler and Ann Daniel. The Sci-Fi Channel. 4 June 1998.

"Healers," *Sightings*. narr. Tim White. writ. Susan Michaels. prod. Joanne L. Fish. Henry Winkler and Ann Daniel. The Sci-Fi Channel. 17 Feb. 1998.

"Height 611." *Sightings*. narr. Tim White. writ. Susan Michaels. prod. Henry Winkler and Ann Daniel. The Sci-Fi Channel. 24 May 1998.

Hopkins, Budd et al. *The Roper Poll. Budd Hopkins*. 1992. <http://www.spiritweb.org/spirit/abduction-roper-poll.html>. 28 Aug. 1998.

Hopkins, Budd. Interview with Larry King. *The UFO Cover-up?* Live from Area 51. A TNT Larry King Special. narr. Larry King. writ. Tom Farmer. prod. Carrie Stevenson. TNT. 13 Sept. 1998.

"Houston, Texas, UFOs." *Sightings*. In the News. narr. Tim White. writ. Susan Michaels. prod. Henry Winkler and Ann Daniel. The Sci-Fi Channel. 28 April 1998.

<http://popularmechanics.com/popmech/sci/9706stmim.html>(Access date: 28 Aug. 1998).

"*Hubble*, Secrets From Space." *Sci-Trek*. narr. Martin Sheen. writ. Mark Brice. ed. Bill Moore. prod. Mark Brice. The Discovery Channel. 2 May 1998.

Huffman, Herbert. Prof. of Old Testament. Duke University. Interview. "*Prophets*: Soul Catchers." *Mysteries of the Bible*. narr. Richard Kiley and Jean Simmons. ed. Duane Tudahl. prod. Brarm Roos. David M. Frank and Gayle Kirschenbaum. The Arts and Entertainment Network. 28 Nov. 1998.

"Hudson Valley UFO Sighting." *Unsolved Mysteries*. The Unexplained. narr. Robert Stack. writ. Raymond Bridgers and Terry Dunn Meurer. prod. Terry Dunn Meurer and John Cosgrove. Lifetime. 1 Oct. 1998.

"Idaho UFO Flap." *Sightings*. narr. Tim White. writ. Susan Michaels. prod. Henry Winkler and Ann Daniel. The Sci-Fi Channel. 2 Feb. 1998.

"Identical Twins." *Strange But True?*. narr. Michael Aspel. prod. Bob Reid. The Discovery Channel. 19 Mar. 1998.

Imbrogno, Phillip. UFO Researcher and Author. Interview. "Extraterrestrial Life." *The Unexplained*. narr. Norm Woodel. writ. Jaime Ceaser. Rollie Hudson. prod. Jamie Ceaser. The Arts & Entertainment Network. 9 March 1998.

Inter Press Service. *CNN/Time Poll*. June 10, 1998. <http://www.nacomm.org/news/1998/qtr2/ cnntime.htm>. 26 August 1998.

International Crop Circle Database. Enigma Publications. 1997. <http://www.interalpha.net/customer/puigay/2base/1997.html>. 26 Aug. 1998.

In the News. *Sightings*. narr. Tim White. writ. Susan Michaels. prod. Henry Winkler and Ann Daniel. The Sci-Fi Channel. 23 Feb. 1998.

"In the Shadows." *Animal X*. narr. Betsy Aidem. writ. Wendy Wilson and Cathryn Garland. prod. Melanie Ambrose and Max Jacobson-Gonzalez. The Discovery Channel. 30 Aug. 1998.

"Joseph McMoneagle." *Doc Hambone*. <http://www.io.com/:hambone/web/mcmoneagle.html>. 27 Jan. 1999.

Kaku, Michio. Physicist. City Univ., NY. Interview. *Invisible Forces*. Science of the Impossible. narr. Michael Goldfarb. ed. Jason Farrow. prod. Chris Lent. John Blake and George Caney. The Discovery Channel. 19 July 1998.

Krantz, Dr. Grover. Interview. "Bigfoot." *Ancient Mysteries*. narr. Leonard Nemoy. writ. Rob Englehardt. prod. James P. Taylor. The Arts and Entertainment Network. 29 March 1998.

Kusters, Jack. Hewett Packard. Interview. "The Mystery of the Crystal Skulls." *The Unexplained*. narr. Norm Woodel. writ. Peter Mihns. prod. BBC. A&E Network. Co-Producers. The Arts & Entertainment Network. 4 June 1998.

Lazar, Robert S. Alleged former Aear 51 and Area 5-4 Research Engineer. Interview. "*Alien Secrets*: Area 51." narr. Bruce Burgess. prod. Bruce Burgess. The Learning Channel. 8 Dec. 1997.

LeBlanc, Benjamin. Interview. "The Search for Dracula." *Science Mysteries*. narr. Eli Wallach. writ. Eleanor Grant. prod. Nicola Valcor and Tom Naughton. The Discovery Channel. 11 Jan. 1998.

Levengood, W.C. Biophysicist and Barry Chamish. Investigator. Interviews. "UFO Encounter: Shikmona." *Sightings*. narr. Tim White. writ. Susan Michaels. prod. Ruth Rafidi and Phillip Lapkin. The Sci-Fi Channel. 18 Feb. 1998.

Life After Life. video cassette. Della LLC. Nashville. Della LLC. 1992. color. 57 minutes.

Lindemann, Michael. UFO Investigator. Interview. "Gulf Breeze Encounters." *Sightings.* narr. Tim White. writ. Susan Michaels. prod. Henry Winkler and Ann Daniel. The Sci-Fi Channel. 10 May 1998.

Lindemann, Michael. ed. *CNI News.*<http://www.cninews.com>. 26 August 1998.

"Loch Ness." *Great Mysteries and Myths of the Twentieth Century.* narr. Michael Carroll. writ. Wendy Wilson. prod. Sharon Gillooly. The Learning Channel. 30 Jan. 1998.

Luck, Steve. ed. *Oxford Family Encyclopedia.* 1st edition. New York. New York: Oxford University Press, Inc. 1997. (84, 167, 178, 183, 246, 320, 408, 435, 467, 488, 567).

"Magic and Miracles in the Old Testament." *Mysteries of the Bible.* narr. Richard Kiley and Jean Simmons. writ. Tracey Benger and Susan Lutz. prod. Bram Roos. The Arts & Entertainment Network. 7 June 1998.

"Mantell Re-Examined." *Sightings.* narr. Tim White. writ. Susan Michaels. prod. Philip Davis. The Sci-Fi Channel. 30 March 1998.

"Mary." Interview. *Sacred Places and Mystic Spirits.* Mysteries of the Unexplained. narr. James Coburn. writ. Robert Gardner. prod. Robert Gardner. The Discovery Channel. 12 June 1998.

May, Ed. Interview. *Invisible Forces.* Science of the Impossible. narr. Michael Goldfarb. ed. Jason Farrow. prod. Chris Lent. John Blake and George Caney. The Discovery Channel. 19 July 1998.

McMoneagle, Joe. Interview. *Invisible Forces.* Science of the Impossible. narr. Michael Goldfarb. ed. Jason Farrow. prod. Chris Lent. John Blake and George Caney. The Discovery Channel.19 July 1998.

Meldrum, Jeff. Primate Anatomist. Interview. *Strange Beings and UFOs.* Mysteries of the Unexplained. narr. James Coburn. writ. Shamus Culhane. prod. Joel Westbrook. The Discovery Channel. 5 April 1998.

"Men in Black." *Unsolved Mysteries.* The Unexplained. narr. Robert Stack. writ. Raymond Bridgers and Terry Dunn Meurer. prod. Terry Dunn Meurer and John Cosgrove. Lifetime. 25 March 1998.

"Mexico Mass Sightings." *Sightings.* Update. narr. Tim White. writ. Susan Michaels. prod. Henry Winkler and Ann Daniel. The Sci-Fi Channel. 2 Feb. 1998.

Michaels, Susan. *Sightings: Beyond Imagination Lies The Truth.* New York: Fireside. 1996. Photoghraphs 58 and 59.

Miller, Kenneth. "Psychics: Science or Seance? A reporter visits the twilight zone." *Life.* New York. June 1998: 88-103.

"Miracles and Sainthood." *Strange But True?.* narr. Michael Aspel. prod. Ralph Jones and Simon Shaps. The Discovery Channel. 12 March 1998.

Modern Marvels. narr. Harlan Saperstein. prod. Bruce Nash. The History Channel. 16 Sept.1998.

Moody, Dr. Raymond A. *Life After Life.* video cassette. Della LLC. Nashville. Della LLC. 1992. color. 57 minutes.

"Monsters of the Lake." *Arthur C. Clark's Mysterious World.* narr. Stanley Anderson. prod. John Fanshawe. The Discovery Channel. 7 June 1998.

"Montreal Mass Sighting." *Sightings.* narr. Tim White. writ. Susan Michaels. prod. Henry Winkler and Ann Daniel. The Sci-Fi Channel. 15 Jan. 1998.

"Mysteries of Alien Beings." *Unsolved Mysteries.* narr. Robert Stack. writ. Raymond Bridgers and Terry Dunn Meurer. prod. Terry Dunn Meurer and John Cosgrove. Lifetime. 4 Dec. 1997.

Natale, Carl. President. UBA Fire Investigators. Interview. "Spontaneous Human Combustion." *The Unexplained.* narr. Norm Woodel. writ. Gaylon Emerzian. prod. Gaylon Emerzian. The Arts & Entertainment Network. 19 Feb. 1998.

"Near Death Experiences." *Arthur C. Clarke's Mysterious Universe.* narr. Stanley Anderson. prod. Adam Hart-David. The Discovery Channel. 3 May 1998.

Nesure, Pam. Interview. "Visions of Heaven." *Life After Death.* narr. Tom Harpur. writ. Tom Harpur. prod. Jim Hanley and David Brady. The Learning Channel. 22 Dec. 1997.

Nesure, Pam. Interview. "*After Life:* Heaven Can Wait." *48 Hours.* narr. Erin Moriarity. prod. CBS Worldwide, Inc.. CBS. 6 Aug. 1998.

"New Mexico UFO Mystery." *Sightings.* narr. Tim White. writ. Susan Michaels. prod. Henry Winkler and Ann Daniel. The Sci-Fi Channel. 1 June 1998.

New Visions of the Future. Ancient Prophecies III. narr. David McCallum. prod. Paul Klein. The Learning Channel. 28 June 1998.

"New York, Marketing UFO." *Sightings.* In The News. narr. Tim White. writ. Susan Michael. prod. Henry Winkler and Ann Daniel. The Sci-Fi Channel. 11 March 1998.

O'Brien, Chris. UFO Researcher. Colorado. Interview. "San Luis Valley. Colorado. Mysterious Valley." *Sightings.* In the News. narr. Tim White. writ. Susan Michaels. prod. Henry Winkler and Ann Daniel. The Sci-Fi Channel. 9 April 1998.

Oxford Atlas of the World. 5th edition. New York. New York: Oxford University Press, Inc. 1997. (2, 18, 130-131).

"*Oz Encounters,* UFOs in Australia." narr. Martin Sacks. writ. Debbie Byrne. prod. Debbie Byrne. The Discovery Channel. 27 Sept. 1998.

Pendergast, Dr. David with The Royal Ontario Museum. Interview. "The Mystery of the Crystal Skulls." *The Unexplained.* narr. Norm Woodel. writ. Peter Minns. prod. BBC. A&E Network. Co-Producers. The Arts & Entertainment Network. 4 June 1998.

"Photography: The Technology of photography: SPECIAL PHOTOSENSITIVE SYSTEMS: Electronic photography." *Britannica Online.* <http://www.eb.com:180/cgi-bin/g? DocF=macro/5005/2/61.html>Access date   07 October 1998.

"Profilers." *Sightings.* narr. Tim White. writ. Susan Michaels. prod. Ruth Rafidi. Michael Kriz. Henry Winkler and Ann Daniel. The Sci-Fi Channel. 4 May 1998.

"Prophecies." *In Search of History.* narr. David Ackroyd. ed. Shelley Stocking. prod. Bram Roos. David M. Frank and Frank Kosa. The History Channel. 13 March 1998.

Prophecies. Unnatural History. narr. Mark Hammill. prod. Andrea Matzke. The Learning Channel. 26 May 1998.

"*Prophets:* Soul Catchers." *Mysteries of the Bible.* narr. Richard Kiley and Jean Simmons. ed. Duane Tudahl. prod. Gayle Kirschenbaum. Lionel Friedberg and Bram Roos. The Arts & Entertainment Network. 28 Nov. 1998.

"Psychic Detective." *Sightings.* narr. Tim White. writ. Susan Michaels. prod. Henry Winkler and Ann Daniel. The Sci-Fi Channel. 7 Sept. 1998.

Purdy, Robert. Retired Emergency Services Coordinator for Essex County, New York. Interview. "S.H.C." *Sightings.* Update. narr. Tim White. writ. Susan Michaels. prod. Henry Winkler and Ann Daniel. The Sci-Fi Channel. 7 June 1998.

"Rachel, Nevada, Area 51." *Sightings.* narr. Tim White. writ. Susan Michaels. prod. Henry Winkler and Ann Daniel. The Sci-Fi Channel. 3 March 1998.

"Rachel, Nevada, Area 51." *Sightings.* In The News. narr. Tim White. writ. Susan Michaels. prod. Henry Winkler and Ann Daniel. The Sci-Fi Channel. 4 March 1998.

Radin, Dean, Ph.D. *Consciousness Research Laboratory.* <http://www.psiresearch.org>. 26 Jan.1999.

Radin, Dean, Ph.D. Interview. *Invisible Forces*. Science of the Impossible. narr. Michael Goldfarb. ed. Hugh Williams and Peter Clark. prod. Chris Lent. John Blake and George Carey. The Discovery Channel. 19 July 1998.

Randle, Kevin. Capt. Air Force Reserves. Interview with Larry King. *The UFO Cover-up?* Live from Area 51. A TNT Larry King Special. narr. Larry King. writ. Tom Farmer. prod. Carrie Stevenson. TNT. 13 Sept. 1998.

Rhine Research Center (Inst. for Parapsychology). <http://www.rhine.org/>.

Rodonaia, Dr. George. Interview. *Life After Life*. video cassette. Della LLC. Nashville. Della LLC. 1992. color. 57 minutes.

Rotem, Doron. and Barry Chamish. Interviews. "UFO Contact: The Holland." *Sightings*. narr. Tim White. writ. Susan Michaels. prod. Henry Winkler and Ann Daniel. The Sci-Fi Channel. 6 Feb. 1998

R. R. Bowker's Books in Print. 97-98 edition. New Providence. New Jersey: R. R. Bowker. 1998.

Rutowski, Chris A. ed. Ufology Research of Manitoba. The 1997 Canadian UFO Survey. Winnipeg. Manitoba. 1998. <http://www.geocities.com/Area 51/rampart/265397 survey. html>. 26 Aug. 1998.

Rutowski, Chris. UFO Researcher. Interview. UFO Encounter. *Unsolved Mysteries*. narr. Robert Stack. writ. Raymond Bridgers and Terry Dunn Meurer. prod. Terry Dunn Meurer and John Casgrove. Lifetime. 19 Sept. 1998.

"Ruwa Re-Examined." *Sightings*. narr. Tim White. writ. Susan Michaels. prod. Henry Winkler and Ann Daniel. The Sci-Fi Channel. 22 March 1998.

"San Luis Valley. Colorado. Mysterious Valley." *Sightings*. In The News. narr. Tim White. writ. Susan Michaels. prod. Henry Winkler and Ann Daniel. The Sci-Fi Channel. 9 April 1998.

"Seizure Alert Dogs." *Sightings*. narr. Tim White. writ. Susan Michaels. prod. Henry Winkler and Ann Daniel. The Sci-Fi Channel. 2 Sept. 1998.

"S.E.T.I. Resurrected." *Sightings*. narr. Tim White. writ. Susan Michaels. prod. Henry Winkler and Ann Daniel. The Sci-Fi Channel. 18 May 1998.

"Shag Harbor Investigation." *Sightings*. narr. Tim White. writ. Susan Michaels. prod. Phillip Davis. The Sci-Fi Channel. 3 March 1998.

Sheldrake, Rupert. Interview. *Sightings*. In the News. narr. Tim White. writ. Susan Michaels. prod. Henry Winkler and Ann Daniel. The Sci-Fi Channel. 23 July 1998.

Sheppherd, Graham. Commercial Pilot. Interview. "Idaho UFO Flap." *Sightings*. narr. Tim White. writ. Susan Michaels. prod. Henry Winkler and Ann Daniel. The Sci-Fi Channel. 2 Feb. 1998.

"Sightings On Line." *Sightings*. narr. Tim White. writ. Susan Michaels. prod. Henry Winkler and Ann Daniel. The Sci-Fi Channel. 2 March 1998.

Sightings. narr. Tim White. writ. Susan Michaels. prod. Henry Winkler and Ann Daniel. The Sci-Fi Channel. 8 Feb. 1998.

Sightings. narr. Tim White. writ. Susan Michaels. prod. Henry Winkler and Ann Daniel. The Sci-Fi Channel. 10 March 1998.

Sightings. narr. Tim White. writ. Susan Michaels. prod. Henry Winkler and Ann Daniel. The Sci-Fi Channel. 15 March 1998.

Sightings. narr. Tim White. writ. Susan Michaels. prod. Henry Winkler and Ann Daniel. The Sci-Fi Channel. 20 Aug. 1998.

"Silent Intruder." *Sightings*. narr. Tim White. writ. Susan Michaels. prod. Philip Davis. The Sci-Fi Channel. 25 March 1998.

Sims, Darrell. Investigator. and Dr. Roger Leir. California Foot Surgeon. Interview. *Alien Hunters*. We Are Not Alone. narr. Colin Stinton prod. Sara Woodford. The Learning Channel. 3 May 1998.

Sky Watchers. We Are Not Alone. narr. Colin Stinton. prod. Sara Woodford. The Learning Channel. 3 May 1998.

"Socorro. New Mexico. UFO Investigation." *Sightings*. In the News. narr. Tim White. writ. Susan Michaels. prod. Rob Morhaim. The Sci-Fi Channel. 25 March 1998.

Sparrow, Lynn. Interview. *Ancient Prophecies*. narr. David McCallum. ed. Michael Andrews. prod. Graeme Whifler and Paul Klein. The Learning Channel. 9 Jan. 1998.

"Spontaneous Human Combustion." *The Unexplained*. narr. Norm Woodel. writ. Gaylon Emerzian. prod. Gaylon Emerzian. The Arts & Entertainment Network. 19 Feb. 1998.

"Spontaneous Human Combustion." *Beyond Bizarre*. narr. Jay Robinston. writ. John Burrud. exec. prod. John Burrud. sup. ed. Kurt Porter. The Discovery Channel. 2 June 1998.

"Spontaneous Human Combustion." *Extremely Weird*. narr. Jay Thomas. ed. Tony Black. prod. Alexander Enright. The Learning Channel. 31 Jan. 1998.

Stefula, Joe. UFO Investigator. Interview. "*UFO Deep Secrets*." narr. Paul Anthony. prod. Jeremy Evans. The Discovery Channel. 4 Jan. 1998.

Stevens, Lt. Col. Wendelle. Foreign Technology Division. Wright-Patterson A.F.B. Interview. "*Alien Secrets*: Area 51." narr. Bruce Burgess. prod. Bruce Burgess. The Learning Channel. 8 Dec. 1997.

"STIGMATA The Wounds of Christ?." *Arthur C. Clarke's World of Strange Powers*. narr. Stanley Anderson. prod. Adam Hart-Davis. The Discovery Channel. 15 March 1998.

Strange Beings and UFOs. Mysteries of the Unexplained. narr. James Coburn. writ. Shamus Culhane. prod. Joel Westbrook. Jason Williams. William Morgan and Steve Eder. The Discovery Channel. 5 April 1998.

Strange But True?. narr. Michael Aspel. ed. David Alpin. Jeremy Phillips. prod. Ralph Jones and Simon Shaps. The Discovery Channel. 18 Feb. 1998.

"Strange Disappearances." *The Unexplained*. narr. Bill Kurtis. writ. Mark Caras. prod. Mark Caras. The Arts & Entertainment Network. 20 Aug. 1998.

"Strange Powers of Animals." *Arthur C. Clarke's Mysterious Universe*. narr. Ed Green. writ. Cathryn Garland. prod. Simon Westcott. The Discovery Channel. 23 Aug. 1998.

Stringdield, Leonard. UFO Researcher. Interview. "What's Inside Hanger 18." *Sightings*. narr. Tim White. writ. Susan Michaels. prod. Henry Winkler and Ann Daniel. The Sci-Fi Channel. 10 Feb. 1998.

Strom, Andrew. International Lecturer and Author. Interview. *New Visions of the Future*. Ancient Prophecies III. narr. David McCallum. prod. Paul Klein. The Learning Channel. 28 June 1998.

"The Abominable Snowman." *In Search of History*. narr. David Ackroyd. prod. Tim Evans. The History Channel. 30 April 1998.

The Belgian Air Force. The Belgian Gendarmarie. Interviews. *Unsolved Mysteries*. narr. Robert Stack. writ. Raymond Bridgers and Terry Dunn Muerer. prod. Terry Dunn Muerer and John Cosgrove. Lifetime. 17 June 1998.

"The Brazilian E.T. Case." *Sightings*. narr. Tim White. writ. Susan Michaels. prod. Philip Davis and Adam Stepan. The Sci-Fi Channel. 26 March 1998.

"*The Living Dead*, Speaking from the Grave." *Sightings*. narr. Tim White. writ. Susan Michaels. prod. Henry Winkler and Ann Daniel. The Sci-Fi Channel. 25 Oct. 1998.

"The Loch Ness Monster." *In Search of History*. narr. David Ackroyd. writ. Steve Muscarella and Melissa Jo Peltier. prod. Melissa Jo Peltier. The History Channel. 27 July 1998.

"The Loch Ness Secret." *Paleo World.* narr. Ted Maynard. writ. Georgann Kane. prod. Alex Graham. The Learning Channel. 6 May 1998.

"The Mystery of the Crystal Skulls." *The Unexplained.* narr. Norm Woodel. writ. Peter Minns. prod. BBC. A&E Network. Co-Producers. The Arts & Entertainment Network. 4 June 1998.

"The Near Death Experience." *Life After Death.* narr. Tom Harpur. writ. Tom Harpur. prod. Jim Hanley and David Brady. The Learning Channel. 22 Dec. 1997.

"The Real Dracula." *In Search of History.* narr. David Ackroyd. writ. Charles Ryan. prod. Charles Ryan. The History Channel. 18 May 1998.

"The Search for Dracula." *Science Mysteries.* narr. Eli Wallach. writ. Eleanor Grant. prod. Nicola Valcor and Tom Naughton. The Discovery Channel. 11 Jan. 1998.

"The Secrets of Alien Abduction." *Sightings.* In Depth and Beyond. narr. Tim White. writ. Susan Michaels. prod. Henry Winkler and Ann Daniel. The Sci-Fi Channel. 14 March 1998.

"*The UFO Cover-Up?* Live from Area 51." A TNT Larry King Special. narr. Larry King. writ. Tom Farmer. prod. Carrie Stevenson. TNT. 13 Sept. 1998.

"*The UFO Cover-Up?* Live." narr. Les Marshak and Mike Farrell. prod. LBS Communications, Inc./Seligman Productions. WGN-TV Chicago. Fall. 1988.

"The UFO Report." *Sightings.* narr. Tim White. writ. Susan Michaels. prod. Henry Winkler and Ann Daniel Productions. The Sci-Fi Channel. 4 Jan. 1998.

"The Uninvited." *Sightings.* narr. Tim White. writ. Susan Michaels. prod. Henry Winkler and Ann Daniel. The Sci-Fi Channel. 11 Oct. 1998.

The Universe. Understanding Festival. narr. Candice Bergen. writ. Dale Minor and Jonathan Ward. ed. Art Binkowski and Walter Cronkite. prod. Ron Bowman. Dan Everett and Jonathan Ward. The Learning Channel. 21 Nov. 1998.

"The Watchers." *Sightings.* narr. Tim White. writ. Susan Michaels. prod. Kim Steer. The Sci-Fi Channel. 13 April 1998.

Thompson, Dr. Richard L. Interview. *UFO's; The First Encounters.* prod. Lionel Friedberg. The Arts & Entertainment Network. 19 July 1998.

"Top Secret Projects." *Sightings.* narr. Tim White. writ. Susan Michaels. prod. Henry Winkler and Ann Daniel. The Sci-Fi Channel. 3 Feb. 1998.

"Trapped in Time." *Sightings.* narr. Tim White. writ. Susan Michaels. prod. Lindsey Paddor. The Sci-Fi Channel. 15 March 1998.

"*Trinity and Beyond:* The Atom Bomb Movie." narr. William Shatner. prod. Peter Kuran and Alan Munro. The Learning Channel. 29 March 1998.

"Tunguska." *Sightings.* narr. Tim White. writ. Susan Michaels. prod. Henry Winkler and Ann Daniel. The Sci-Fi Channel. 17 May 1998.

"*UFO* - Above Top Secret." dir. Yin Gazda. prod. Yin Gazda. Conolis Films. 1991.

"UFO Confrontation: Iran." *Sightings.* narr. Tim White. writ. Susan Michaels. prod. Philip Davis. The Sci-Fi Channel. 19 Feb. 1998.

"UFO Confrontation: Mansfield." *Sightings.* narr. Tim White. writ. Susan Michaels. prod. Philip Davis. The Sci-Fi Channel. 14 Jan. 1998.

"UFO Contact: The Holyland." *Sightings.* narr. Tim White. writ. Susan Michaels. prod. Henry Winkler and Ann Daniel. The Sci-Fi Channel. 6 Feb. 1998.

"*UFO* Deep Secrets." narr. Paul Anthony. prod. Jeremy Evans. The Discovery Channel. 4 Jan. 1998.

"UFO Encounter at 30,000 Feet." *Sightings.* narr. Tim White. writ. Susan Michaels. prod. Henry Winkler and Ann Daniel. The Sci-Fi Channel. 14 July 1998.

"UFO Encounter: Shikmona." *Sightings*. narr. Tim White. writ. Susan Michaels. prod. Ruth Rafidi and Phillip Lapkin. The Sci-Fi Channel. 18 Feb. 1998.

"*UFO* Great Balls of Light." narr. Paul Anthony. prod. Jeremy Evans, The Discovery Channel, 23 Jan. 1998.

"UFO Investigation." *Sightings*. narr. Tim White. writ. Susan Michaels. prod. Henry Winkler and Ann Daniel. The Sci-Fi Channel. 8 March 1998.

"*UFO* Reason to Believe." narr. Paul Anthony. prod. Jeremy Evans. The Discovery Channel. 8 Dec. 1997.

"*UFO* Uncovering the Evidence." narr. Paul Anthony. prod. Jeremy Evans. The Discovery Channel. 4 Jan. 1998.

"*UFO's*: Above and Beyond." narr. James Doohan. writ. Chris Wyatt. prod. John Goodwin. The Learning Channel. 16 July 1998.

"UFOs: Japan." *Sightings*. narr. Tim White. writ. Susan Michaels. prod. Henry Winkler and Ann Daniel. The Sci-Fi Channel. 19 March 1998.

"UFOs over FDR." *Sightings*. narr. Tim White. writ. Susan Michaels. prod. Henry Winkler and Ann Daniel. The Sci-Fi Channel. 3 June 1998.

"*UFOs*: The First Encounters." prod. Lionel Friedberg. The Arts & Entertainment Network. 19 July 1998.

"*UFOs*: The 100 Year Cover-up." *Sightings*. In Depth and Beyond. narr. Tim White. writ. Susan Michaels. prod. Henry Winkler and Ann Daniel. 1 Jan. 1998.

"*UFO's II* Have We Been Visited?" narr. Michael Dorn. prod. Lisa Bourgoujian. The Arts & Entertainment Network. 22 Feb. 1998.

Umepeg, Vicki. Interview. "Visions of Heaven." *Life After Death*. narr. Tom Harpur. writ. Tom Harpur. prod. Jim Hanley and David Brady. The Learning Channel. 22 Dec. 1997.

Unsolved Mysteries. The Unexplained. narr. Robert Stack. writ. Raymond Bridgers and Terry Dunn Meurer. prod. Terry Dunn Meurer and John Cosgrove. Lifetime. 4 Dec. 1997.

Unsolved Mysteries. The Unexplained. narr. Robert Stack. writ. Raymond Bridgers and Terry Dunn Meurer. prod. Terry Dunn Meurer and John Cosgrove. Lifetime. 24 Feb. 1998.

Unsolved Mysteries. The Unexplained. narr. Robert Stack. writ. Raymond Bridgers and Terry Dunn Meurer. prod. Terry Dunn Meurer and John Cosgrove. Lifetime. 3 June 1998.

Unsolved Mysteries. The Unexplained. narr. Robert Stack. writ. Raymond Bridgers and Terry Dunn Meurer. prod. Terry Dunn Meurer and John Cosgrove. Lifetime. 17 June 1998.

Unsolved Mysteries. The Unexplained. narr. Robert Stack. writ. Raymond Bridgers and Terry Dunn Meurer. prod. Terry Dunn Meurer and John Cosgrove. Lifetime. 19 June 1998.

Unsolved Mysteries. The Unexplained. narr. Robert Stack. writ. Raymond Bridgers and Terry Dunn Meurer. prod. Terry Dunn Meurer and John Cosgrove. Lifetime. 30 June 1998.

Unsolved Mysteries. The Unexplained. narr. Robert Stack. writ. Raymond Bridgers and Terry Dunn Meurer. prod. Terry Dunn Meurer and John Cosgrove. Lifetime. 27 July 1998.

Unsolved Mysteries. The Unexplained. narr. Robert Stack. writ. Raymond Bridgers and Terry Dunn Meurer. prod. Terry Dunn Meurer and John Cosgrove. Lifetime. 19 Aug. 1998.

Unsolved Mysteries. The Unexplained. narr. Robert Stack. writ. Raymond Bridgers and Terry Dunn Meurer. prod. Terry Dunn Meurer and John Cosgrove. Lifetime. 15 Sept. 1998.

"Vampires." *Unnatural History.* narr. Mark Hamill. writ. Anne McGrail. prod. Michael Tetrick. The Learning Channel. 26 Jan. 1998.

"Waiting Room of the Soul." *Sightings.* narr. Tim White. writ. Susan Michaels. prod. Henry Winkler and Ann Daniel. The Sci-Fi Channel. 10 Feb. 1998.

Walker, Paul Robert. Interview. *Stories of Miracles.* narr. Devon O'Day. writ. Peter Shockey. prod. Peter Shockey. 25 Dec. 1998.

Webster's Encyclopedic Unabridged Dictionary of the English Language. Deluxe ed. rev. New York. New York: Gramercy Books, a Division of Random House Publications, Inc. 1996. (206)

"What's Inside Hanger 18." *Sightings.* narr. Tim White. writ. Susan Michaels. prod. Henry Winkler and Ann Daniel. The Sci-Fi Channel. 10 Feb. 1998.

"Whitley Strieber's Breakthrough." *Sightings.* narr. Tim White. writ. Susan Michael. prod. Philip Davis. The Sci-Fi Channel. 4 March 1998.

"Winchester, England, Crop Circles." *Sightings.* In the News. narr. Tim White. writ. Susan Michaels. prod. Kim Steer. The Sci-Fi Channel. 4 March 1998

"Without a Tracc." *Sightings.* narr. Tim White. writ. Susan Michaels. prod. John Bayliss and Ruth Rafidi. The Sci-Fi Channel. 8 March 1998.

Young, Beth. Interview. "Visions of Heaven." *Life After Death.* narr. Tom Harpur. writ. Tom Harpur. prod. Jim Hanley and David Brady. The Learning Channel. 22 Dec. 1997.

Z., Ryan. *Atomic Bomb.* <http://darter.ocps.k12.fl.us/classroom/who/darter1/atomic.htm>. Access date 22 Nov. 1998.

COMING IN THE YEAR 2000!

The second volume of the Millennium Series

Dance of the Renaissance

Near-death experiencer Pam Nesure uttered these words upon her return from the realm beyond physical death:

> "Somehow it was all connected."

Elizabeth Robinson spoke these words after her experience in the presence of intelligent beings from another world:

> "They've come to help us awaken."

Dance of the Renaissance explores the significant meaning of these eleven words and picks up where *The Magic of Our Universe* ends. The book delves into the delicate dance humans now perform upon an environmentally challenged Earth in the midst of the following:

• The exponential explosion of human population and technology.

• The environmental impact of this trend and the top ten responsibilities each and every human can and should assume to help preserve the Earth.

• The expanding interactivity between extraterrestrial and human life, and the genesis of mainstream scientific research into the phenomenon.

• The attractiveness of human characteristics to extraterrestrials to warrant DNA transfusions.

• The proximity of humans to living within the realm where fiction and non-fiction become one.

• The interconnectedness of the Universe including: recent discoveries in psi research and life beyond death; the powerful omniscient force of love; consciospiritualism in the context of the world's major religions; the implications of fractal geometry.

• The prophecy of the Maya and others both historical and contemporary: that "time" as we know it may soon end.

• All of these astounding revelations are occurring within the same current period of human history.

• The great library of television is once again researched for *Dance of the Renaissance*.

• For further information visit the internet site of Camelot Productions and Kent Davis Moberg at: **http://www.camelotpublishing.com**